THEIR POLITICS AND

Text

Thanks to dialectical and historical materialism, Marx and Engels placed at the disposal of the human race the possibility of extending their scientific method to the analysis of history and society. This is already an extremely important result; but Marxist science is much more than that. Applied to human society, Marxist science explains the processes that make communism a historical necessity, allows the scientific definition of the strategy for the communist revolution, and ensures the superiority of the proletariat over the other classes, a superiority ensured solely by this scientific strategy.

All the Marxist literary works are born as weapons in the revolutionary battle for communism and are only able to survive as such. In one and a half centuries, the fighting of numerous generations of Marxists has led to the accumulation of a scientific patrimony that unfortunately is little known and even less used today.

Arrigo Cervetto, who considered science as the salient feature of Lenin's party and founded his attempt to transfer the Bolshevik experience from tsarist Russia to post-WWII imperialist Italy on this hypothesis, defined the patrimony of Marxist science as a largely unexplored lode.

To bring a part of this theoretical treasure trove back into the light for the English-speaking reader is one of the tasks our publishing house has set itself, not with the aim of spreading culture but with the aim of providing the theoretical weapons with which to fight the revolutionary battle for communism.

The reality of this 21st century as a whole reveals how much of scientifically-founded revolutionary strategy was contained in the final appeal of the "Manifesto" – *Workers of all countries, unite!* An international proletariat that has swollen to huge dimensions has more than ever an urgent need to rediscover Marxist science and, in view of its future battles, to anchor its revolutionary preparation in it.

The work that lies before us is immense. Our catalogue is the measure of the contribution that we, as the Èditions Science Marxiste, have succeeded in making so far.

Renato Pastorino

Their Politics and Ours

A New Communist Generation in Europe

Science
éditions Marxiste

Marxist Science Pubblications

Text

For information about our publications please contact
Éditions Science Marxiste SARL
10, rue Lavoisier – 93100 Montreuil-sous-Bois – France
e-mail: info@sciencemarxiste.com
http://www.sciencemarxiste.com

Translated from Italian
First published as: *La loro politica e la nostra*
Edizioni Lotta Comunista, Milan, Italy

ISBN 978-2-490073-36-8

Publisher's note:

This volume collects articles published in the newspaper *Lotta Comunista* between January 2007 and May 2020, translated into English for the newspapers *Internationalist Bulletin* between March 2007 – November 2018 and *Internationalism* between April 2019 – June 2020. Apart from the correction of misprints, they are presented integrally.
The division and chapter headings are the work of the editor.

Contents

Preface

"Lenin wrote in *What Is to Be Done?*: 'Every question *runs in a vicious circle* because political life as a whole is an endless chain consisting of an infinite number of links. The whole art of politics lies in finding and taking as firm a grip as we can of the link that is least likely to be struck from our hands'. Thus, concluded Lenin, it will be possible to take 'possession of the whole chain'.

In *Our General Task,* Cervetto starts from this concept and indicates that link is to be found in organisational work: 'the organisational plan, systematic work as the guarantee and necessary condition for being able to face turns of events, social explosions and political complications'. There is no doubt that the *pandemic of the century* represents an unexpected turn of events, which we have dealt with precisely with 'systematic work' among our supporters".

This reference to organisational theory in Lenin and Cervetto forms part of the last article in this book, which draws the conclusions from the political battle fought by our workers' circles in order to face the *pandemic of the century crisis.* The cross reference to the "general task" of our *party-plan* is completed by another crucial concept, again anchored in Lenin's theory:

"Cervetto concludes the editorial *The Dialectics of the Political Crisis* [October 1988] quoting Lenin: 'The experience of war, like the experience of any crisis in history, of any great calamity and any sudden turn in human life, stuns and breaks some people, but enlightens and tempers others.' Cervetto comments: 'Sometimes we have not reflected enough on the fact that the same events that stun and break certain political currents enlighten and temper others. This is a lesson of the materialist conception of politics'".

We believe this reflection best represents the spirit of this book, *Their Politics and Ours*. As in *The Unprecedented Task*, which collected texts published from 1996 to 2006, this new volume collects articles of the last fourteen years, from 2007 to 2020, all written in relation to political battles or moments in the life of our party. Whence their particular value, the systematic attention paid to the practical translation of theoretical reflections and general political analyses.

How many times have we quoted Lenin's *What Is to Be Done?* in some report, and how many Cervetto's *Our General Task*? And yet, perhaps never as in the *pandemic of the century* battle have those concepts turned out to be a living, almost tangible thing: our workers' circles have indeed been "the link" seized in order to lead back to the whole chain; our network of supporters has allowed us to speak to the "deep strata" of our class in the working-class districts; the structures of our circles have found themselves being the headquarters from which to organise thousands of volunteers, drawing in new energies in a sudden and unpredictable fight. And again, really and truly, the crisis has "enlightened" and "tempered" our militants, since the challenge was such as to impose the greatest intelligence, will-power, energy and also *scientific fantasy* in facing it.

All of this is connected to another common feature of the articles of this book: they open and close with two major crises – the one we defined as the *global-relations crisis*, which began in 2007, and precisely today's *pandemic of the century crisis*. All of these articles were written to the rhythm of tensions and partial crises among the powers, which mark the "stormy times" of the *new strategic phase*. We need only think of China's definitive irruption as a global power, American decline, the contradictory steps forward of European imperialism, the wars in the Middle East, the "external collision" of the migration flows in Europe and the United States, and the "voter revolts" with which the frightened petty bourgeoisie and intermediate strata reacted to the uncertainties of the new epoch.

Here too, in every battle, the vantage point is at the crossroads between theory and political analysis on the one hand, and party battle on the other. Let's consider for example the internationalist battle, with its chain of wars in the Middle East, the protraction of the conflict in Iraq, the so-called "Arab Springs", and the wars in Libya and Syria. In the Middle East, we wrote in January 2007, we see "the urgency of the unity of the Arab and Israeli proletariat, and not only them", against the various regional bourgeoisies that exploit the national, ethnic or religious pretext in their contention. A political conclusion stems from the internationalist principle. "Our internationalist force is the only one that waves this class flag"; "We well understand what force the unity of the Arab and Israeli proletariats and of all the nationalities working there could have against the Israeli bourgeoisie, the Palestinian bourgeoisie, the avid Arab bourgeoisies and the imperialist powers that use them and support them".

The internationalist battle is not therefore the mere preaching of a principle: that class flag that only Lotta Comunista waves also expresses a real practical need, which arises from the connection between the Middle Eastern proletariat and old Europe. The Mediterranean is "Europe's *banlieue*", we wrote in February 2011 when the *Arab Springs* first flared up; youths of the Middle East and North Africa look to Europe; they will be taken hostage by the bourgeois fractions and factions if they do not find "a solid anchorage in a Leninist Party firmly entrenched in the European metropolis". Furthermore: "many North African youths animate our initiatives and frequent our workers' circles, and various of them participate in our militant activity"; more organised force is needed "for our strategic elaboration to become a solid reference point".

This is the immediate practical sense of the internationalist battle. Certainly, in the future, class unity in the revolutionary strategy of the Middle Eastern proletariat will sabotage all the games of the imperialist powerhouses and local bourgeoisies. But in the meantime, tens of millions of wage earners in Europe have their roots in the southern shore of the Mediterranean. To defend the internationalist principle in the Middle East means fighting also in Europe against ideologies and fanaticisms that would like to divide proletarians; to claim the class principle for the Middle Eastern proletariat means asserting it for the European worker. There are more and more youths in our circles who find in this simple idea of internationalist unity the solution to a conundrum that nationalism generated and is therefore unable to resolve.

Let's think, moreover, about the contraposition between "their" politics and "our" politics, another leitmotif of many articles. Certainly, the starting point is the crisis of and confusion in the ruling ideology, exacerbated in recent years by the crisis in liberal ideology. The big bourgeoisie is running out of breath, we wrote in January 2020, "in its attempt to force disappointed, resentful petty-bourgeois and intermediate strata that are gripped with fear to see reason, a strategically-founded reason".

Our denunciation concedes nothing to the superficial fashion of *anti-politics*, the populist vogue leading to the xenophobic and racist demagogy of the League or to the statist and pro-South amateurism of the Five Stars. The crisis in "their" politics is rather an opportunity for commitment: "Disillusionment and disorientation are tangible, we know, and our positions penetrate more easily" [February 2014]. When the key ideas of "imperialist Europeanism" arrive, we will fight them, "but for the moment their politics is in difficulty all over Europe"; "this is the moment to strike the hardest blows, it is the moment of our politics, starting from those millions of workers and youths who do not listen to their politics, who do not vote" [April 2018].

It is not therefore by chance that another leitmotif of the articles collected in this volume is our organisational battle, which is the real field in which every result can be safeguarded, preserved and hence transmitted. This brings us to a final aspect, which is the attention we must pay to a *new generation*, drawn to politics precisely in the crises and upheavals of the last fifteen years. Moreover: if *The Unprecedented Task* was the book of the *third generation* of Lotta Comunista – the one drawn to politics starting from the crisis in the Soviet Union and won over in the internationalist battles of the Iraq War, the wars in the Balkans and the second Gulf War – in many respects, this new volume is the text of the *fourth generation*, precisely the one that had and will have its defining political battles in the two 2007 and 2020 crises.

Within a few years, our *fifth generation* will appear. It will contribute to facing the *new strategic phase* in its most convulsive developments, the 2020s and 2030s characterised as can already be glimpsed by the rearmament race between China and the emerging Asian countries and the powers of the old order. The link of class organisation needs to be gripped more firmly than ever.

Chapter One

OUR LENINIST BATTLE IN THE CRISIS OF GLOBAL RELATIONS

A revolutionary policy in the Middle Eastern crisis

A Historical Lesson for the Internationalist Struggle*

The Middle East, with the Persian Gulf, has been a crossroads of international tensions from time immemorial. A crucial area because of its oil production and energy reserves, it has become even more crucial since it started to fuel the strong Asian development; an area where a still ongoing decades-long game is affecting the balance of the relationship among the great powers.

The order of imperialism

In the book *L'Europa e la Guerra* [Europe and War] it was pointed out that "in one century the imperialist struggle for oil has been intertwined with the struggle through oil" [1]. It was the power relations among the powers that decided, over time, how the oil was to be shared out, but those divisions, the agreements among the big groups, and the cartels have become weapons in the world contention. This is now a more than one-century-long clash of capital, investments and financial flows which has regularly led to military clashes. Lenin argued that "the opportunity for revolution is born of the incapacity of capitalism to maintain a world order" [2]. The Middle East is an example of this thesis on a regional scale, but at the same time it is also an example of what their order, the capitalist order, really is.

Egypt was occupied by the British from as early as 1882 to 1922, and they remained in Suez until 1955. Jordan was under British mandate until 1946, while Lebanon was under French mandate until 1943. This was also the case of Syria: as late as 1945 the French air force bombed Damascus, which the French had to leave the following year. In the case of Iraq, the British mandate lasted from 1920 top 1932. Then the country remained under the strict control of Britain, which reoccupied it militarily in 1941. As regards Palestine, the British mandate lasted until 1948 when the UN resolution, backed by the United States and the USSR, sanctioned the birth of the state of Israel, which then led to the start of the Arab-Israeli wars. Even a "poor man's imperialism" like Italy's had its colonial adventures in Libya and the Horn of

* *Internationalist Bulletin,* March 2007

Africa, and a bloody repression did not even spare those populations from the use of gas.

The new national bourgeoisies

Colonial rule did not prevent the development of voracious national bourgeoisies. On the contrary, it stimulated it: as they grew stronger, they claimed a growing share of the booty appropriated by the powers. As a consequence, during the period of decolonisation the struggles for national liberalisation and for the formation of new states sprang up, becoming the tools of those new bourgeoisies. In accordance with Lenin's instructions, these struggles were immediately supported by the internationalists, not because the national question for us Marxists was a question of principle, but because the formation of national states with the unification and expansion of their markets, agrarian reforms, industrialisation, and the development and concentration of the working class worked to the advantage of the struggle of the international proletariat. That cycle of struggles for national liberation led to formation of most of the states in the world we know today.

In 1982, when he was analysing the clash between Britain and Argentina over Falklands, Arrigo Cervetto observed: "Most of the states recognised by the UN have sprung up in the last thirty-five years. Nearly all of them have incorporated populations of different ethnic origins and have acquired their rights to national sovereignty by the use of that violence which colonialism and imperialism has used against them. Many of these states have inherited borders drawn administratively by the old powers"[3].

The cycle of struggles for national liberation practically ended in the 1960s with the Vietnam War. The United States which, with a keen eye on developing Japan, had taken over in Indochina from the old French plunderer, was forced to withdraw in haste, a defeat which still affects the US and which, not always appropriately, is being recalled today by various experts in connection with what is happening in Iraq.

The national pretext in the Middle East

The process of decolonisation ended up leaving various ethnic groups without a national state of their own and without being included in plurinational states. This was the case of not only the Armenians, the Kurds and the Palestinians.

"Dozen of nationalities in dozens of states find themselves in their condition. There is no state that, in its formation, has not included national minorities, often by coercion. [...] What is true of the states which formed in the past centuries, in Europe for instance, is even more true of the states which have formed in Africa and Asia in the last few decades. This means that national factors are being used in the struggle among the states and will be ever more in the future"[4] [A. Cervetto, *Il pretesto nazionale nella poltica mediterranea* (The National Pretext in Mediterranean Politics), 1985].

The national pretext has been used and abused in the Middle East during these decades. With the end of that historical phase, the intervention of the great powers has continued and, if possible, has increased in the struggle with no holds barred for spheres of influence. Every single power is at work to keep the different national bourgeoisies, their fractions and often their factions tied to itself and to its big groups. It is a struggle whose aim is to open up the markets and to favour one's own investments and financial flows in order to limit or condition the influence of rival powers. Moreover, these interventions have multiplied, also in the military field, using every possible pretext, and the national one in particular.

Unity of the Arab and Israeli proletariat

Since 1960s the sole objective for us Marxists has become the development of the internationalist struggle in every sector of the world proletariat. It is no longer a question of supporting struggles for national liberation, but of carrying on and sustaining the unity and autonomous struggle of the proletariat with all our might and in every corner of the capitalist world.

This last applies to the bloodstained Middle East, where we do not see struggles of national liberation to sustain, but the urgency, of the unity of the Arab and Israeli proletariat (et al.) against the various national bourgeoisies and the powers supporting them. Does this mean we are indifferent to the Palestinian or Kurdish question, or that we accept the persecution of national minorities, ethnic groups or even religious minorities? Absolutely not, and it is even ridiculous to think so: the defence of the oppressed and of the weakest has always been written on our banners. It does mean, however, that we believe only the struggle of the united proletariat, beyond all differences of nationality, ethnicity and religion, is the only barrier against the persecution and oppression of very minority, and, at the same time, the tool for the only progress possible today: the struggle for communism.

Millions of immigrants and wage earners in the Middle East

Our internationalist force is the only one carrying this class banner. One needs merely to think that in years and years of political and ideological campaigns on the Middle East, no one has ever considered the over two-million-strong Israeli proletariat, which has thus been delivered into the hands of its own bourgeoisie. What a force against the Israeli bourgeoisie, against the voracious Arab bourgeoisies, and against the imperialist powers that exploit and support them the unity of the Arab and Israeli proletariat and of all the nationalities working there might be! There are millions of immigrant workers, exploited in the country-sides, in the factories and in the oilfields of the Middle East. There are about seven million in Saudi Arabia, over one million in Kuwait, roughly two million in the United Arab Emirates, one million three hundred thousand in Oman, and around half a million in Israel. In the six countries of the Persian Gulf alone are reckoned to be no fewer than 13 million. They come from India, Bangladesh, Pakistan, Egypt, the Philippines, Palestine, Sri Lanka, other Arab countries, and Eastern Europe, and are exploited together with their Arab and Israeli companions. Here is the real barrier against the oppression and exploitation of the minorities at the hands of imperialism and of the various national bourgeoisies!

No one ever mentions this working class, which in actual fact is international, except in arid tables of statistics, and yet it is these workers and these technicians that enable oil to pulse in the energy artery of the Persian Gulf. No one mentions this class reality because everyone fears a force of millions of workers who, if united in a class struggle, could really clog that energy artery. For us, this is the only real coalition possible in the Middle East, this is the reference of our internationalist battle, a battle against unitary imperialism driven by the never-ending struggle for the division of the world market.

Budapest and Suez in 1956

Last November, in a series of well-attended internationalist demonstrations, we paid homage to the Hungarian students and workers crushed by the tanks of Russian imperialism fifty years ago. However, that autumn of 1956 was also a key moment for the Middle East, when France and Great Britain opposed the nationalisation of the Suez Canal, but whose military intervention was blocked by the converging pressures of the United States and the USSR, on that occasion allies. The withdrawal of the French and British paratroopers from Suez became the symbol of the downsising of France and Britain in this area, in the face of rising American and also Soviet influence.

Budapest and Suez were two only apparently distant crises, intimately connected with the struggle for the division of spheres of influence among the imperialist powers. No one paid heed to Budapest's cry for help except for small minorities of internationalists. Why did the United States, the bastion of "Western democracy", not lift a finger? The reason is both simple and ruthless: in the division of the spheres of influence sanctioned at Yalta after the Second World War, Eastern Europe had become the appanage of the Soviet Union. Meanwhile American imperialism, the de facto ally of the USSR as it put down the Hungarian revolt in blood, was forcing France and Great Britain to abandon Suez.

Opportunists and Stalinists against the workers

Those crises of the autumn of 1956 provided a terrible and tragic verification of the role of opportunism, and it is also for this reason that the sacrifice of the Hungarian youths and workers will not have been in vain, as long as that lesson is assimilated and passed on from generation to generation. The Stalinist parties, with the PCI in the lead, aligned themselves with the Russian tanks that were massacring the Hungarian workers. Despite all the ideologies of the "Cold War", they therefore also supported American imperialism which, allied with the Soviet Union, was kicking the Anglo-French out of Suez: this is the logic of unitary imperialism.

In the last few months, clearly penitent and apologising profuse, the children and grandchildren of yesterday's opportunists took part in the commemoration of the Hungarian revolt. They said that at that time they did not know exactly what was going on and that in any case, as the world was than divided into two camps, it was necessary to take sides. It is true the world was divided into two camps, but on one side there was the proletariat and on the other the imperialist bourgeoisie. On their political choice was imperialism. Those who wanted to know knew what was going on. The men who founded *Lotta Comunista*, a group of young workers with modest means at their disposal, wanted to know and sided with the proletariat against unitary imperialism.

No more alibis

Today the unstable Middle East is offering a tragic repetition, and now that they cannot but know, now that the alibi of the "Cold War" between the USA and the USSR is no longer valid, and now that the contention among the powers in the world is multipolar, they, the opportunists, have again sided with imperialism. With all their strength they are supporting and sustaining Europe, which has never forgotten the humiliation of Suez. They have sided with European imperialism which, by virtue of the constant changes in the power relations among the powers, is trying to capitalise on the failure of the Bush Doctrine and the erosion of American influence in the Middle East.

It is for this reason that, today more than ever, the watchword of our policy is "proletarian opposition to European imperialism".

Scientific clarity in the struggle against the ideologies of imperialism
"To Study, Propagandise and Organise" *

Throughout the history of imperialism, all the interventions of the great powers, including their military ventures, have been justified by the ideology of the bourgeoisie with the noblest of motives. Every season had had its myths, from ideas of national greatness to dramatisations of humanitarian interventionism.

Myths of peace and democracy

In today's struggle for spheres of influence and the division of the markets, the recurrent justifications are those of "peace" and the "development of democracy". Iraq is an example of this: in the past it was one of the best customers of the Russian, French, American and also Italian armaments industries, especially during the long war with Iran. Various Arab bourgeoisies backed it against Tehran and it was bankrolled particularly by Egypt and Saudi Arabia.

According to the most conservative estimates, the latest military intervention in Iraq for "peace and democracy" has so far cost the lives of more than 60,000 persons, roughly 50,000 of whom civilians. There are estimates which, counting also "indirect" casualties, arrive at a total of over half a million war dead. The three Gulf Wars have cost about 600,000 lives. If we consider the conflicts in the whole of the Middle East since 1945, the final count is of roughly one million war dead. This is the peace of the powers of imperialism, and this the price of their democracy.

European Imperialism within Multipolarism

Today the failure of George W. Bush's *political war* is before our eyes. The United States is having to submit the negotiations it had wished to impose on the other powers, with the relative and inevitable prices to pay. Its rival powers, in primis Russia, China and Europe, are getting ready to take advantage of the erosion of US influence in the Middle East. They will certainly leave no stone unturned in order to increase their share of the loot.

"Unitary imperialism is considered as a dialectic between general and common interests and the particular interests of the international capitalist class [...]. Unitary imperialism is a 'den of thieves', as Lenin defines it, thieves organically united in stealing the loot and thieves irremediably divided in its share-out"[5]. And in their struggle for the share-out the thieves of today will certainly use the various Arab bourgeoisies and their factions, all the national pretexts possible, and all the feuds and struggles of the factions, just like the past. In these clashes European imperialism

* *Internationalist Bulletin*, April 2007

is sharpening its weapons and spreading its ideologies. Dominique Moïsi, director of IFRI, the French Institute for International Relations, argues that a tectonic upheaval is under way in the international system, with the passage from the unipolar to the multipolar world.

These are many people today who are discovering the multipolar world after years of debate on the sole American superpower or hyper-power. It is worthwhile to note how Arrigo Cervetto's book *Il mondo multipolare* [The Multipolar World] was published, alas posthumously, more than ten years ago. Moïsi goes on to say that the EU is the only natural ally of the USA as far as values are concerned, and that it is the European Union which can make multipolarism work. He adds that in some ways the end of the unipolar world might be the striking of Europe's real hour.

The scientific clarity of marxism

In all the capitals, and not only in the European ones, situations are incubating where "peace" and the "development of democracy" will once again become the ideological myths brandished in the power struggle. This is why Marxist scientific clarity becomes an imperative. It is indispensable for getting to minds as well as to hearts, indispensable for opposing the misdeeds of imperialism, and indispensable for gathering round our communist policy an ever vaster and more solid sphere of influence which may act as the sounding board of our internationalist positions among the masses.

All of this requires great clarity. For us, peace among the powers, when it is not a mere pretext, is simply an interval between the wars of imperialism. History demonstrates this, and the Middle Eastern tragedy is an extremely clear example of it. Democracy is the political shell through which the economically dominant class exercises its power, leading to times of peace and times of war. We communists are not "democrats"; we are, precisely, communists.

The title of the first article published by a young Sergio Motosi in our newspaper in 1972 stated: "Democracy is bourgeois, communism is proletariat". Democracy is the tool used by one class to dominate another. This has been true since it first saw the light of day in ancient Athens. With the advent of capitalism democracy has become its best, most useful and most efficient shell: useful for settling the perennial conflicts among the various bourgeois fractions, efficient in subjugating the proletariat through the state and it is more than ever so today in the forms of imperialist democracy. These are the basic reasons why we are unwilling to be enrolled in the wars "for peace and democracy" to which the imperialist world periodically gives birth.

The essence of communist policy

How then can the succession of crises be faced, how can the ventures and wars of imperialism be opposed? There is only one concrete way today: a commitment and a ceaseless struggle to make the proletariat aware that those crises and those wars are not accidents of history, but rather the inevitable product of capitalism in the stage of its imperialist maturity.

It is necessary to make the proletariat aware that those crisis points in Iraq, Korea, Lebanon, Afghanistan, Iran, Chechnya, etc., which seem to be distant from and disconnected with one another, are actually linked by a multiplicity of threads, threads which compose a "web of communicating vessels" originating in the permanent struggle among the powers. Bringing that awareness to the real movement is the essence of communist policy for today because it means working in depth among the masses in order to prepare and organise the vanguard of our class so that, when the contradictions of imperialism result in world catastrophe, it will be able to lead the masses towards the only possible way out: the proletarian revolution. We are revolutionaries precisely because we know that the alternative the future reserves for the whole of humanity lies between this revolution for a classless society and a new imperialist war, a war in which "the state of present things" would be perpetuated, as it already has been in the past.

The force of the dominant ideologies

Bringing this awareness from the outside cannot be done by preaching, nor can it be effected through a scholarly university course. It requires a struggle – often bitter – against the ideas of the ruling class among the masses, against the ideologies through which imperialism seeks to bind the proletariat to itself in order to perpetuate its domination and to exploit the work, strength, capacity and brains of the working class in its struggle for spheres of influence and the conquest of the markets.

In *L'Europa e lo Stato* [Europe and the State] it is pointed out how ideologies are not mere fantastic inventions, and it adds: "Their strength lies in distorting and overturning reality in its deepest sense, while founding themselves, however, on the partial truth of a fragment of that same reality. In short, ideologies [...] have on their side the strength of appearances, of popular perceptions, and of reality as it seems to rise to the surface of the historical and social dynamic" [6].

This is the reason why our struggle to make the masses aware needs a scientific analysis of reality, whose deep meaning must be grasped in order to understand how much is changing and the trace the trends that are establishing themselves. In other words, it needs the science-party, "a political body centralised and disciplined around the dividing line of strategic analysis" [7]. Otherwise, with a mere repetition of principles or, even worse, of one "clever" idea after another, bourgeois ideology will get the upper hand and impose itself as, unfortunately, has been the case.

The deep meaning of our "Unprecedented Task"

Lenin provides very clear guidelines on how to carry out this task. Three years before writing *What Is To Be Done?* he wrote: "We do not believe in conspiracies, we refuse revolutionary actions devised to overthrow the government; the practical watchword for our work is provided for us by the motto of Liebknecht, the veteran of German Social Democracy: "*Studieren, propagandieren, organisieren*" – to study, to propagandise, to organise – and the fulcrum of that activity can only and must only be constituted by a press organ of the party" [8].

We too, together with Lenin, have made this motto ours. An entire generation of militants has grown up and trained itself by following those guidelines. They remain an apt synthesis of our policy in the present counter-revolutionary phase, conditioned by a widespread social passivity. The effectiveness of the German internationalists' motto has been verified by the facts. The clearly demonstrated proof of this effectiveness is to be found in the succession of the generations of Marxism and in the history of our party right up to its most recent development.

If at the beginning of the third millennium copies of the *Manifesto*, of the fundamental texts of the Marxist school and of our analyses are circulating among the masses, it is by virtue of the fertility of that motto, a fertility which ensures that hundreds of young people hear about Marxism every day and that they have, at the same time, the possibility of seeing the vitality of communist policy for themselves. "To study, to propagandise, to organise" is, essentially, the deepest sense of our unprecedented task, which is to embed in the heart of imperialist Europe a science-party able to indicate a prospect of practicable internationalist struggle, looking at the future unfolding of the struggle among the classes.

A struggle steered by strategy

This struggle of ours is based on the scientific analysis of reality, and is therefore able to grasp the dynamic of imperialism and of the constant changes in the power relationships. This is so that events do not take us by surprise, leaving us behind and so pushed to the margins of social reality, unheard, isolated and reduced to waffling, to insignificance. It is strategic analysis which lends efficacy to our policy and our internationalist struggle fought above all against our imperialism. We were born during the struggle against Italian imperialism, which we fought all by ourselves when everyone at that time maintained Italy was an American colony: this is a struggle we continue to fight every day, in the factories, in the workshops and on the wharves, but also in offices and schools, the breeding grounds of imperialist ideologies. However, precisely because our struggle against Italian imperialism was based on the scientific analysis of reality, we were able to grasp its deep sense in time. We were able to trace the tendency towards the multipolar world and the formation of new powers in both Asia and the

Old Continent. This enabled us to deal with the tortuous process of the formation of a European imperialist power and of its institutions, seeing the new ideologies of imperialist Europeanism unfold at the same time.

The European Union, the new beacon of the continent's left wing, is bound to be an imperialist power. We have not been left behind or taken by surprise. Now that Europe is sharpening its weapons, it is more than ever necessary "To study, to propagandise, to organise" in order to make the proletarian opposition to European imperialism effective.

The challenge of the new strategic phase

A Patient and Persevering Task *

In February, quoting the option of a large number of analysts, the *Financial Times* reported that the post-*cold war* world by now dead and buried. Their thesis was that America has lost both power and influence, and so a "new, uncertain era" is about to begin. The City's newspaper published an evaluation by Madeleine Albright in which she argued that we seem to be going towards a "systemic" change that would lead to a multipolar world where China and India increase their influence while America's declines.

This trend is emerging not only in America's attempt to break out of its impasse in Iraq by internationalising the crisis, as is demonstrated by the recently opened conference in Baghdad, but also in the renewed assertiveness of both Beijing and Moscow, and in Germany's initiative during its presidency of the European Union.

A new strategic phase

These thorny problems show tangible signs of an about-turn that is now underway in the imperialist contention, and which is causing "tensions and conflicts in the state system"[9]: an about-turn that opens a new strategic phase calling the Marxist school to make a further effort in the field of theory and scientific recognition; an about-turn which, starting with our growing influence and increased responsibilities thanks to our development of the last few years, commits our party to pitting itself against new and more complex problems in order to face the ongoing tensions and contradictions. Hence, it is once again necessary to pause to reflect on this world-shaking about-turn that is now taking place as a result of China's emergence as an imperialist power.

The book *L'Europa e lo Stato* underlines the fact that "every year [registers] a 1% shift of the Chinese population from rural to urban"[10]. We have written that this fact concentrates in itself the essence of the general trend now underway. Indeed, the nature and the rhythm of an extraordinary and absolutely unprecedented process in the history of the world are condensed in those 12 million peasants who migrate from the countryside to the towns every year.

This process marks the definitive shift of the barycentre of world development to Asia: China had a 10.7% growth rate in 2006, with a 24% increase in capital formation. "Le Monde" observed in January that, according to official estimates, roughly 300 million Chinese will leave the

---

* *Internationalist Bulletin*, May 2007

rural areas in the next 25 years. In 2016 China's working-age population will be equal to the working population of all the developed countries.

L'Europa e lo Stato also highlights how the population of modern-day China is equal to that of the entire early-twentieth-century world, with an even greater economic weight than the world product of that time. It is worth recalling that that world was under the lens of Lenin's analysis in his detailed study of imperialism. This is the about-turn now underway, and it is no accident that Arrigo Cervetto, when dealing with this phenomenon beforehand, recalled the sixteenth century, with its passage from one epoch to another, which shifted the fulcrum of the world economy from the Mediterranean to the Atlantic, with everything this meant for the rise and fall of the powers of that time. The old *Middle Kingdom* is the engine of the world-shaking about-turn of this historical phase of imperialism in which we are operating, but it is not the only thing that characterised this new strategic phase.

China and Europe

Alongside China, we have said, there is Europe. The other unprecedented element of the change underway is the acceleration the process of European unification has undergone since the collapse of the "Russian empire" and Germany's reunification. Today a sizeable part of the countries of the former Warsaw Pact has crossed the Union's frontiers and, with the adhesion of Romania and Bulgaria, it has become an EU with 27 members, with a single central bank, the euro by now an international currency, and a single market now extended also to the workforce. The driving force behind this process is the irruption of China as a power: these are the communicating vessels that are in action.

The analysis of the process of formation of a European imperialist power is crucial to our revolutionary political struggle. So far we have succeeded in dealing with this process thanks to the analyses done by various generations of the Marxist school, with Cervetto ably took up again, developed and passed on to us. After the acceleration it has experienced since Germany's reunification, European unification has been forced to slow down because of the French and Dutch noes to the process of national reunification of the constitutional treaty. Now, after little less than two years, the phenomenon is witnessing a new acceleration under the driving force of the German engine, as was already the case in the past.

We have never thought that Europe's process of imperialist unification could be a procedure of peaceful and gradual rise towards a goal decided upon by diplomacy. This is simply because this unification is the outcome of an imperialist struggle, and of the clash among the great powers and among the interests of the ruling class's fractions and big groups. Before the French and Dutch noes, in June 2004, we wrote: "In no way do we minimise the crucial step of the constitution, neither do we exclude that a torturous political process in the long struggle for ratification may open up again" [11]. And this has been the case.

Pro-European general line

Today the pro-European general line of the continent's big groups has recovered its strength, urged on by the strong German recovery. Angela Merkel has given herself the goal of setting the course, by June, for the ratification of a new treaty. Mention is being made of a slimmer version of the text that may be ratified via a parliamentary vote, thus avoiding the danger of referendums: a new struggle with many obstacles to overcome, including the divisive actions which Washington, despite its difficulties, is showing it does not wish to give up.

Hence, China and Europe: we have written that the essence of the present epoch may be seen in these two entities. Of course the imperialist contention does not only lie in the European-Chinese dynamic. A total version of the contention, which would enable us to grasp its tensions and contradictions, requires a scientific effort to observe the whole spectrum of the great powers, their mutual relationships, the constantly shaken regional balances, and the medium and even small powers in the areas of crisis. However, Cervetto teaches us, there are always sensitive points and crucial questions in the history of imperialism which give meaning to a historical phase of the world contention. Today these crucial questions are precisely China and Europe. It is not for nothing that we have written they are "a challenge for the Marxist theory of the state, for the Marxist science of international relation, and for the Leninist theory of imperialism".

The world-shaking about-turn now underway has inevitable consequences for our revolutionary strategy. First of all, it means a huge increase in the world proletariat. China is emerging because year by year it is transforming millions of peasants into workers. With the development of the modern proletariat in Asia, the development of the class struggle and of the contradictions generated by it is inevitable. The *inflammable substances* of the world revolution therefore increase.

Secondly, China's emergence has forced Europe's bourgeoisie to unify the labour market after it had already unified the goods and capital markets. This means there is now a single European proletariat without any national barriers and without any legal impediments to the free circulation of the workforce, an age-old demand of the workers' movement. This is the contradictory element of the process of European unification: to counter Asia, European imperialism is being forced to unify and concentrate its antagonistic element, the European proletariat. This is an objective advantage for our struggle, to be considered with great attention, in an imperialist contention that is now taking place among great continental powers; a clash in which Europe is and remains one of the most important links in the state system of unitary imperialism.

175 million wage earners, 50 million workers

Here, then, is the key to the consequence for our revolutionary order of the about-turn underway. The shift of the economic centre of gravity to Asia, which is also the shift and disproportion of the class forces, offers, dialectically, a historic opportunity for entrenching the Leninist Party in the European metropolis. If we consider the present EU-27, we find before us a labour market of over 175 million wage earners, to whom a few million unregistered workers should be added. This is a young class, with more than half below the age of forty, and which boasts over 50 million workmen, employees and skilled industrial workers in the strict sense of the term.

It is a proletariat which is not uniformly distributed on the European market, but which is dislocated in a number of big urban and labour-market concentrations. International statistical analyses, circulated in the last few months also in the European press, consider Paris and the Île de France – with over 11 million residents – and the great metropolitan area of Milan – with a total of 7.4 million inhabitants – as the two leading megalopolises in Europe. Milan is considered to be equal to London, while other OECD analyses put the vast Rhine-Ruhr area before Paris and Milan.

This big European labour market with its megalopolises is the necessary point of reference for our unprecedented task of entrenching our party; an unprecedented and arduous task on which the delay accumulated by the generations of Marxism in the development of the revolutionary party continues to weigh. This is a delay we have never been willing to submit to, not even when everything seemed lost beneath the material, political, and even ideal rubble of the Second World War, with Stalinism at the height of its influence over the working class.

The choice of being communists

The first generation of *Lotta Comunista* committed itself to a Herculean counter-current task without letting itself be intimidated by the delay and the enormity of the unprecedented task of the time. Having tied the thread of theory again, commitment to a ceaseless organisational work throughout the generations has enabled the party to develop and, together with it, to bring Marxism back to the masses. This is, at root, the essence of our being communists, a conviction and a life choice which inspire a spirit of conquest which to most people may seem fool-hardly. It is with this spirit that we face today's unprecedented task, fully aware that the impact of a historical delay continues to weigh heavily on it.

In *The Difficult Question of Times* Cervetto wrote: "[...] one can seize the link of the party's historical delay and work concretely to decrease its negative impact. From this point of view, the 'question of times' is translated into the constant work of educating and organising the proletariat, day after day, without impatient waiting for exceptional opportunities" [12].

Iron will and organisation

The past decades have provided compelling evidence of this thesis. Cervetto added: "Organised strength [cannot] be improvised, and requires decades of anonymous, patient, incessant work to be selected, build, trained, and tested".

Throughout the past decades that anonymous, patient, incessant work has selected the organised strength which has enabled the party to overcome its historical delay and face the new epoch now unfolding in a thriving condition. This has set the conditions whereby the decades of the new strategic phase may allow us to seize the historic opportunity to entrench the Leninist Party in the European imperialist metropolis. The sole guarantee lies in a strategic analysis equal to the new times, integrated with a constant, incessant organisational work, bearing well in mind that "there cannot be organised work without an iron will, but there cannot be an iron will without organised work" [13].

Scientific marxism vs. bourgeois illusions and defeatist ideologies

Certainties for a Conscious Struggle*

The storm looming on the horizon of the world markets is bringing "political economy" back to the centre of attention. In 1859, in the foreword to his *Critique of Political Economy*, Karl Marx anticipated some of the conclusions of his labours with his well-known synthesis of our materialist concept, summarising how, in the course of their development, the forces of production inevitably clash with the relations of production: "From forms of development of the productive forces, these relations turn into their fetters. Then begins an epoch of social revolution" [14].

The wars and crises of imperialism

That scientific prediction has come true: to such an extent that the twentieth century, with its appalling devastation of two world wars and of countless partial conflicts, has been characterised as the age of imperialism, but also as the "age of social revolution", opening with the Russian October Revolution of 1917.

Marx would clarify how the growing incompatibility between the forces and the relations of production reveals itself in "contradictions, crises, and violent convulsions" [15]. This is happening during these months. The big banks have been so hard hit by the bursting of the American housing bubble that they have been forced to drastically write down the securities registered in their financial statements. A credit crunch is threatening the global economy and the dynamic of the world cycle. The marked devaluation of the dollar is giving growing cause for concern, and is re-opening the conflict over its international role. It is rumoured that a new structure based on "monetary bipolarism" is being prepared: a sign of the further decline of American power.

Unknowns in the old and new powers

Troubled times are looming for unitary imperialism. The present partial crisis is weighing on power relationships and disturbing their balance. Our newspaper has written: "The real tectonic force generating these imbalances is to be found in Asia. This characterises the crisis, both economically and strategically" [16]. The deflationary effect of years of Asian development has contributed to swelling the American housing bubble, but Asia's "thirst for energy" has raised the price of a barrel of crude to almost 100 dollars.

---

* *Internationalist Bulletin*, February 2008

The capital which is buying up shares in the big western groups comes from China and Asia. Capital exports are the salient feature of imperialist maturity, and we can be sure that Blackstone, Bear Sterns, Barclays, Fortis, Standard Chartered, and UBS are only the first step.

If the old capitals of imperialism are torn between confirmation of the liberist cycle and demand for regulations and protective tariffs, not even the new powers can consider themselves immune to the crisis: the problems of how much a recession in the US would penalise China, of the unknown factors of Asian inflation, and of the new speculative "bubble" swelling in Shanghai. All of this lends a much darker tint to the face of globalisation, until now painted in the colours of placid optimism.

The new strategic phase confirms the irruption of the Asian giants. Europe is reacting to the contraction of its margins of action by strengthening itself politically. The ECB has passed the test of its first great financial storm, coming out of the trial strengthened and more authoritative.

Alongside this, the Treaty of Lisbon is nearing ratification in a process that promises to be smoother than the last. It is a choice that looks towards higher levels of efficiency in the political and institutional instruments with which the EU will have to face the new strategic phase.

A wave of transformism

The political reinforcement of Brussels weighs on the European capitals, and particularly on the confused situation in Rome. EU protections, restrictions, and obligations were all mentioned in the debates on the budget and on welfare. What is also significant is the halt Europe has called to the shabby campaign against Romanian immigrants, the ill-chosen debut of the PD [Democratic Party] secretary.

The long agony of the government in Rome is being exacerbated by a new wave of transformism. The fundamental currents representing the big Italian groups hope that the objective pressure of the EU will push the Italian political system towards two main formations on the European model, which can alternate in power, thus guaranteeing political turnover and stability. This prospect, however, hangs on a number of unknown political factors, and on the countless pitfalls of parliamentary cretinism, beginning with the negotiations for a new electoral law.

The desert of imperialist society

A debate dominated by electoral engineering to gain an extra few tenths of a percentage point is all but incomprehensible to the masses, and not only to them. We are heading for a phase of great turbulence on the world markets, with inevitable repercussions for international relations. All of this will overlap with the convulsions of Italian politics, in a huge media and ideological muddle. In order not to get lost, the compass of Marxist scientific analysis will be more necessary than ever before. The need for clarity, but also for orientation, will increase. Which side to take? Which party to vote for? This will involve each and every worker, but particularly the young.

Bourgeois society, especially in its imperialist maturity, is pervaded by parasitism and by rampant corruption. It is a society corroded by moral decay, and it is natural that it should repel the young who want participation.

Bourgeois politics, *their politics*, labours to express fundamental ideas and values capable of attracting the young. No doubt the young will be again drawn in, at some future point when, in the case of a profound crisis or of mobilisation for war, bourgeois politics will ensnare the masses with the spectres of hatred and fanatism, but today it has very little to offer. At this point, religion steps in, coming to the aid of the ruling classes with its "respect-for-values" ideology. The Church's hold on the younger generations is today is a well-known and clearly observable phenomenon.

A patient task

Marx clearly explains what religion is able to offer: "Religious suffering is, at one and the same time, the expression of real suffering and a protest against real suffering" [17]. It is not only a question of material poverty. In fact, in Marx's opinion, "Religion is the sigh of the oppressed creature", and only in this sense is it the "opium of the people", the palliative for the sufferings of social oppression. Benedict XVI's latest encyclical is indicative of this, right from its very title, *Spe salvi* [Saved By Hope].

Marxists have always confronted the question of religion very seriously, despite their firm opposition, as dialectical materialists and hence atheists, to all religions and to all Churches, which today are inevitably tools of bourgeois reaction. In an article of 1909, Lenin returned to the question, recalling Engel's repeated condemnation of those who wished to insert atheism – as a declaration of war on religion – in the programme of the workers' party, observing, among other things, how this was the way to "revive interest in religion and to prevent it from really dying out" [18].

The workers' party must "have the ability to work patiently at the task of organising and educating the proletariat". Lenin underlined the necessity of getting to the root of religious feeling, which is not to be found in the "ignorance of the people", as "the bourgeois progressive, the radical, and the bourgeois materialist" maintain. Its roots are social, buried deep "in the social oppression of the masses [...] and in their impotence in the face of the blind forces of capitalism". In the patient work of the party it is against those roots that our energies are concentrated – in developing the class struggle which "in the conditions of modern capitalist society will convert Christian workers to social democracy and to atheism a hundred times better than bald atheist propaganda".

A cliché of bourgeois ideology

In his encyclical, Joseph Ratzinger criticises both the Enlightenment and Marxism, though he appears to think quite highly of the latter. However, his basic thesis on scientific materialism is frankly disappointing, in that it indulges in many groundless clichés of anti-Marxist ideology. Marx is seen as committed to progress towards "a definitely good world" that can be realised by scientifically conceived politics capable of showing the way towards revolution. However, the success of the revolution underlined Marx's basic mistake: he did not indicate how to proceed to the building of the "New Jerusalem". This is why, without these signposts, Lenin's dictatorship of the proletariat ended in failure.

To reduce Marxism to the prophecy of a "New Jerusalem" is a groundless attempt which attributes to scientific communism the mere aspirations of "utopian socialism". Criticism should be directed, if at all, against those Catholic currents of thought which theorise "liberation theology". It is they who, in their "Third Worldism", are the true heirs of the illusions and economic romanticism of those utopias. In *The German Ideology*, Marx and Engels recall that "Communism is not a state of affairs, an ideal to which reality will have to adjust itself" [19].

According to the reasoning of the encyclical, Marx's mistake derives from his materialism, from seeing human beings as the product of economic conditions alone; but this is an astonishing simplification. A letter of 1890 from Friedrich Engels to Joseph Block deals precisely with this mechanistic distortion. Dialectical materialism has never stated "that the economic factor is the only determining factor" [20], Engels averred, listing the plurality of factors influencing the economic basis.

1917 and the war

In conclusion, the encyclical contains an unacceptable statement: that the "intermediate phase" of the dictatorship of the proletariat in Russia left "a desolate waste" behind it. It is no coincidence that this judgement coincides with that of an exponent of lay thought, Eugenio Scalfari, who, in his critique of the encyclical, states that the "earthly paradise" championed by Marxism led to the "unspeakable horrors" of Stalinism. This is not just a question of deliberately ignoring the difference between Stalin's counter-revolution and Lenin's Bolsheviks, themselves victims of Stalinism. There is also a crucial omission: no mention is made of the fact that the October Revolution originated in the carnage of the First World War, with its price of million of lives.

The great European powers prepared for that catastrophe by mobilising all the political currents of the bourgeoisie, from nationalism to the interventionism of the intellectuals, including, in Italy, many renowned fathers of lay thought. Only revolutionary Marxism opposed the conflict, first breaking with the leaders of the Second International who had voted for war loans, and then, with the October Revolution, imposing peace on the eastern front. We Marxists do not forget that the German Catholics of the Zentrum voted for war loans in the Reichstag, together with the followers of the renegade Kautsky, nor can we forget the support of the French Catholics for the *Union Sacrée* in that August of 1914. It was they who began the conflict, and it was we internationalists who ended it, at the point at which the strength of a conscious organisation could offer an alternative to the proletariat sent to rot and die in the trenches.

The relevance of Marxism

In the encyclical, concern is expressed about the fact that Karl Marx's work, "thanks to the acuteness of its analysis and to its clear indication of the tools of radical change, has fascinated and continues to fascinate". This is true: Marxism still fascinates because it is capable of offering much more than a hope in future redemption. Marxism is able to offer scientific certainties about the future of society and mankind, certainties that allow us to live in the present as conscious fighters in the class struggle, a struggle we wage with heads held high for a cause involving the whole of humanity.

Our leninist battle in the crisis of global relations

An Opportunity for Revolutionary Clarity*

The capitals and institutions of unitary imperialism are being hard pressed by the crisis that is shaking both world markets and world relations. But for our class, the crisis brings us back to the vitality of Marxism.

Insoluble contradictions

With scientific perseverance, our school of thought has continued to underline that our society "has entangled itself in an insoluble contradiction; it has split into irreconcilable antagonisms that it is powerless to eliminate" [21]: a contradiction between production, which is increasingly accentuating its social nature, and appropriation, which remains private. This is reflected in market anarchy, which generates crises of varying intensity, during which huge productive forces are destroyed.

The credit sector was the first to be hit by the present crisis. Mind-boggling figures are doing the rounds. For America's *subprime* mortgage – backed securities alone – the easy credit that swelled the housing bubble – estimates range from 400 to 700 billion dollars. At the end of January, Merrill Lynch had written off 24.5 billion, Citigroup 19.9, UBS 14.4, Morgan Stanley 9.4, Bank of China an estimated 8 billion, and so on. These losses are being continually updated, with the biggest world credit giants at the top of the list. These groups have at their disposal hundreds of analysts, first-rate financial consultants, all the living Nobel prize-winners in economy, and professors from the best universities. These big banks have state-of-the-art data processing systems and some of the most sophisticated calculation programs. Yet all of them, without exception, fell victim to the present crisis; all those high-powered instruments of knowledge proved to be powerless.

Lenin and crises

The same was true of the central banks and of the various market regulators: what better example of their impotence in the face of the insoluble contradictions of capitalism? Obviously, the world has obviously changed since the days of Marx; Lenin himself had to study the birth of the imperialist phase of capitalism. Today, imperialist society itself is constantly spawning new developments: one needs only to think of the role of the central banks. But our Marxist school has not only discovered the laws of

* *Internationalist Bulletin*, April 2008

movements of capitalist society: it has also put at our disposal the tools with which to study its continual transformation.

Who on the *board* of Merrill Lynch or of Citigroup could object to what Lenin wrote exactly one century ago? "Reality soon showed the revisionists that crises have not had their day: prosperity was followed by crisis. The forms, the order and the physiognomy of the single crises have changed, but crises continue to be an integral part of the capitalist regime" [22]. Arrigo Cervetto commented on this highly topical observation of 1908: "Lenin says that the forms, the physiognomy and the order of the single crises change. Science is what is capable of analysing this social process and its historical rhythms" [23].

Liberism and statism

The rest is part of the smokescreen of ideologies. For years, they have even shamelessly celebrated the splendours of the free market and of globalisation. In these last few months we have witnessed the massive interventions of the central banks in the markets; in the best tradition of state interventionism, the Bush administration has launched a plan for fiscal stimulus to the tune of over 160 billion dollars.

Western banks are opening up their capital to Asian or Middle Eastern sovereign funds. Both in the City and in Germany, we have witnessed de facto state rescue of struggling banks. This is anything but free competition - letting the markets regulate themselves and so on. Our old school has long known that liberism and statism are the two guises of capitalism. As we have already said, one for sunny days, and the other for when cold winds start to blow, as in these last few weeks.

In the course of the crisis, the attitude of the American Central Bank differed from that of the ECB. Mr Trichet, who is also more than willing to inject liquidity into the markets, has, however, steadfastly refused to reduce the cost of money by cutting interest rates. His argument is that economic conditions in Europe are different from those on the other shore of the Atlantic.

The forces of Asia

The ECB has even threatened to raise interest rates should there be signs of a wage-price spiral in the EU. This is a declaration of war on any pay rises not welded to productivity. In fact, the strong inflationary pressure is mostly generated by increases in the prices of raw materials, especially of food and petroleum products: an increase caused, above all, by growing Asian demand, fuelled continually by the extraordinary growth rates of China, India and Asia. We have previously written that the real "tectonic force" generating the present imbalances is to be found in Asia, and that this "characterises the crisis, both economically and strategically" [24]. In this sense, the present crisis is also "the sign of American decline and of Asian irruption". The symbol of this situation is undoubtedly China, the imperialist power of this century.

Half a century of scientific investigation

We have been following the development of Chinese state capitalism since the 1950s, well before European intellectuals became infatuated with Mao Zedong, and without falling into their childish self-illusions: it was young capitalism that was growing in China, and certainly not an impossible national socialism. We have studied the great imperialist leap that, in fifteen years, has allowed China to become the second manufacturing exporter in the world, filling its coffers with dollar currency reserves.

We are not surprised by this phenomenon: we carefully study its accelerated pace. For half a century, the world roles of China and India – together with the prediction of a long cycle of capitalist expansion on the world market, and on the Asian in particular – have been written in our "strategic constitution" that of the *Theses on Imperialist Development* [25], formulated in 1957.

Over the years, we have fought our internationalist battle on the basis of that formulation, and those "Theses" have made possible our development and the renewed dimensions of our entrenchment. Undoubtedly, today we are fewer than we would like to be, and especially fewer than we would need to be, and the international dimensions of the present crisis are a harsh reminder of this. But the presence of our internationalist stance, its growing influence and increasingly solid roots, also point to the concrete possibilities of continuing the process of entrenching our party in the European labour market. The present crisis offers us further possibilities of and opportunities for growth, provided that we succeed in grasping the deeper meaning and the perspective of events, including Italy's umpteenth political crisis.

The new strategic phase

In the last decades, the trends outlined in that far-off 1957 have unfolded. Capitalist development in Asia has proceeded, and from those then backward markets, China, with its continental dimensions and its monumental demographic power, is emerging today as an imperialist power, a force that can aim to condition access to its own market, and that can insist on a new world division more in keeping with its weight. A new strategic phase is about to begin.

The present crisis has seen the emergence of sovereign funds, Middle Eastern and Asian state investment funds, with China in the lead. These funds, which, just two years ago, were rejected by the American government, have acquired substantial shares in Western banking groups. A swift process, favoured by the crisis, investing, by our calculations, 40 billion dollars in 40 days. The *Financial Times* reports that 93% of these investments come from China, Singapore, Dubai, Abu Dhabi and Kuwait. In this way, substantial shares of Morgan Stanley, Citigroup, Merrill Lynch, UBS, etc. have ended up in the hands of these sovereign funds. Today, struggling banking groups, perhaps on the brink of bankruptcy, welcome the export of capital from imperialist China. Both in India and in Russia, there are those who point to China as their model in this field.

But this reserve flow of capital, from East to West, is beginning to cause concern. Some analysts are demanding transparency, while others are calling for joint regulations in the US and the EU: a Euro-Atlantic defensive move that is not quite protectionism. The markets are still open, but it is clear that many are reconsidering the issue. It is also in this sense that China's irruption is now forcing Europe and America, the old imperialist powers, to take up a defensive position.

A political battle

We have written that our analytical difficulties arise from the fact that we are in a kind of "grey area" in which the previous cycle has not yet completely exhausted itself. The Asian markets offer Western capital ample space for investment, but China today, and India tomorrow, are gradually restricting this possibility. China, above all, may begin to impose conditions. Thus, the present crisis is turning into a crisis of a new strategic phase which is beating out the rhythms of Asian rise and Atlantic decline, "the first battle in another war, in which Europe and America face emerging China" [26].

A partial crisis, certainly, but one which reveals the profound contradictions of unitary imperialism. With both a strategic analysis equal to the task, and renewed dedication, our Leninist battle may be furthered by it.

Our leninist battle in the crisis of global relations - II
The Moment of Conscious Commitment*

The rise of Asia and the decline of the Atlantic beat out the rhythms of the crisis in global relations. Our paper is no newcomer to America's decline; immediately after the Second World War we witnessed the re-emergence of the defeated powers, Japan and Germany, though the latter was divided. That process inevitably reduced the weight of American imperialism on world production; and that phase of uneven development also gave rise to a partial contradiction: the restructuring crisis of the mid-1970s.

In the subsequent quarter-century, with the irruption of the Chinese giant, a phenomenon of totally unprecedented dimensions, Asian development has once again underlined American decline.

The USA and Europe face to face with China

This is the essence of the strategic issues Washington's future administration will have to face, but the problem of decline also concerns the other shore of the Atlantic. Europe, too, is hard-pressed by the emergence of China, and by Asian development, and is reacting with the tools of its imperialist power. The monetary power of the ECB, the European Central Bank, represents the real federal dimension of the Union. During the crisis, this has made the euro a concrete alternative to the dollar, to such a point that a phase of "monetary bipolarism" between the two currencies has even been suggested.

The strength of Europe is also reinforced by a single labour market considerably enlarged to the East: an area whose industrial tradition and cheap labour force have allowed continental restructuring to expand. In the motor vehicle sector, if Turkey is included, delocalisations and new plants have shifted up to one-fifth of Europe's production to the "Eastern Detroits". But the ECB, the euro and the continental market are not enough. European imperialism needs political tools for its power struggle: these are the stakes in the current ratification of the Lisbon Treaty.

In Italy, the crisis in global relations overlaps a political crisis. This can be understood only in a European scenario, where Rome's crucial choices are subject to the guardianship of the ECB and of the Brussels Commission. This is what allows Roman politics to present its umpteenth electoral show without paying too high a price.

---

* *Internationalist Bulletin*, May 2008

Global crisis, Italian swings

Clearly, the repercussions of the American recession will reverberate in Italy too. The forecasts for 2008 and 2009 place it bottom of the EU, with near-zero growth rates. If these forecasts are confirmed, problems for the most vulnerable production sectors are inevitable. But the fall of the Prodi government is not directly linked with these processes: it is the result of old and new internal imbalances. This most recent failure of the centre-left also marks the end of a political cycle – the final defeat of a coalition formed in the early 1990s.

The end of a cycle

We may add that this also represents the failure of a political generation: that of the so-called PCI [Italian Communist Party] "colonels" who, twenty years ago, ousted Alessandro Natta as Secretary of the party and led the "great renunciation", resulting in the dissolution of the PCI in 1991. A political generation that would play the leading role in the final attack on Craxism and that after disposing of the new party Secretary, Achille Occhetto, would come to power along with the Prodi government of 1996.

Ten years later, the second chance for Mr Prodi and the left wing against Mr Berlusconi has lasted less than twenty months: a heavy defeat. During these weeks of the carnival of parliamentary cretinism, an interesting aspect has emerged: the debate on the need for a bipartisan agreement, grand coalition style or not, between Messrs Veltroni and Berlusconi over a number of reforms. The Italian system has to adapt itself to the times of European politics by tackling its imbalances. To this end, the repeated interventions of such a *grand commis* of European imperialism as Mario Monti are significant. According to many sources, an agreement between the two main political alignments is already in the making, and is motivating the electoral choices of the two major parties, aided and abetted by the winds of US recession that are swelling the sails of national unity at the workers' expense.

The end of illusion

A cold wind is blowing in centre-left circles: the failure of the Prodi government weighs heavily, the campaign of the Italian Episcopal Conference on respect of moral values is an exacerbation, and the prospect of a post-election agreement with Mr Berlusconi is turning into a nightmare. Those who had deluded themselves or had hoped that there would be an end to Berlusconism find themselves faced with harsh reality, and with a disturbing outlook for the future.

In the course of our battle over spheres of influence, we must reflect on this political psychology. It is not a question of trying to work on a disillusioned and at times desperate Left. At issue is our own sphere of influence and our internationalist position within the working class, where some of these hopes and illusions circulated. It is inevitable that some of that youth, those workers, these pensioners, should look to us today with renewed and increasing interest. We represent the only real, the only concrete alternative to the impotence of opportunism, and to the profound crisis of parliamentary government.

The practical sense of our strategic battle

We have already had occasion to underline how, within our concept, every theory has always a practical sense. Strategic analysis, the analysis of the crisis in global relations, dictates the times and the forms of our political struggle, and of our internationalist battle in the unfolding of the Italian political crisis. We are an inevitable part of the European proletariat, and we are its conscious part, aware of the nature, times and possible repercussions of the current crisis. This lays great responsibilities upon us, but it also offers us considerable possibilities, which imperialism's difficult moments always offer the conscious minority of the real movement. We are able to carry on our struggle in the most highly concentrated industrial area of Europe: here are the manifest contradictions of the stock exchange, the major banks, the euro, inflation, and the wages issue.

We do not expect great social reaction in the heart of European imperialism: that is not the point. But what needs to be very carefully considered is that in this part of the European market, today far more than yesterday, our internationalist position has a sphere of influence, an organised sphere, which acts as a link between the party and the vast strata of wage earners. It is the result of decades of battles, and on it we can work intensively.

The 1970s crisis

In our recent history, we have already found ourselves working during the course of a serious enough international crisis. In the middle of the 1970s, a restructuring crisis shook unitary imperialism – a crisis that debilitated the working class, but benefited its party. Those decades of restructuring delayed the advent of wage stratification, the phenomenon of the corruption of our class, and the diffusion of the ideologies of imperialist affluence. In this sense, they offered additional time for our unprecedented attempt: time put to good use in the entrenchment and development of our party during subsequent years.

We faced that crisis with few forces, with a very small sphere of influence, and a core of activists with only a few years of political experience. It was in those years that the PCI and the DC [Christian Democrats] were at the height of their influence over our class.

A greater responsibility

Today, we face the present crisis with an entrenchment of unparalleled dimensions, with a much wider and more solid sphere of influence, and with accumulated experience. The Democratic Party, and Mr Berlusconi's PDL [People of Freedom Party] are parties in the making, or in a phase of transformation. But they are also the debris of the failure of the First Republic's political formats. Finally, there is the irruption of the Chinese giant into the world balance, a completely new fact in terms of dimensions and power. In this crisis too, sections of our class will inevitably pay a price: just how high remains to be seen. But today, as in the past, the crisis may benefit our Leninist party. It is no longer a question of fighting for time against the phenomenon of the corruption of our class, which has proceeded by leaps and bounds in the last few decades. These objective difficulties have not prevented our entrenchment, nor have they pushed our party to the margins of society. And this is not all: our communist battle has shown, even recently, that it is capable of successfully attracting all wage stratifications.

Today, we must consider the unprecedented dimensions and the specific nature gained by our sphere of influence in these last few decades: a sphere of influence made up of concentric circles of workers who gradually come to have a closer link with our party. The boundaries of these circles are not clear-cut, and the passage from one circle to the next does not occur gradually, but by leaps. There are struggles, contradictions, defeats, and even disappointments that have to be analysed, and that cause individuals to move their position. They can draw them closer to the party or alienate them, as has often happened: one need only think of the difficult years after 1905.

Strategic abstentionism and conscious political commitment

The present crisis can benefit our party by helping our supporters to make a leap forward in their relations with our international battle. There are hundreds of individuals willing to work for our cause: we have to know how organise them. For many of them, in the present crisis, our abstentionism can become a moment of concrete refusal of passive delegation; it can become the choice of a conscious commitment to a concrete class policy: a commitment perhaps made up of very small, simple actions, but of actions indispensable to the communist cause.

Opportunism, Leninism and the 'Northern question'

A Battle of Strategy and Organisation*

The present time will go down in the history of imperialism as that of the crisis in world relations, a crisis that for the past nine months has strongly affected the international scene. This international crisis intertwines with – and influences – both the continental and the national dynamic in Italy. The defeat of opportunism – currently in the shape of the Democratic party – has once again been marked by the "northern question".

The issue is the recurring difficulty that opportunism, in its various forms, experiences in electorally representing the requirements of northern Italy: a key area, with the highest level of industrialisation, an efficient financial network, and a wholly "modern" social stratification as well as an area that is an integral – and important – part of the European Union's industrial core. It is here that the centre-left has proved incapable of winning over voters, an incapacity that has been the subject of fruitless debate for fifteen years.

A long-standing weakness

In fact, this issue has formed part of the Italian electoral dynamic for decades. In the north, the Stalinist Communist Party of Italy (PCI) has always run into difficulties in any confrontation with the Christian Democrat Party (DC). In the 1963 elections, after restructuring and in the middle of the economic boom, the PCI polled 19.9% of valid votes in the north, as against 38% in central Italy, and 24.4% in the centre-south. Despite a number of enclaves in the industrial north, the PCI's problems were evident in Veneto (15% of votes), Friuli (17.3%), and Lombardy (20.1%). The situation was better in Piedmont (23.2%), while Liguria stood out with its 28.4%, still a long way from the Tuscan-Emilian peaks of 38.5% and 40.7%. At that time, the PCI was Italy's 'Russian party', polling 25.3% of the votes in a country with a 90% turnout of voters. Five years later, in 1968, with a growing overall electorate, the PCI polled 27% of valid votes, confirming its weak points in the north.

It was the cycle of workers' struggles at the end of the 1960s, and not the "primacy of politics", that was to stir up those somewhat static electoral pools. Indirectly, these struggles triggered the tendency towards the two-party system (DC-PCI) that was first sanctioned in the regional elections of June 1975. With the decline of trade unionism, the recovery of the inter-class parties was "almost automatic". In July of that year, Arrigo Cervetto wrote: "In a few years, the defeat of the divided and fragmented

* *Internationalist Bulletin*, August 2008

DC trade-union wing by that of the PCI has been clearly evident. Being back in the driving seat favoured the PCI in the elections" [27]: This was a voting shift from the DC to the PCI that we estimated as "made up of about half blue-collar votes, about one third white-collar, and about one sixth petty-bourgeois" – an upheaval of about one tenth of the voters, with the north as the epicentre of the shift among blue-collar workers.

At the time, the effect of a wave of workers' struggles began to resolve the northern Italy issue, and the PCI polled 33.5% of the votes. As we shall see, this was a transient phenomenon. The 1976 election confirmed the two-party-system trend, with the PCI reaching its historic peak at 34.49%.

Electoral rise and fall

But within that vote, a counter trend was already underway. In July 1976, Sergio Motosi *La marcia verso il bipartismo in Italia* [28] [The march towards the Two-Party-System in Italy] underlined that, if in 1975 the new votes for the PCI came from the north, in 1976 60% of them came from the south: "In essence, the PCI is at a standstill in the north". After analysing the votes of the industrial zones, Motosi wrote that "in essence, in 1976, the flow of industrial workers' votes to the PCI dried up, and the DC also clawed back the industrial workers' vote from the smaller parties". His assessment was correct: the electoral decline of the PCI can be dated from that very moment. A parenthesis: after changing its name three or four times, after an alliance with part of the Christian Democrats, and over thirty years later, Walter Veltroni's Democratic Party (PD) failed to reach that 34.4% of the pro-Russia PCI led by the rather grey figure of Enrico Berlinguer.

The PCI's downward trend began in 1976, and ten years later, in 1987, it polled only 26.6% of the votes, the same percentage as in the early 1960s. In 1992, after the fall of Berlin Wall and of the Soviet Union's false socialism, after the PCI's abjuration and under a new name, the PDS [Democrats of the Left] stuck at 16.1%, with Lombardy at 12% and Veneto at 10%. From the mid-1970s to the end of the 1980s, Italy was shaken by a profound restructuring process resulting from the international crisis of that time. The PCI faced that process at the height of its strength and at a voting advantage due to the previous cycle of workers' struggles.

The question of the "bourgeois workers' party"

But that cycle of struggles also brought with it a poisoned chalice for the PCI. A generation of petty-bourgeois intellectuals, spawned by the students' movements of that time, flowed into the PCI, forming a political personnel that gathered increasing weight in the party leadership, giving birth to a kind of mutation.

Since we were forced to deal with dreams and delirium, our strategic analysis duly picked up that trend - that mutation. In March 1975, Cervetto presented a paper on the restructuring crisis of world imperialism, its aspects in Italy, and its possible consequences for the Leninist party – the political translation of a strategic elaboration. In fact, in the conclusion, Cervetto presented a detailed analysis, breaking it down into sections dealing with the PCI, recruitment to the FGCI [Italian Communist Youth Federations], the party leaders, and the changes taking place in this opportunistic party.

What emerged was an inter-class PCI that, with blue-collar workers accounting for 47.2% of its members, accurately reflected their weight in the population: 47.8% at that time. White-collar workers, at 5.2% of party membership, compared with the 17% of their social weight, were under-represented. This was also true, but to a lesser extent, of the petty bourgeoisie, accounting for 15% of PCI members, as against 29.4% of the population. In the recruitment analysis, there emerged an FGCI that, after the damage caused by 1968, had not yet returned to the recruitment levels of the early 1960s. Moreover, for a number of years influx had stagnated, revealing difficulties in recruiting young workers: hence, the youth section was becoming a student organisation, a poor training ground for worker cadres. For us this was an important development to note, not from the point of view of exalting the working class per se, which has never affected our thinking, but because "the levels of the danger of opportunism in a party can be gauged by opportunism's grip on the working class".

Intellectuals and state capital

An important part of Lenin's analysis regards, precisely, the question of how opportunism takes root in the workers' movement – the classic issue of the "bourgeois workers' party".

Cervetto's analysis of the PCI leadership clearly showed the trend within the party. Intellectuals accounted for 3% of the party members, but for 25.5% of the federal committees, 29.5% of the executive committees, and 30% of the secretariats: a clear, controversial tendency within the PCI which we noted as an element of the party's weakness and of relative advantage for our revolutionary minority. The party's intellectual component continued to gain in importance, and directed the PCI as it rode the rough waves of restructuring.

Towards the end of the 1980s and now published in the book *Forze e forme del mutamento italiano* [The Forces and Forms of the Italian Transformation], Cervetto drew up a first balance sheet of Italian restructuring, which was having "both a profound and an extensive [effect] on the body of society". He estimated that about 30% of the population changed their jobs. But he singled out the main element of the process as the "reduction in the overall weight of state capital" [29].

Three superstructural phenomena sprang from that structural element. A Christian Democrat Party, expressing Catholic liberism, had adapted itself to reducing the role of the state. The PCI on the contrary, was finding it difficult to adapt to the process: for the party of opportunism, state capitalism was one of the mainstays of its beliefs, representing as it did alleged real socialism. The third phenomenon to emerge from restructuring, Craxism, not so closely linked to state capitalism, and therefore more "unscrupulous and adaptable", was a potential threat to the PCI. In fact, there were many who, at that time, expected the PSI [Italian Socialist Party] to overtake the PCI.

The 1989 catastrophe

In the same book, in October 1988, Cervetto expressed his opinion on the PCI crisis: "The crisis of the PCI has deepened, reflecting the relative weakening of two of its economic and ideological cornerstones: the co-operation of Emilia-Romagna, and state capitalism. At the same time, the social effects of restructuring have led to a greater deterioration in the organisational apparatus of the opportunist party – its number swollen by petulant and decadent intellectuals – and have frayed its traditional trade-union drive belt" [30]. A year later, the Russian empire imploded, and the party's Moscow headquarters closed down. The PCI was cast off like an old coat, and the PDS set off on its uncertain voyage.

The "clean hands" cyclone swept away the DC and the PSI, but by no means settled the northern question. Walter Veltroni's PD will have no choice but to tackle this issue again.

A Bolshevik model in Europe's industrial heartland

To conclude: all this is cause for reflection. Opportunism is struggling in northern Italy, in a strategic area for European imperialism, an area of the greatest development and entrenchment of our Leninist and internationalist stance. This only apparently contradictory phenomenon is no casual achievement. It is the result of a choice imposed by the dislocation of the class forces. But it is also the product of our concept of the science-party, of the strategy party. At the same time, our party model is the result of a long struggle against opportunism, fought precisely where its class roots were deepest: in Genoa, capital of state capitalism, with its high concentration of skilled workers in state-controlled factories, and with the transport capital of its port, then also state-controlled.

Our struggle has always been fought in the strategic awareness that we needed to go beyond this, entrenching the party in Italy's industrial triangle, in the Milanese megalopolis, and then within the concentrations of the European labour market. After that trial run, our Bolshevik model has proved to be a tool capable of leaving its mark on the large metropolitan areas of northern Italy – and not there alone. Hundreds of young people, including students and intellectuals, have placed themselves at the service of the working class, in a militancy that is necessarily expressed in the hard work of organisation among the masses.

In these years of hard work, the influence of our Leninist stance has spread. It is now possible to pose ourselves the problem of further increasing this influence. We know that there are hundreds of people willing to work for our communist cause; it is our responsibility to organise them. In this way it will be possible to turn our eyes towards the European metropolis, in the full awareness of the still heavy weight of the party's historical delay. It is undoubtedly an unprecedented task, but we do not lack science, organisation and the strength of our class.

The crisis and the revolutionary party

A Theoretical, Political, Orientational and Organisational Battle*

The crisis continues to rock the metropolises of unitary imperialism. We have followed its development with particular attention, and with the aim of setting the co-ordinates of our strategic Leninist battle among the masses, shaken and hard hit by the crisis. Our party had never found itself fighting in such a violent storm. The reaction to its effects reveals concrete possibilities of making contact, as well as considerable possibilities of development, and therefore of an at least partial catching up on our decades-long historical delay. Crises always represent an abrupt rupture with the previous balances, with consequent major repercussions on the dominant ideologies.

In the confusion created by these moments of rupture, our Marxist science can unleash all its power, and our school can offer guidelines that do not regard only the revolutionary minority, but also the conditions of millions of people.

The tendency towards state capitalism

After the catastrophic collapse of the investment banks, the crisis had hit industrial production hard: the prospects for 2009 are worsening and, according to current estimates, most pundits expect a recovery only in 2010. We know very well how "political" the figures in forecast are, but there is one sure fact from which to start: the crisis has not yet touched rock-bottom, since the financial system is far from being stabilised. And this despite substantial state intervention.

A renewed tendency towards state capitalism is under way, particularly marked in America and the UK, the areas hardest hit by the crisis of the financial institutions. It will not be long before the ideological repercussions of this tendency era felt. It is easy to imagine that the regulatory role of the state will somehow come back into vogue, since the ideologies of the self-regulating capacity of the market have failed miserably. Old ideas in new forms: our Marxist school has a well-furnished theoretical arsenal of these.

Let us not forget that the tendency towards state capitalism comes at the price of heavy government borrowing. This new dimension of debt will soon weigh in the world contention: fears of future inflationary tensions and repercussions on currencies are already circulating.

---

* *Internationalist Bulletin*, March 2009

A second consequence is the big restructuring processes that will involve the international groups. We have dealt with these exhaustively in these pages, and these battles will keep us busy in the near future.

A third, more immediate, effect of the crisis is the one that is hitting the labour market today, with particular virulence in the manufacturing sector. Employment is falling everywhere, social security cushions are being put into operation and, for various sectors, dismissal procedures. The wage stratifications are being variously hit. The army of illegal workers with its numerous immigrants has been decimated; after them, the hardest hit are workers with atypical, temporary, etc. contracts. These are the first to be left at home [for example in Italy] without any social security whatsoever. Then the employees of small factories. And, after them again, the workers, clerical employees and technicians of the big factories, where redundancy pay covers roughly half the normal wage. And then, finally, the big public service sector, whose jobs are perfectly safe.

The crisis is therefore affecting the wage-earning stratifications in different ways, with objectively divisive effects that make our already difficult defensive struggles even more complex. Starting with the big industrial concentrations, we are deployed in the front line of these struggles, with the aim of extending guaranteed wages to everyone and, at the same time, of defending salary levels: a difficult struggle in the wage field that requires ceaseless effort in order to act accordingly in the political field.

The multipolar clash among the powers

The crisis is heavily affecting the balances among the powers. The very measures for tackling restructuring and unemployment are tools in a growing multipolar clash: an internationalist response becomes absolutely vital. The current crisis is not the first international crisis we have come across. The restructuring crisis of the mid-1970s had similar motivations to those of the current crisis. At that time, it was the defeated powers in the Second World War that were pressing on the "old order". Today, it is a continental giant like China, on a world market changed by over 30 years of strong development, that is pressing on the "old order". This is why we have written that today's upheaval has a "multiplied seismic intensity" [31] with respect to that of the 1970s.

Our battle in the 1970s' restructuring crisis is a frame of reference for our choices of today that should not be taken for granted, because we must not forget that two new Leninist generations that did not live through that crisis or that battle are now fully engaged in the field. For the young generations who breathe new life into our workers' circles [Marxist Study Centre's], the current crisis is important above all on the education front, and its magnitude, much greater than the crisis of thirty years ago, allows them to acquire considerable knowledge and experience in a relatively concentrated time. It is above all in this sense that we see fertile times ahead for our class organisation: Commenting on Lenin about the effect of war and crises, Arrigo Cervetto observed: "Sometimes, we have not reflected enough on the fact that the same events that bring down and numb the minds of certain political currents strengthen and educate others. This is a lesson of the materialist concept of politics"[32].

Our response to the restructuring crisis is defined in this newspaper in *Il compito generale* [Our General Task] of September 1975. How were we to respond to that critical juncture? How were we to tackle the complications of the crisis? With our "organisational plan and systematic work as the guarantee and necessary condition that allow us to face critical junctures, social explosions and political complications"[33].

Assimilating the theory

This similarity with the 1970s makes sense if we take into account "the multiplied seismic intensity" of the current crisis, and if we consider how much has changed at a subjective level. What we must bear well in mind is our current, unprecedented, organisation development, i.e. our development during the intervening years, the growing dimensions of our work, and a spreading of our influence.

The development of the last thirty years – and history will judge whether it has been sufficient – has meant a precious accumulation of experience, and a process of assimilation and education of a new generation now being put to the test: a development that is also the verification of the analysis and choices of the 1970s. In 1986, as he considered the questions of training and rooting in theory, Cervetto wrote: "There are cycles of theoretical assimilation with twenty-and thirty-year deadlines, cycles that can be faced thanks to our accumulated Marxist patrimony. Our commitment to analysis forges ahead thanks to this patrimony"[34]. This has also been the case with our analysis of the 1970s' restructuring and our elaboration of today's crisis in global relations. The development of these years and the new dimensions of our revolutionary activity must be examined with attention at the very moment in which the crisis is accelerating, highlighting considerable possibilities and fresh, important prospects for the development of our party: above all, the development of our Marxist science and of our strategic analysis. We have been educated in the knowledge that we cannot live on our name in this field: "There are no shortcuts along the main road of the historical emancipation of the proletariat, and hence of humanity. To think that the hard curves of science, of scientific assimilation and scientific struggle can be cut means going straight on to crash into the wall of maximalism, verbalism and nihilism"[35]. This is a lesson that we have learnt and that we endeavour to apply with rigour and continuity: the demonstration of this lies in the facts, and, to date, this is an encouragement.

The ideological crisis

In the second place, the development of the party means a continuous relationship between the masses and the science-party. Marxism is a science for revolutionary action; without action in the class struggle it ceases to live, it becomes barren, withers away and dies. The relationship between the masses and the science-party is, essentially, struggle: struggle to influence the working class, to win over growing numbers of workers to internationalist positions, and to organise this sphere of influence, a real interconnecting circle between the party and the masses. Fighting against the ideas of the ruling among the masses is a ceaseless struggle, a battle that we have fought over the decades and that has made sure that internationalist sphere of influence of sizeable dimensions is present in today's crisis. This is a qualitative difference with respect to the 1970s that should be taken into account in assessing our prospects.

In these weeks, the crisis, involving industry, is draining the strength of the wage-earning strata as it increasingly puts jobs and wage levels at risk. Inexorably, fear, fear for the future, a real psychology of uncertainty with material bases, is spreading. The collapse of the ideologies of globalisation, with all their illusions about continuous progress, growing affluence, and ever more widespread homeownership corresponds to this. In these conditions, the search for a sure handhold in the midst of the storm becomes a necessity for many. Opportunism and Left, shaken by their difficulties, are not able to offer one of even a maximalist kind.

All of this makes the propaganda of our science-party more effective. Our daily militancy among the masses undoubtedly spreads our Marxist science, but at the same time it also conveys certainties, stability, pride, and even a sense of reaction: a reaction to the crisis which is possible through our internationalist battle. This, then, is why the crisis is arousing growing attention and greater preference for our science-party.

The Bolshevik model

The current trend is destined to last longer than the crisis itself. It requires both greater engagement in our organisational work and, therefore, cadres equal to the times and to the new tasks. The process of training these cadres in the third essential aspects of our party's development. We have fought a historic battle to establish the Bolshevik model of cadre party within the Italian worker's movement. In August 1902, Lenin answered the letter of an anonymous correspondent; the subject is clearly the recently published *What is to Be Done?* "You write that I haven't indicate how a rigidly centralised revolutionary organisation can come into touch with the mass of workers"[36]. Lenin points out to his correspondent that he has fallen into contradiction and misunderstanding, and goes on to say: "From the small group of professional revolutionary (centre), a nucleus of a highly centralised and limited nature, to the 'organisation' of the memberless masses there is a whole series of links". And he dwells on the intermediate links: "I stress (yes, stress) the need for those intermediaries who [...] obviously stand between the organisation of the revolutionaries and the 'organisation' of the masses". This is our party model: the organisation of the revolutionaries, wholly devoted to the cause, with deep social roots in the factories and working-class districts thought thousands of sympathisers and supporters". A sphere of influence that can act as a link with the mass of readers, subscribers and admirers, with the "organisation" of the "memberless" masses. And, as Lenin observed, as its mass nature grows, so must the organisation become less rigid.

A new generation

In the course of decades-long battle we have given concrete life to this Bolshevik model. It is obvious that the engine of this series of circles is the restricted nucleus ["centre"] of revolutionaries, a "centralised and limited" group of militants, always ready to contribute to resolving the problems posed to the party by the class struggle.

These are the cadres of our party, engaged in all the activity the struggle requires, but mainly engaged in the organisational work. At the height of the crisis, at the very moment when our influence is growing, revealing important prospects for development, it is necessary to reflect once again on the need to further increase our process of cadre-training. The history of the revolutionary movement teaches us that a very large part of the energy required has always come from the younger generations. This was markedly so for the Bolshevik Party, hand has been so for our party. The storm of the crisis can allow our systematic work among the young, whether workers or students, to considerably increase the ranks of "internationalist youth": from there can come our new cadres, essential to managing, directing and controlling a new phase of development and entrenchment.

Cervetto observes in *The Political Shell* that the proletariat is a historically recent class that can increase its preparation and enlarge its experience only by turning to Marxist science. "Only in this way can the proletariat form its cadres, who will be able to defeat the cadres of the bourgeoisie.[...] There is only one example in history of such an achievement – the Bolshevik example, which unfortunately was limited to Russia and thus inevitably succumbed. By prevailing only in Russia, the Bolshevik cadres could not offset the overwhelming predominance of the international bourgeoisie.[...] A suitable instrument exists, and it is revolutionary Marxism. The tasks to be accomplished are therefore those of pushing our way forward"[37]. These are tasks that do not frighten us.

The crisis and the organisational battle
The Communist Choice for a New Generation*

For two years now unitary imperialism has been lashed by the crisis in global relations.. As forecast, 2009 is turning out to be the hardest year: in the last few months the crisis has affected industry, putting pressure on employment and on the living conditions of many levels of wage earners. As we have said, the crisis is the tangible sign of a structural change in relations among the powers. The irruption of a power of continental dimensions such as China has shaken the existing world order: we are, in fact, witnessing "the first battle ... in which America and Europe are confronting emerging China"[38].

Our formulations are the result of in-depth work on the nexus between the crisis and the changes in power relations. An essential part of our strategic vision is that these changes will lead to tomorrow's world cataclysm.

A giant global restructuring

This work necessarily starts from the immense world market, with scientific investigation of the relations between classes, and between the fractions of the ruling class that dominate it. The crisis is the result of three decades of liberist imperialist development, and the restructuring which this has brought about has profoundly changed relations between classes and fractions. The driving force has been the disintegration, on a gigantic scale, of the peasantry in the emerging areas. In Asia, Africa and Latin America, hundreds of millions of peasant farmers have gone to swell the ranks of the urban proletariat. Part of this human river has overflowed into the old metropolises, in America and in Europe, filling the void left by the fall in the birthrate. The relative size of the classes has changed, and the working class has increased significantly throughout the world.

This giant restructuring is what has allowed China to set itself up as a new power among the powers, shaking the old order. It has changed the relations between the bourgeois fractions in the old powers, increasingly differentiating the situation of continental Europe (and of Germany in particular) from that of America and Britain. In these pages we have already highlighted how in Germany industry is a much more important part of the overall economy than it is for the Anglo-Saxon world[39]. Conversely, in the United States and Great Britain, the financial services benefited more from development during those decades. Anglo-Saxon banks and insurance companies became

* *Internationalist Bulletin*, August-September 2009

stronger, and today carry considerably more weight in the class structures of their metropolises than they do for continental Europe.

This is definitively a global crisis, striking at all the powers, but with differing degrees of intensity because of the differing balances between the share of social capital and the relative strengths of classes and fractions in the individual areas of the world market. For this reason, we believe that the crisis will be translated into an even more pronounced change in the balance of political power, which will exacerbate existing tensions, preparing the way for yet more devastating crises.

State capitalism returns, transformed

In the last two years we have witnessed the massive return of the State to the economy: state intervention in the control and regulation above all of finance, but also the entry of the State to the capital shareholdings of the big financial and industrial groups flattened by the crisis. This has caused a sudden increase in public debt that will take years to be reabsorbed: an increase that differs between parts of the world and between States which is outlined in "The three faces of the crisis in the debt cycle". On the basis of provisional IMF figures, we have estimated that in most of the metropolises the debt will rise to around 100% of Gross Domestic Product, while in the emerging metropolises it will remain at around 1/3 of GDP. However, two differing types of debt are coming out of the old metropolises: the debt associated with Anglo-Saxon financial liberism is growing more rapidly than that associated with the Rhineland industrial model.

A gigantic public debt is being created, the highest of the postwar period. Its burden, which each and every power will have to shoulder, will influence the imperialist contention for at least the next decade. After years of sermons about the virtues of the minimalist State, we are therefore witnessing a return of State capitalism, with new forms and new relationships. We have already written of the need to go back to the Marxist theory of State capitalism, first laid out in the work of our teachers such as Engels' thesis on "The State as Collective Capitalist"[40]. We have contributed significantly to this field of analysis, thanks to the work of Arrigo Cervetto. This scientific contribution was motivated not only by our fight against Stalinism, which tried to pass off Russian state capitalism as socialism, but was rooted in the struggle to establish our party in the Italian metropolis, with its massive presence of state capitalist groups closely linked with the trade unions and with the opportunism of the Italian Communist Party.

Growing abstentionism

State capitalism is a historical tendency that the cycle's countervailing climate of imperialist liberism had slowed down and overshadowed. The crisis has brought it back to the fore in the old metropolises, and the ideological and political spin-offs are beginning to be felt, as in the recent European elections. The first fact to emerge from this consultation exercise was the massive levels of voter abstention: nearly 60% of the citizens of Europe deserted the polling booths. The increase in abstentionism, exacerbated by an Eastern Europe unused to such processes, is common to all the old metropolises of Europe, and is more marked in those areas with high working-class concentrations. In as crucial an area of the EU as Île-de-France, abstentionism has reached 58%, but in working-class areas such as Seine-St. Denis, the level is 67%, with peaks of over 70% in some specific districts.

The second political fact that emerges from the European elections is the heavy defeat of all the currents of European socialism: the collapse of Labour in England, the defeat of Zapatero in Spain, the downfall of the PSF, the SPD at its historical lowest ebb, the significant fall in support for the PD in Italy. As we wrote: "today every single one of them has been cast adrift"[41]. The crisis caught them by surprise, found them unarmed, and wrong-footed them with the massive re-entry of the State to the economy.

Defeat of opportunist transformism

There is a tragic irony in these defeats. Exactly twenty years ago the Berlin Wall fell, triggering the state collapse of Moscow's empire. The defeat of Russian state capitalism sent its seismic shocks throughout the whole of Europe. The debris of the Wall have swept away the statist ideologies that had spread throughout the Old Continent in the postwar period. All the ideologies about the superior nature of a State economy, of public planning and intervention, etc, were treated with ignominy, and banned. This thinking had formed a large part of the ideological armament of the socialist, social democratic and so-called communist parties of Europe. Such parties had to come to a long and difficult accommodation with the ideologies of imperialist liberism that were becoming current – this is the story of European political opportunism over the last twenty years. As often happens with converts, they were exaggerated in their praise of free market competition, the driving power of market forces, of excellence and flexibility, of individual rights pushed to excess. Just when they thought they had accommodated to the new paradigms, and to have cleverly regained respectability, along came the crisis, and state intervention became all the rage.

The Centre-Right, grouped around the European People's Party, was ready, under pressure of the emergency, to become the champion of public spending and of a return to borrowing. With notable pragmatism, it led the great injection of public capital, presenting itself as the defender of the home ground in the face of the crisis, even as far as support to families and jobs via welfare payments. For European socialism, it was a dramatic case of "Those orders have been countermanded, comrade" which has exacerbated disaffection, disillusion and recriminations – all registered by the European elections. For the PD, it was the last stage of the long transformist labour pains of Italian opportunism, a hard knock aggravated by defeat in the local elections – a heavy blow which has seen the PD lose control of almost all its councils in the North of Italy.

Opportunism in chronic crisis in Northern Italy

This aspect is worth considering, since it touches on our struggle to establish our party in the European metropolis, of which Northern Italy is a crucial area: an area in which big industrial and financial groups are present alongside a consistent and concentrated working-class. Our fight is against all counter-revolutionary political forms. We fight against all parties that represent the bourgeoisie, its fractions or its groups. But the bitter and tragic experience of history has taught us that the most dangerous form is that which succeeds in infiltrating the heart of the working-class movement. Hence today we fight against opportunist parties large and small, those parties which don a "progressive" garb and which hold out the promise of a well-organised, solid capitalism.

The fact that Italy's home-grown opportunism is seeing its crisis worsen in the North represents an unexpected advantage for our strategic prospects. We must remember that this might not necessarily have been the case: at any rate, not to the same extent. The crisis is a testing-ground for all political movements, ours as well as theirs: firstly in terms of our scientific analysis, and secondly in terms of our consequent strategic formulations. So far, the facts have mercilessly confirmed our position, and in the course of the crisis this has allowed us to conduct a vigorous battle which has resulted in some interesting results.

A wide-ranging battle

It is a battle fought wide and deep among the proletariat, a battle which does not aim to detach the odd disillusioned individual among many from the PD or from the crumbling Left. Our commitment is instead to pull members from the masses, out from apathy and helplessness. In 1873 Engels wrote to Bebel that the members of the workers' movements in Germany "still only form a very small minority of the German working class". He suggests that "the correct tactic is not to draw away a few individuals and members here and there from one's opponent, but to work on the great mass which remains apathetic. A single individual whom we have ourselves attracted from the crude mass ... is worth more than ten Lassallean renegades, who always bring the seeds of their false tendencies into the Party with them"[42].

It is in this spirit that we have always fought, and most of all in these months during which we have redoubled our political initiative. Members have come to us from the masses, both adults and young people with the capacity to be trained and to give a growing contribution to our party's struggle.

Strengthening the Leninist party

Imperialism will come out of its crisis: there is talk of signs of a recovery in 2010. This is by no means unanimous. One thing is certain: a future recovery will brew up even more devastating crises. The important thing is that the Leninist party should come out of this crisis stronger: the current trend can and must be consolidated. Two convulsive years have opened up future opportunities for the internationalist position, new opportunities to be exploited even more energetically than we have in the past.

It is worth remembering the words of Engels: we still represent a very small minority of the European working-class movement. But we are a vital and growing minority, and a well-organised, cohesive Leninist minority, with a strategical analysis equal to the times, can aim at future conquests. It can aim at leading the working-class movement, in a tomorrow when conditions will force the masses to make vital choices. This is not a question of luck, but of a concrete possibility, though obviously not a guaranteed development, since this will depend on the outcome of the struggle. The historic example of Lenin's party, which can never be erased, shows us that this is the case. The Bolshevik party originally represented a very small minority of the Russian proletariat, but was able to gain the leadership of it, transforming an imperialist war into a proletarian revolution. This is the strategic perspective within which we are working, and its outcome will depend largely on today's battles.

The militant way

A new generation is taking its first steps in revolutionary struggle, in the full spate of this crisis. In a short time, it is accumulating a wealth of important experiences which, if accompanied by commitment to the study and assimilation of our formulations, must shape its future development. These young people have started on their way by meeting our newspaper at the factory gate, on street corners, in front of their schools or at the doors of their homes. Among the masses there are thousands asking themselves where our world is going, where the future is taking them, what it will be for them. We must give them the chance to choose, to make the communist choice – the chance that we have all had.

We can do it: and on this, too, depends the outcome of the battle we have been fighting for generations.

Militancy and conscious commitment in the unknowns of the global recovery

Our Communist Party Policy vs. the Squalor of Their Parliamentary Government*

The great recession caused by the crisis in global relations has now bottomed out, ant there are numerous signs of an about-turn in the cycle. The economic recovery is viewed with great prudence and caution: there are still those who fear that another relapse is possible. The problems threatening recovery are various, but one of them stands out above all: the huge public debt accumulated by the states during the crisis.

Their large-scale public intervention has shown results: it has protected the banks and financial institutions from possible collapse, and has helped the big industrial groups via direct interventions. Incentives, and social shock absorbers, thus promoting the restructuring processes. These many interventions have attenuated the effects of the crisis in the old metropolises, and have allowed the emerging powers to maintain stable growth rates, as in the case of China with its + 8%. But the price that has been paid is that of increasing a public debt that has now become enormous.

The long debt-cycle

The International Monetary Fund (IMF) has estimated that debt of the advanced countries will reach 115% of GDP in about 2014. Great effects will be required for 15-20 years to bring it back to acceptable levels, i.e. to about 60% of GDP. We have written that a debt cycle is about to begin, a cycle that will heavily engage all the metropolises for years, leaving its mark on the struggle among the powers.

In Europe, the seriously ill state is the UK, but what is worrying the world is the mountain of debt burdening the US, the epicentre of the crisis.

The American federal budget forecasts an about 100% of GDP debt for 2013. We have seen in these pages that the federal estimates are thought to be over-optimistic. In fact, estimates that predict a US debt of about 150% of GDP are doing the rounds[43]. There is a evident fear that the only exit strategy for the American government is that of inflation and of dollar devaluation. There is heated debate about the decline of the greenback, its role as reserve currency, possible rival currencies, and eventual currency baskets to replace it. Monetary weapons are once again being brandished in the world contention.

---

* *Internationalist Bulletin*, December 2009

Recovery tensions

Despite all this, at the first signs of recovery the motto that spread quickly from one capital to another was: "the worst is over"; a very short-sighted view that sees the repercussions of the crisis die out in the economic cycle alone. In an article of October 1976, Arrigo Cervetto reflected on the economic recovery that followed the restructuring crisis: "The counterblows of the recovery, of the opportunities for expansion and, above all, for the testing of their respective restructurings will inevitably form part of the relations among the great powers. Hence, the big problem of capitalist recovery, the great clashes of imperialist competition, and the first changes in the power relationships among the states are looming ahead"[44]. Cervetto added an observation of particular interest and topicality: "A partial knowledge of the capitalist cycles sees the greatest imperialist tensions in phase of depression. On the contrary, the opposite is true. The greatest tensions break out precisely as a consequence of the uneven development of capitalism, and when some powers are ascending and others declining. [...] This bill in the world register of the imperialist powers has not yet been presented, but it will be in the next year and in the years to come". This is the case also today, and with even greater intensity. In this sense, the worst is yet to come.

Crisis and competition among the powers

These are considerations that send us back to our Marxist conception of crises as "crises of socio-economic capitalist formation", in which the contradictions and oscillations provoked by the crises themselves cannot be dissipated in their connection with the economic cycle alone. It is necessary in every crisis, to take into account its social, political and institutional connections, and especially its connection with relations among the powers.

In May 1981, some years after the mid-1970s crisis, while Cervetto was analysing the *Tendenze profonde nella nuova contesa* [Deep Trends in the New Contention], he observed: "The 1970s were characterised by the restructuring crisis of the world's industrial apparatus. The struggle among the various imperialist metropolises to face it, resolve it, and exit it, as well as the increasing competition on the world market, derive from this . The general slowdown and the differences in the growth or slowdown rates are the sign of the changed relations of force between the old the young powers, and among the whole spectrum of powers in their mutual relationships"[45].

This is the crisis of socio-economic formation. This is the grasping of the connection with the relations among the powers that allows us to perceive the exacerbation of the clash in the world contention.

The price of unemployment

The worst is definitely not yet over for the workers. The Organisation for the Economic Co-operation and Development (OECD) predicts that there will be a further jump in unemployment next year. About 9 million new unemployed workers will swell the ranks of the 16 million who have already lost their jobs thanks to the crisis. This is the combined effect of the restructuring and concentration processes that the crisis itself has triggered. It is a bitter price that our class is called upon to pay once more. There is no doubt that the worst is yet to come in this field. But this is also true of the other ramifications of the crisis, and especially of its repercussions for the relations among the powers.

The United States is facing a new phase in its decline, demonstrated by the crisis in an extremely explicit way. The Obama administration has very difficult choices to make, starting from the country's internal problems, which all require an urgent solution: financial restructuring and regulation, the deadlines for unpostponable industrial restructuring and health care reform, and, above all, budget policies to deal with the mountain of debt. These are demanding tasks that call for political resolution, while the critical point on the international chessboard, from the Middle East to Afghanistan, demand urgent solutions.

As regards Asia, the Chinese Dragon, together with the other emerging countries, was granted recognition at the G20, and was even given formal commitments that sanction its status as a power. China emerges from the crisis as the new, great, Asian power that dwarfs Japan's efforts to come out of its long lethargy. Debate is going on about an East Asian economic area, interpreted by each regional power in its own way. It is hard to think that this may be the solution to Tokyo's strategic conundrum, faced as it is by Beijing's overwhelming power.

The era of continental power

Europe is on the eve of seeing the Institutional Lisbon Treaty* come into force. The new powers of imperialist Europe, the conclusion of a process that has taken half a century to unfold, are about to see the light. The global crisis has simply accelerated the final leg of that long march, and has weighed decisively in the Irish referendum, the last real obstacle to the treaty.

A new phase is beginning for European imperialism, a phase that will mean renewed commitment to our internationalist struggle. A sign of the times is the speech made by the British foreign minister at a conference held at the London international Institute for Strategic Studies. David Miliband argued that: "the continental era has begun", and added that, in the "multipolar world" in which the continents move, "power is gathering round a number of regional centre". According to the British minister, it

* The Lisbon Treaty came into force on December 1st 2009

follows that "in this modern world dimension", Great Britain, with its 60 million inhabitants, cannot be a major player in world affairs. His conclusion is particularly significant: "Europe is our continent". In our internationalist battle we have been analysing multipolarism for decades, as well as studying the emergence of continental powers and contextualising the process of European unification from that perspective for years. For Miliband, it was a belated attempt at adaptation, but foe us, it is the confirmation of years of work and struggle against European imperialism.

Counterblows for Italian imperialism

The current trends and future choices of Asia, America and Europe will give birth to the, "inevitable counterblows of the recovery": "the big problem of capitalist recovery, and the great clashes of imperialist competition" are to be found in this choices. This is also true of Rome, dragged into the acceleration of the European process. The Berlusconi government's public intervention in the crisis was minimum, a choice imposed by the weight of the debt accumulated in previous years.

Despite this, the re-organisations, restructurings and regulations imposed by the recovery are also on the agenda of the big groups of Italian imperialism. The same is true of the vast sectors of small and medium-sized business shaken by the crisis. The debate on exit strategies is highly topical in Italy. Too, where its choices are held in a vice-like grip between demands for tax cuts and the pressure of accumulated debt.

Our communist battle

These troubled weeks have often dragged Italian politics down to the typical low levels of back-alley dives. The mud slung in these months has not even spared some of the top economic groups, and has even sullied the good name of the Avvocato* the venerable patriarch of Italian capitalism. These events bring to mind the words spoken by Lorenzo Parodi at a moment that was a difficult as it was sad for us : the funeral of comrade Cervetto, words later published in our March 1995 editorial. "In the light of Italy's political decay, already glimpsed twenty-five years ago in the 'Theses' on the Italian imbalance formulated by comrade Cervetto, we may have been guilty of overestimating the capacity of the bourgeois ruling class to provide itself with a suitable political staff"[46].

Parodi concluded: "Comrade Cervetto, I agree with you – you mentioned it to me recently –. that we have overestimated the ability of these Italian exponents of the ruling class in the course of our long years of analysis and study".

---

* "Avvocato": a nickname often used for Giovanni Agnelli (1921-2003), the main shareholder and CEO of Fiat.

These recent months have given us strong confirmation of this, a confirmation of the squalor of their politics. This is yet another reason to put even more energy into our internationalist battle and into our policy, based on revolutionary passion upheld by sound, scientifically based principles. A passion that fuels a militancy that requires commitment, rigour, discipline, and awareness of the important role of collective work: a communist tradition unfailingly handed down from one generation of Marxism to another.

Chapter Two

A NEW REVOLUTIONARY GENERATION

The challenge of the new strategic phase

A New Battle for the Organisation of Our Class*

In these months the difficult recovery of the world economy has continued to plod along. The IMF estimates that China will grow this year at an over 10% rate, followed by India with 9.7%. The rates of the old powers will be much lower, with the euro zone at 1.7% and the United States at 2.6%. The speed of the German recovery – at about 3.5% - stands out, clearly better than the US economic dynamic. This divergence has reopened the debate over the particular characteristics of the "German model", about which we have often spoken in these pages. These particular characteristics are rooted in the strength of its industrial structure and in the competitiveness of its big industrial and financial groups. But even the "Rhineland model", which has so far exited the crisis victoriously, has its weak points. We have highlighted one of them: the seriousness of the "demographic decline" that is already making itself felt.

Germany and China

Berlin is competing with Tokyo for the fall in the birth rate prize. This is a "senile illness of imperialism" that afflicts all the old powers. The German strain of this virus is particularly aggressive. The progressive decline in the new generations means that even today Germany is experiencing a lack of skilled workers, technicians, and engineers, all of them particularly necessary to German industry: a challenge to Rhineland industrialism that may reserve bitter surprises in the not so distant future. Thanks to its technological efficiency and its productivity, German industry excels in quality exports. This has allowed Germany to couple itself in time to Asia's rapid recovery, an advantage that is not only undermined by the demographic factor, but is also in thrall to an insoluble contradiction that will make competition on the world market much fiercer. Germany exports to China and Asia machinery and plants that contribute to strengthening the Asian companies that will be competing with the German groups tomorrow, with the advantage of being able to exploit cheap labour. At the end of August, the German newspaper *Der Spiegel* published a long report to which it

---

* *Internationalist Bulletin*, November 2010

dedicated its cover with the eloquent headline *Die Rivalen*. The theory expounded is that China already has industrial groups able to compete with the Germans.

A few weeks later the French *Le Figaro* argued that a world battle in the high-speed train sector is already being fought. The traditional groups of the sector, Alstom, Siemens, Bombardier and Kawasaki, now have to reckon with two state-owned Chinese groups, CSR and CNR, which are capturing increasing shares of that market. At the end of September the *Financial Times* reported that the groups that traditionally work in the high-speed train sector have been forced to sign partnership agreements with Chinese groups in order to have access to that lucrative expanding market in China. As these old groups are all in competition, they were eager to hand over their technologies to the Chinese groups. In fact, this technology transfer was a prerequisite to the signing of the joint agreements with the local groups: a kind of competition in technology transfer to those who have now become rival groups. It's like selling rope to tomorrow's hangman, but this is the unavoidable logic of the capitalist mode of production. The City daily adds that, as the old competitors cannot beat the new arrivals, they are said to be considering alliances with them in projects in which the Chinese producers are gaining ground: in Brazil, Saudi Arabia, Turkey and... California.

Asian rearmament

The debate on American "reindustrialisation" can assume many aspects. In these weeks, attention in the capitals of imperialism has been focused on exchange rate tensions, but, in the last few months, the clash of monetary weapons has been echoed by that of real weapons brandished in the China and Persian Gulf seas. Their huge public debt pressure is braking military expenditure in the old powers. This is not the case with Asia, where rearmament trends are marching to the tune of Chinese modernisation and, above all, of its naval projection.

Perhaps over-egging the pudding, Robert Kaplan writes that the greatest geopolitical development of the decade has been China's rising naval power: a rise that is undoubtedly causing concern. In mid-September *Le Monde* reported that the Indian prime minister, Singh, had publicly announced that China intends to gain a foothold in South Asia: "It's hard to tell what this'll lead to. So it's important to be prepared". Meanwhile, there are obvious signs of rearmament in the Persian Gulf, where the US will be selling 123 billion dollars' worth of arms in the next few years: we already spoke about this in last month's issue of our newspaper[47]. An energy artery that is essential to Asian development runs between the Asian seas and that of the Gulf, an artery that the United States controls with its military presence in Iraq. Monetary gunboats and aircraft carriers are crossing on the seas of imperialism, and are inevitably paving the way for tomorrow's storms.

European restructuring

Today, more than ever before, internationalism becomes the only sure landfall for the proletariat. The Italian metropolis is inevitably buffeted by the crisis-generated waves, but parliamentary politics seems unaware of this and continues to stage a farcical and yet melancholy show. Showmanship, muckraking, and opportunism are its main ingredients. It really takes a great effort of will to deal with it: the only way is to return to the foundations of our concept of politics. "At root, we Marxists are materialistically generous: according to us, it is the economic process that changes ideas, rather than bad faith and shabby behaviour, of which there is certainly no lack"[48] [Arrigo Cervetto, 1976]. Today the economic process is obliging all the old metropolises to tackle the problems of productivity and wage levels. At the same time, in view of the sluggish pace of recovery, the need to get out of crippling debt makes drastic cuts to public spending inevitable.

The European Union is exerting strong pressure, and the revision of the Stability Pact will be a further coercive factor. The competitiveness and wage issue reached Italy in the wake of the world car battle. The Fiat-Chrysler line has won the day, dividing the trade unions and finding a minimum of resistance only in the FIOM-CGIL positions, a defensive battle to which the Leninist workers continue to contribute. Among other things, the need to deal with one of the highest public debts in the world obliges Italy to reduce financial aid to its southern regions. This is a very old problem, and it is no accident that we have recalled Giolitti in these pages.

As European pressure has grown and "federalism" has become a concrete factor in the transfer of funds, the demands of the southern regions have taken on fresh force. This is basically what is agitating the waters of politics and of parliamentary arithmetic, with Gianfranco Fini trying to make himself the champion of spending on and the transfer of funds to the South. This is what led to the clash between the premier and the speaker of the Lower House, and to the crisis in the majority, with its relative shifts from one parliamentary group to another. Significantly, after the executive quickly approved the Stability Act (the former budget), despite the protests of various government departments, Giulio Tremonti, the treasury minister, stated: "Now everything's changed. Now numbers come before politics. It isn't true that I put the government under the administration of an external commission [...] the truth is that we're all under the administration of the Brussels external commission".

A degrading political show

This is the real novelty of Italian politics, a novelty that further contributes to depriving parliament of its authority, sinking it ever deeper in the vortexes of parliamentary cretinism.

The forms of the political-parliamentary clash are those typical of the Italian-style political show. For over a year the "political debate" has been animated by muckraking campaigns. If we were a small group of spectators we could even laugh carelessly at the degradation of their politics. But we must not forget that we have a serious practical task: to steer and educate a growing number of supporters and sympathisers, and especially to train the younger generations who, attracted by Marxism, flock to our workers' circles and their initiatives.

An extra effort is required of us to push all those who are seeking a meaning beyond fallacious outward appearances to face the essence of the political facts, to lift their heads and look out to the world, to the forces and forms that really count in the class struggle. It means steering them towards the study of our materialistic conception, towards the deepening of our strategic analysis, in a militancy that is a daily struggle among the masses of wage earners, to speak on their behalf and to represent them. In far-off 1979, Arrigo Cervetto wrote: "In Marxist analysis we must not let ourselves be distracted by single episodes and by the personality cults that the economic and political struggle inevitably generates. We have to go deeper and see what really lies behind the single characters. It is easier to create a scene with only a few actors than to examine the structure that makes them act and dance; it is easier, but useless"[49].

A vital party

Actors and dancers undoubtedly abound in the Italian political scene and we are also obliged, out of a sense of duty, to observe them. But woe to us if we let ourselves be distracted, especially in this new phase in which the contradictions of unitary imperialism call the science-party to new demanding tasks. The crisis has put an end to the thirty years of the cycle of imperialist liberism generated by the mid-1970s' restructuring crisis: a global crisis that, in its turn, had put an end to a cycle of great development, the "thirty glorious years", as the French would say, or, in Italian terminology, the "economic miracle". Two thirty-year cycles in which the struggle of various generations was fought to entrench a party on the lines of the Bolshevik model in one of the citadels of imperialism: a tough struggle to see that our revolutionary Leninist positions were not pushed to the sidelines of an imperialistically mature society; a historically unprecedented task, and, on the whole, a challenge met.

The Leninist Party is alive and kicking, has no longer been a small group for years, has succeeded in being handed down from generation to generation, and is becoming rooted in one of the nerve centres of European imperialism, even crossing old frontiers. Unlike many, to look back on the past can also be gratifying for us. But in the revolutionary struggle this makes sense only if it permits us to better assess and weigh up our future tasks and steps. Reflection on our past progress is useful only if we concentrate on what could have been done and was not done, and on the critical analysis of our shortcomings and mistakes, to draw from them ideas and stimuli for the further development of the party, a long road still lying before us today.

The new chapter to write

A new phase in the relations among the powers has begun, a phase fraught with tensions, clashes and potentially catastrophic contradictions, and at the same time fraught with totally unprecedented phenomena. New continental powers are challenging the old balances and the old powers, now immersed in a long debt cycle, debt of a size never before seen in "peacetime". It is inevitable that the social-democratisation processes with which we clashed in the "thirty glorious years" should enter a declining phase, with social and political effects that still have to be measured. Our own revolutionary task has greater dimensions that, in themselves, set us more demanding tasks. As we have written, for our revolutionary minority this will be "a new chapter for our revolutionary science and a new battle for the organisation of our class"[50]. We have already begun to write this new chapter. We are able to do it since we have a decisive scientific advantage, a decades-long analysis on which to draw. But it requires a renewed effort at every level: the mere repetition of what we have acquired is not enough to face the unprecedented and to plot a course for our future struggles.

There are also the objective and subjective conditions to face a new battle for the organisation of our class, a battle that, however, requires more creative energies. Some of these are already available, but an effort is required to employ them fully in our organisational plan. The influx of the younger generations continues with regularity, and this is the best guarantee. In this sense, the "demographic deficit" is not affecting the organisation of our class. Interest in and openness to our internationalist positions are considerable in our sphere of influence in the various districts, as well as in the factories and the workplace. This is a particularly important aspect, since it enables us to extend our battle to the wage earners that nobody represents today. It is possible to build up a much vaster network of activists and supporters of our positions in the workplace, a network that can spread out from the workers' circles, and whose mesh is linked through our newspaper. This would be the first fight in the new battle for the organisation of our class.

An organised force for our internationalist battle

A Struggle against Time*

The world economy has begun to grow again: by 5% in 2010. But this is a global trend that hides a great difference between the old powers that, weighed down by debt, grew by 3%, and the so-called emerging powers that forged ahead at a rhythm of 7.6%.

Once again the engine has been the powerful Chinese locomotive that has continued to grow by over 10%: at almost four times the rate of America, and at almost six times the rate of the euro area, engaged in rigorous fiscal consolidation. Germany, with its +3.6%, thanks to its exports, stands out in Europe. Despite this, Germany has so far recuperated only 73% of what it lost during the crisis.

The liberals and war

Martin Wolf, the *Financial Times* economic editor-in-chief, observes that the difference between the growth rhythms of the "advanced" and "emerging" countries corresponds to the "great convergence" between their incomes. This is a world-shaking change that, according to Wolf, poses two problems: the future availability of raw materials and the change in world power. If the transfer of power is not successfully handled, "it could lead to war".

This admission is worth noting, since the *Financial Times* editor-in-chief was one of the champions of globalisation, which, via economic development, would have led to "great convergence", with emancipation from poverty, peace and democracy all over the world.

Today the Chinese power, now a key player in the struggle to divide up the markets, is painting globalisation in much gloomier colours. Even one of the best bourgeois newspapers is beginning to think that the uneven development between the old and the new powers could lead to a world war. This is what we have always thought.

Wages in the old and new powers

Uneven development in the economic dynamic produced by globalisation and exacerbated by the crisis has also had an effect on wages. Even before the crisis, the strong economic growth in the emerging powers had led to tensions in the labour market that, generally speaking, the crisis has not attenuated. We have witnessed wage struggles, notable increases in minimum wages, and the development of trade unions in old and new forms in

* *Internationalist Bulletin*, March 2011

China and the whole of Asia. Meanwhile, for the same basic reasons but going in the opposite direction, the conditions for pay restraint that the crisis has greatly exacerbated are now emerging.

The tendency towards falling wages in the mature metropolises is a product of globalisation with its uneven economic development: an underestimated phenomenon that Arrigo Cervetto dealt with in his last labours in the early 1990s. In an article of December 1993 he examined a Credit Suisse First Boston study. This highlighted how the entry into the markets of millions of Chinese and Indian workers with very low labour costs would have the effect of squeesing those of the advanced countries. Cervetto added: "Marx formulated his wage theory taking into account the cost of subsistence that had been lowered by corn imports. In the present world wage cycle the drop in prices could also already have an effect"[51]. A month later he returned to the subject: "There is no commodity and workforce price monopoly. If development trends continue at a world level, the workforce price will fall because the prices of its subsistence will fall"[52].

The price for the younger generations

The trend that Cervetto observed has now been hit by the crisis: the rapid rise in unemployment and income support has put further pressure on wages. In the United States, the epicentre of the crisis, the General Motors agreement, which we have already mentioned, was hailed with great enthusiasm. This agreement guarantees 60% of the older workers 28 dollars an hour, but envisages halved pay for the remaining 40% of newly-hired younger workers: a contractual double standard that reduces wages via a sizeable cut in the starting wage. This double standard that hits the younger generations hard has become ever more widespread in Europe through such contractual institutions as apprenticeships or agency work. One of the secrets of the "German model" is to be found in the diffusion of apprenticeships, while, reports *Das Handelsblatt*, the number of agency workers has tripled since 2003. This phenomenon is also spreading in Italy, arousing much less protest than the Pomigliano and Mirafiore agreements.

The French labour minister estimates that there are 2.3 million minimum wage earners in France. The same source maintains that there are at least the same number of workers with wages very near the SMIC. Altogether there would be at least 20% of French workers at those wage levels. These lower levels of the wage scale generally regard immigrant and younger workers, two partly overlapping groups that have paid the highest price in the crisis, also in terms of unemployment.

It is in Spain, still in recession in 2010, that one of the highest unemployment rates (over 20%) is to be found. The Spanish labour minister estimates that this rate stands at 18.2% for Spanish workers, and at 30.2% for the foreign. In France, according to the INSEE, unemployment among foreign workers is 1.5-2 times higher than among the indigenous. The hardest hit are reportedly the Maghrebi workers.

As regards the young, the International Labour Organisation (ILO) estimates that 81 million youths are unemployed. It observes that the pace of the youth unemployment rate in the crisis years has exploded to 35 times the average of the pre-crisis years. The ILO reports that this explosion is located in the more developed countries, with youths as the main victims. The latest ISTAT figures for Italy put the unemployment rate for youths between the ages of 15 and 24 at 29%, a 2.9% increase.

The pressure brought to bear by the crisis on wages and employment has not provoked particular social reactions in the advanced metropolises, including Italy. The consequences of the crisis have been mitigated by so-called family welfare, i.e. by combined family incomes and the assets accumulated over the decades. This is less so in the case of immigrant and single-income families, and even less so in single-adult families, that are on the increase due to the ageing of the population and the rise in legal separations. Always according to the INSEE, in France the children living with a single parent rose from the 6% of 1968 to the 16% of 2005. 90% of them live with their mothers. Here the crisis has hit hard, and the number of children living below the poverty line has greatly increased. This, too, is happening in modern, opulent Europe. Cervetto had already warned us of this in his study of American society over twenty years ago[53]. [*Vecchi e bambini nella ristrutturazione sociale* – "The Elderly and Children in Social Restructuring" – April 1989].

Assets and family welfare

Generally speaking, however, family welfare has worked. This is particularly true of Italy, where high savings rates correspond to high asset levels. The Credit Suisse research institute has published a monumental study on family wealth in no fewer than 160 countries. For average per capita wealth (financial and real-estate) Italy is seventh in the world and second in the G7, behind its French cousins. It is third in the world for median (the value that divides the scale in half) wealth per adult, and first in the world for the lowest number of adults with assets below 10,000 dollars: only 3% as against 27% in the US. The high asset level of Italian families is largely due to the widespread diffusion of home ownership. This is also why Italy has suffered less from the crisis-induced erosion of wealth. The Edison Foundation estimates that, from 2007 to 2010, average wealth fell by 1.5% in Canada, 3.8 in Italy, 4.8 in Germany, 6.6 in France, and 13.4% in the US, the epicentre of the crisis.

In the light of these considerations the role of family welfare as a shock absorber of the social effects of the crisis is evident, even if deferred wages cannot be ignored in any assessment of globalisation and the wage crisis. Pension cuts have been drastic, hitting not only age limits but also reducing future pension cheques. There is no doubt that the younger generations will retire later than their parents and with lower amounts.

The Mediterranean, a European banlieue

This is the shape of the declining phase of social-democratisation in the old powers. But in this trend towards wage reductions there is a possible countertrend: the effects of the *demographic deficit*. In Germany in 2010 there were also talks of pay rises, and some wage-earning sectors obtained partial results. There is no doubt that economic recovery played a role in this, but many observers see the lack of skilled labour as one of the reasons. It is difficult to reduce wages if there is a lack of labour force on the market.

In the European *banlieue*, without the protection of the euro and family welfare, the wage squeese, food price inflation and high unemployment have triggered social protest, as has been the case in North Africa. This is an area in which there has been a 65-million population growth in twenty years, with the great interweaving of social mobility and huge processes of peasantry disintegration, urbanisation and large-scale migrations. These are markets that were put under great pressure by the crisis. The local industries, already suffering from Asian competition, were hit; the migratory outlets towards Europe were suddenly reduced; migratory pressure from the heart of Africa increased; and the emigrants' remittances fell. The increase in raw material prices during the economic recovery has inevitably involved food prices, and this was what triggered off the social explosion.

In the front line, yet again, the younger generations, paying their toll in human lives: a young proletariat plagued by unemployment and wage reductions, young holders of diplomas, university graduates, and also secondary school students, who see no future prospects; a youth dazzled by the images of Paris and Rome broadcast on satellite TV that has also seen its way out via emigration closed to it. The crisis made the privileges of the ruling classes of corrupt regimes that, with their clan ties and close-linked networks of cronies, controlled considerable shares of the economies of their countries, even more hated: a condition that links many states on the southern shore of the Mediterranean, born of the struggles for national freedom of the '50s and '60s. This is an area that is closely interlinked with Europe, a veritable *special zone* of European imperialism, now forced to weigh up the delay of its foreign policy, since the planned Mediterranean Union, with its free trade area, is still largely on the drawing board.

A class force

But this delay also regards our class and our internationalist stance. The young North Africans look towards Europe, whose TV images offer prospects of a better life. We know that for many of them this will only be a mirage. The bright lights of Paris and Milan hide inequalities, exploitation, unemployment, precariousness, and, above all, deep uncertainty, the same uncertainty about the future from which those youths want to escape. The welcome offered by Europe's ruling classes hides – barely – the will to use their labour and brains to fill in the gap that ageing and opulent societies have created. They think that they will be able to use them in their plans to capture markets and in their power politics that do not exclude eventually enrolling them in a future European army.

As they look at Europe those youths should be able to discern a true welcome based on solidarity and class unity, offering the prospect of emancipation and freedom that only the struggle for Communism can give. They have seen in their countries that the sheer weight of numbers can also break up the existing order. But if that sheer weight is not to end up hostage to the bourgeois fractions and factions it needs to be able to find a firm anchorage in a Leninist party that is deeply entrenched in the European metropolis. We are not yet at that point, and this is the measure of our historical delay. Our regret is all the greater since that prospect is now much less remote than in the years when we supported the struggles for national freedom in their countries.

Today, in a nerve centre of Europe, a Leninist minority is fighting with great determination to recuperate that historical delay. Moreover, many North African youths attend our initiatives and come to our workers' circles, while a number of them take part in our militant activity among the masses. If our strategic analysis is to offer a solid frame of reference, we need a strength that is not yet sufficient today; organised, conscious strength that can offer that frame of reference, that leads to reflection, and from there to militancy. We need to quicken our step. Basically, ours is a struggle against time. And time is not at our disposal. Today its rhythms are being beaten out by the contention among the great powers.

An orientation-organisation battle

Our "Scientific Order" vs. the Degradation of Their Politics*

In the summer of 2007 there were the first signs of the crisis in the heart of American imperialism. Four years later, in spite of a torturous economic recovery, the alarm is again sounding in the capitals of the old powers as they face the slowdown in growth and the first counterblows generated by public debt, greatly swollen in the crisis years.

For four years, therefore, instability, uncertainty, and fears about the future have been on the agenda, four years in which threats and restrictive measures, accompanied by unemployment and precariousness, have been offloaded onto the wage-earners, four years in which the capitalist crisis has been under the eyes of the world. After over sixty years of illusory eternal development and welfare ideologies, and after twenty years of hymns of praise to globalisation-fuelled progress, this mode of production is more than explicitly demonstrating its unsolvable contradictions ... and with them the weakness and impotence of its ruling classes.

An uncertainty-filled future

The intensity with which all of this has happened has not been experienced since the war years. Never since then has the failure of the bourgeois ideologies been so evident and the restoration of an ideological framework equal to the times so difficult and demanding. Even more than the effects on present living conditions, which are in any case being felt, it is how future expectations will be affected that is the big question in the old metropolises. There is a growing feeling of disillusion, disappointment, and even fear for the future among the masses. And amidst the great confusion resentment and impotent rage are also emerging, accompanied by widespread social passivity.

The continuing crisis has shaken the reliability of the ruling class's institutions, not to mention the credibility of its representatives and their politics. True, this is not occurring everywhere with the same intensity: in the Italian metropolis these phenomena are exacerbated by long-standing and unresolved imbalances.

The task of the science-party is to apply itself to studying the ongoing transformation, to weigh up the factors and underlying forces that have led to the present situation, and to spot the trends that are emerging in order to trace, as best it can, what this phase is hatching. In the interim, it is more than ever necessary in our battle among the masses to focus on "the present

---

* *Internationalist Bulletin*, November 2011

state of things", such things as how the continuing crisis is affecting social reality and particularly the more susceptible part of our class.

Italian weaknesses

Italy's is a very particular case: it has a weak Establishment, one of the highest public debts in the world, one of its lowest growth rates, politicians that, generally speaking, are not equal to their task, and a political struggle that has degenerated into vulgar muckraking, insults and rows all blown up by the media.

This is a specific state of things that we need to ponder with great attention, (1) because it offers our struggle to entrench our party more time; (2) because a scientific vision of the situation is becoming more than ever necessary; (3) because we can restore order to the widespread confusion through our scientific newspaper; (4) because with our organisation we can offer an anchorage and a future prospect against disillusion and disappointment; and, finally, because we can transform resentment and impotent rage into revolutionary passion.

Leaflets and mass meetings are not enough to do this. We need to carry out our analyses in great depth; we need a clear, objective vision of the objective situation that only a scientifically based analysis can provide: a scientific vision that alone can fuel revolutionary passion, militancy and that indispensable spirit of conquest without which we risk being unarmed prophets.

Imperialist Europeanism

Faced with the crisis and the debt cycle, imperialist Europe is getting its arsenals ready. A Europe strengthened by more efficient means to face not only the debt crisis, but above all the future development of the world contention may emerge from this. We have already issued a warning in these pages: a stronger Europe means an imperialist power that is better equipped for the struggle to carve up the markets. On the domestic front this implies a more efficient and captivating imperialist Europeanism. With greater centralisation the European Union will be better able to combine the stern, hard face it has shown to Greece with the reassuring face of a force able to protect the various social stratifications alarmed by the first shocks of the debt cycle. We have written: "We have to know who we are dealing with"[54]: this is indispensable to our internationalist struggle against European and unitary imperialism.

As the political storm over Europe's public debt intensified, Italian state bonds became an almost inevitable target. This obliged the ECB to come to the markets' rescue. At the same time it imposed a series of urgent measures on the government, measures contained in the unusual and by now famous letter signed by Trichet and Draghi, subsequently published by *Corriere della Sera*. The Italian government implemented them. All of this testifies the extent of the handing over of the sovereignty of the national governments to the euro institutions: a process that our analysis anticipated and has studied for years. The implementation of the measures gave rise to a just below sixty billion euro budget package, which aims to anticipate balancing the public budget to 2013, as requested by Frankfurt.

The whole budgetary birth process was agonising, as always happens when cuts are involved, and not distribution. The unwise handling of the debate, with almost public bargaining over the fiscal measures, heightened the impression of quarrelling among the executive and of the incapacity of the majority. The media brandished everything in an anti-government campaign. The European authorities accepted the budget package and continue to defend its content. Their support was not sufficient to counter the growing criticism of a greatly weakened government.

The epilogue of "berlusconismo"

What has mainly contributed to this situation has been the deterioration in the figure of the premier, which has considerably worsened in the last few months, particularly as a result of the Cavaliere's irresponsible private behaviour, which is doubtless the consequence of Berlusconi's unpolitical trait, but which has fuelled the discredit and ridicule of his leadership of the executive.

Another contribution to all of this is the growing imbalance between the state powers, accompanied by glaring media coverage. Every newspaper without exception has spared no ink in publishing wiretaps (obviously "private and confidential") of very embarrassing and often astonishing telephone conversations. This, too, is a feature of the political circus. And then sticking one's nose into other people's business, especially if it is titillating, boosts circulation: something that should be well known to whoever holds an official position, and even more so if he/she comes from the worlds of information or show business.

The Italian media campaign soon spilled over into the international press, making Silvio Berlusconi the scapegoat for all Italy's problems and the symbol of this metropolis's untrustworthiness in the international context. We know very well that appearances are deceptive. We know the long history of this metropolis's international untrustworthiness; we know where its huge debt comes from and we are well aware of the inconsistency of the Italian Establishment. It is an old bourgeois trick to offload all the responsibility onto a single figure. But when the banner head line of the German economic daily *Das Handelsblatt* reads "The Italian Deficit Is Called Berlusconi", it means that appearances, images, have the same weight as real facts.

We have already dealt in these pages with the epilogue of the long political season dominated by the figure of Berlusconi, who has held in check an ineffectual and divided Opposition for fifteen years. Similarly, we covered the particular characteristics of the political cycle that opened with a billionaire owner of one of the big groups of the Italian bourgeoisie taking the field.

The question today is no longer whether that political cycle is drawing to a close; for their politics, the question has become how to exit that cycle. Since December 14th the Opposition has repeatedly tried to do this via a vote of no-confidence in parliament – ending up regularly defeated – with the latest repeat performance of this overworked script now, in October. Parliament has been the theatre of episodes of parliamentary cretinism verging on the ridiculous. And this is supposed to be the temple of democracy! There is no denying that democracy deceives the exploited classes.

The ambassador Sergio Romano and *Corriere della Sera* tried to propose a way out of the crisis: Berlusconi's renunciation of standing as a candidate for the premiership, plus an early election in 2012, in exchange for a "soft" exit and an orderly transition. The proposal was not accepted and the situation is an objective deadlock. The foreign press has noticed this. In *Die Welt*, Clemens Wergin attacks Berlusconi and his government, and observes in a somewhat disconsolate tone of voice: "besides him there is no one either on the right or on the left" that can form a new government. He adds that the whole of the eurozone risks being held "hostage by a political class that revolves first of all round itself".

Indeed, it is now more than two years that the political debate, their politics, has spiralled in Italy into a clash between the majority and the Opposition wholly based on muckraking, in a flood of abuse and insults always in eager anticipation of further wiretaps. Meanwhile the world is moving on, the crisis is pressing ahead, debt is exerting its pressure, and the next vote count is being prepared in Montecitorio*, while the post-Berlusconi jostling for positions is beginning.

Catholics in movement

It is inevitable that the approaching end of the long Berlusconi political cycle should set the Italian situation in movement again, adding, if possible, yet more confusion. The big business groups shaken by Sergio Marchionne's initiative, which has considerably weakened the Confindustria, are in movement. The Church has started to reflect on future prospects. It is a Church hit by scandal, but still active. The reflection that began in Todi excludes the reconstitution of the Catholic party. If anything, it is the role and weight of Catholics in the future Italian political alignment, starting from the current relative majority party, that is at the centre of debate.

There is no trace of a similar discussion in the main opposition party. Since its inception, it has always been a greatly divided party, in which vastly different positions intermingle. Today it is revealing great difficulty

---

* Montecitorio is a palace in Rome that is currently the seat of the Italian Chamber of Deputies.

in facing a political prospect that will be under the sign of the primacy of the European constrictions and of the repercussions of the debt cycle. It is amazing to hear its national leaders attack the ECB, a "technostructure", because of its interference in the national sovereignty of a state, seen as an attack on democracy. This was the position of Stefano Fassina, of the party's national secretariat, and of other party leaders who openly declared their opposition to the Franco-German line and Europe's neo-liberist formula. On the contrary, its national deputy secretary, Enrico Letta, argues that the post-Berlusconi era will have to set off from the ECB letter that sets targets that, in his opinion, are unavoidable.

Massimo D'Alema has a more thoughtful approach. He points to Europeanism as a new unifying principle. At least he is reflecting on a strategic prospect, thus standing as a candidate to become one of the trumpeters of imperialist Europe.

Defence in restructuring

Meanwhile restructuring is pressing ahead. After the car industry it is the turn of the shipbuilding sector. The divided trade unions bow their heads: they have not even succeeded in imposing a defence for the whole of Fincantieri. Site-by-site agreements are already a defeat in themselves. The determined defensive battle of the Genoa-Sestri shipyard, difficult and with uncertain prospects of success, demonstrates, however, that there are workers and engineers willing to fight with determination. The fact that numerous immigrant contract workers are fighting alongside our comrades is a special piece of news, as are also the sympathy strikes of other Genoese factories: a circumscribed episode, which, however, points the way for future struggles.

The particular Italian situation opens up opportunities for our internationalist battle. Outrage leads nowhere. We need to take the field in our battle for communism among the masses, speaking first of all to the youths who are repelled by "their politics" and looking with greater attention to the banked down energies in the factories and workplaces. Our Leninist party can come out of the transitory moment of the crisis even stronger than before – a further incentive for every militant communist.

The lesson of the crisis in global relations
A New Revolutionary Generation*

"The Topicality of the Revolutionary Way"[55]: this was the headline of our March 1967 leader. The 50th anniversary of the October Revolution was drawing near, and we were reflecting on the lesson to be drawn from 1917 – more than ever necessary since everyone "was vying in the competition to demolish every idea of revolution among the working masses".

Arrigo Cervetto observed that we found ourselves "at one of the lowest points of the working class situation, at one of those points that characterise the counter-revolutionary phase", and added: "as Leninists, we are not afraid to recognise this". The defeat of the noble 1917 attempt weighed on the proletariat. That first assault remained isolated and the European proletariat was unable to follow Lenin and the Bolshevik party. The reaction was harsh, "the greatest defeat of the international proletariat in its history".

It was necessary to set off again from the awareness of that defeat: "Weeping over present conditions is useless. [...] Saying that we find ourselves in a counter-revolutionary phase today does not mean saying that there is nothing to do. On the contrary, there is much to do! The proletarian forces for the revolution have become too numerous to be counted, they have become an infinite army. We need to give them political consciousness, Leninist consciousness".

Change in the 1960s

This was the guideline that the generation of the founders of Lotta Comunista drew up for the youths who were entering the struggle at the end of the 1960s, in a whirl of illusions and exaltation that was almost incredible. Widespread wage struggles and student movements, the product of the spread of education, gave birth to strikes, sit-ins and marches. Some people took all of this for a revolutionary process.

This newspaper told those youths that this was not the case at all. Those workers' wage struggles did not pose the problem of power. There was no way that the students could be taken for a revolutionary class, especially since, at the time, they were most of them the children of the petty bourgeoisie. No revolution was imminent, but this did not mean that there was nothing to do ... on the contrary! Those youths had their eyes opened: they placed themselves at the service of the working class as they set up our workers' circles.

At the time the world was represented as being divided into two camps: one capitalist and dominated by the US, and the other socialist, with Moscow

* *Internationalist Bulletin*, February 2012

as its capital and extending as far as China. There were parties in Europe that insisted on defining themselves as communist. They were actually the heirs of the Stalinist counter-revolution, for which they were fully responsible. At the time the PCI was a force to be reckoned with and, although it was an interclass party, had its roots in the working class. It was not easy to oppose what was really a worker-bourgeois party. And when the first contrasts arose in Asia between Russia and rising China, some of them praised Mao and his particular socialism to the skies. There were a good few youths who thought at the time that they had found their answer in those parties and ideologies.

Crisis in the 1970s

Shortly afterwards, in the mid-1970s, the regular crisis occurred: a crisis of international restructuring that was not as drastic or long-lasting as the present. Various factories closed down, and then as now the workers lived on unemployment benefit and redundancy payments. This proved to be a precious experience for the younger generations in the field who saw with their own eyes that the life of capitalism is really a continual succession of phases of development and crisis. The subsequent development was characterised by imperialist liberism that stepped up the pace of the contention among the world powers, a pace that Moscow could not keep up with.

At the end of the 1980s, the walls that marked the boundaries of the so-called "socialist camp" and that kept Europe divided began to fall. False socialism broke on the rocks of the new contention from the Caucasus to the Balkans; countries that had been Russian satellites for decades were pulled into the orbit of European imperialism, greatly strengthened by Germany's reunification. Hungary, Poland, the Czech Republic, Slovakia, Latvia, Estonia, Lithuania, Bulgaria and Romania are now part of the European Union after having been under the heel of Moscow and its tanks for decades, with the complicity of the Western powers: once and for all, a new imperialist division archived the one that had been decided upon at Yalta at the end of the war.

The collapse of the USSR and globalisation

In the upheavals of those years a new generation of twenty-year-olds began to take an interest in the revolutionary struggle. And, after having seen the violence of war, those youths had to deal with the new ideologies and illusions spread by the ruling classes. With the implosion of the Russian empire, the bourgeois ideologues decreed the defeat of "communism" and the final victory of the market economy. Capital invaded the markets of Eastern Europe, Asia and Latin America. This marked the worldwide triumph of capitalism: globalisation. This newspaper told that third generation of Leninists that this was not the case at all. That capital invested in the new markets was nourishing new voracious competitors and new well-prepared powers.

That triumph of capitalism was preparing further and more serious crises. Just a few years later, amidst the celebrations of globalisation, development and growing affluence, the crisis exploded in the heart of imperialism, at the very core of American finance. It is the most serious crisis in over sixty years.

It was the summer of 2007, forty years after that 1967 leader. The crisis in global relations recalled the "topicality of the revolutionary way" with even greater impact.

The crisis and the long debt cycle

Today world capitalism is still struggling in the spiderweb of the consequences of the crisis.

Those who have been singing the praises of the free market have changed their tune, state intervention in the economy is again welcome, and the old German-style "social market economy" is gaining points. The infusion of public capital in the course of the crisis has determined a marked increase in the debts of the old capitals of imperialism. A long debt cycle, followed by our newspaper in every detail, has begun. The United States and Europe are struggling to deal with it; it is particularly virulent in the Old Continent and in Italy.

With unemployment and wage freezes, it is the wage-earners that have mainly paid for the crisis. The price paid by the younger generations has been particularly high.

In the 2008-2010 two-year period, employment in Italy fell by 2.2%, but in the 15-29 age group by 13.2%, six times as much. Today one youth out of three between the ages of 15 and 24 is unemployed, and temporary employment is greatly on the increase. Fabrizio Saccomanni, the director-general of the Bank of Italy, has spoken of an "excluded generation". In his opinion, a youth that breaks into the labour market has a 55% chance of being offered a temporary job. Youths are becoming increasingly dependent on their families. In 1980 16% of thirty-year-olds lived with their parents; now this figure stands at 40%. Much has been said about "mummy's boys", and in fact there are a good few of them, but little account has been taken of the role of family welfare in the crisis.

Imperialist Europe

At the beginning of the crisis in November 2007, we wrote that the emergence of new powers would shrink the market space, creating "more difficult conditions for dealing with crises and partial clashes"[56].

With its one billion three hundred million population, China is imposing itself on the world markets and is forcing the United States and the old European powers onto the defensive. Taking advantage of the crisis and of its competitors' problems, China is increasing its foreign investment. In annual flows it has already overtaken Japan and the United Kingdom in this field, and is in fifth place behind the US, Germany, France and Hong Kong. Beijing sources maintain that Chinese capital is present in 16,000 companies in 178 countries.

Washington is attempting to react by brandishing the dollar, still the leading reserve currency, although threatened by the euro and tomorrow by the Yuan. And it is exploiting its military power, so far unrivalled but it, too, threatened by America's huge debt: in fact, Barack Obama envisages a reduction in defence spending and a review of the US military presence abroad.

The European Union is reacting with a battle to strengthen its powers and political institutions. Its aim is to create a "power Europe", masked by the rhetoric of peace and the brotherhood of the European peoples. After the decisive step of the single currency, it is now the turn of fiscal unification. The crisis has accelerated the European process. We have given Europe's December decisions on fiscal and budgetary policies a strategic value. It is not hard to imagine that after the single currency and a single fiscal system it will then be the turn of a single army. The battle is being fought, and the way towards fiscal union requires firm budgetary discipline and a determined struggle against excessive debts.

A fresh challenge

In our in-depth work among the masses we meet with veiled resentment, worry, disappointment and even resignation. Some tell us that by now there is nothing more to do. This is not the case: on the contrary, there is much to do. And we say this especially to the youths who have joined our revolutionary struggle during the crisis years: a generation that is not at all "excluded" for us. Indeed, this is a lucky generation since it is taking to the field at a time when crisis is not a fixation on the part of us communists, but a fact ... and glaringly evident moreover! This is a precious experience for the fourth generation of Leninists. Furthermore, this is a lucky generation since it has chosen communism at a time of great changes in the power relations that will lead to further clashes and to deeper crises. Finally, this is a lucky generation since it can take its place in the struggle alongside three previous generations with all their accumulated theory, experience and organisation.

Our Leninist positions are stronger today, even if the way ahead is still long and full of obstacles. But today we know, much better than we did yesterday, just how passable it is. A Leninist party in Europe is more than ever necessary. It is for this that we are fighting, well aware that the revolutionary way is more than ever topical today.

A precious theoretical and political continuity for our battle in European restructuring

"Those Who Have More Passion Will Prevail in the End"*

More than anywhere else, it is in the old powers that the crisis has left unpleasant after-effects. The IMF estimates that world growth for 2012 will be about 3.3% - almost one per cent below its previous assessments. Growth in the "advanced countries" will be poor, +1.2%, while the emerging countries will slow down to 5.4% as against last year's 6.2. With 1.8%, the United States will maintain its 2011 rhythm, while the eurozone will experience a slight slump, -0.5%, which will be much more marked in Italy, -2.2%. China is expected to slow down to +8.2% with respect to last year's +9.2%.

The old powers' slow pace continues to favour the rise of China, which has already benefited from the crisis.

Further European restructuring

According to a BNP-Paribas research, Beijing's share of the world's manufacturing production, which stood at 8.3% in 2000, rose to 14.1% in 2007. In the crisis years it made a further leap ahead, arriving at 21.7% in 2010. All of this was at the expense of the old powers. In fact, the US fell from 24.8% in 2000 to 18.2% before the crisis, and to 15.6% in 2010. These are figures that are causing concern in the old capitals of imperialism. In the first decade of the century, no fewer than six million jobs in manufacturing were lost in the United States: about four million before the crisis, and two million in the crisis years. There is talk about reindustrialisation and insourcing, themes that have been boosted by the presidential election campaign.

In Europe, the reaction to the rise of Chinese imperialism continues to have its strategic aim in the unification of the Old Continent. This took an important step forward in the latest European summit that moved in the direction of fiscal unity. Under pressure from the Franco-German axis, not only the debt battle is going on in Europe, but also radical political, economic and social restructuring.

The federalisation process means that the nation-states will have to yield more of their sovereignty to the EU institutions. The national parliaments are gradually losing their prerogatives, and basic issues are being decided in Brussels, in the European Council, Commission and Central Bank combination. The irremediable crisis of the parliamentary form of government is growing worse in the single states, thus further fuelling every form of

---

* *Internationalist Bulletin*, March 2012

parliamentary cretinism. This is a process that is reflected in the political parties, still anchored to visions limited to their own national confines. Their ideological basis is being severely shaken, and there is no doubt that political restructuring is taking place. This will hold many surprises, but its general direction is that of European imperialist democracy.

The German way for Italy's big business groups

At an economic and social level, this new restructuring brings to mind the recurrent debate about the German industrialist model, about which our analysis has much to say.

The other capitals are viewing the German way, which has imposed itself on the continent thanks to the weight of debt. Berlin is reaping the harvest of having faced a number of the thorny problems of competitiveness and the labour market in advance, with the assimilation of East Germany acting both as a precedent and as a testing-ground.

The balanced budget constriction, which will be imposed by law, obliges Southern Europe in particular to tackle protected socio-economic orders with low general productivity and poor efficiency, nourished by generous flows of government deficit spending. To this are added fiscal reforms that favour indirect taxation, also with the aim of reducing the tax burden on companies and labour: this is the case with Sarkozy's so-called "social VAT", part of the theme of industrial employment in France that he is brandishing in a controversial election campaign.

And finally, interventions in the labour market that take into account that in part of Eastern Europe – in Bulgaria and Romania – wages are by now close to those of Mexico or the coastal areas of China. On the one hand, these interventions regard the containment of labour costs, but on the other, the rapid ageing of their populations and the need to increase their working populations.

The measures passed by the Monti government in Italy are seen by the big business groups of Italian imperialism as implementing the "German way" of European restructuring. The "Save Italy" decree is in force, paid for mainly by wage-earners and pensioners. Now the liberalisation measures involve long-term unresolved problems of the Italian metropolis: first of all, the persistent dualism between a North that is fully integrated into the industrial heartland of Europe, and a South that is similar to the peripheral areas of Mediterranean Europe. The history of the "Southern issue" in Italy is long, and is now being transformed by the European restructuring process. In the South of Italy today industrial districts coexist with vast areas of black economy with a prevalently immigrant workforce and low wages, and with generous flows of parasitic public spending, all of which holding together a social compromise with general low productivity. European restructuring in Italy has an extremely intricate problem to resolve in the South, as has been demonstrated by the first reactions of the petty bourgeois sectors that feel under threat. Meanwhile, the reform of the labour market finds the trade unions divided, weakened, and sorely tried by company restructuring, from Fiat to Fincantieri.

The generations of Leninism

Significant changes are taking place, and there is widespread growing confusion and palpable bewilderment. This is very fertile soil for the Marxist School, offering further opportunities for our work among the masses and the younger generations.

But our struggle is growing more complicated: for reasons linked to the unprecedented phenomena generated by the new strategic phase, but also for subjective reasons. The development of recent years and the diffusion of the influence of our Leninist positions within the working class make our organisational work more complex. The influx of another revolutionary generation and the growing commitment of our Leninist militants in significant episodes of the workers' defensive struggles complicate the work of the party plan. A further effort is required of us. The tool to be used is the accumulated theory, experience and organisation at our disposal.

Over sixty years have gone by since the 1951 Pontedecimo Congress, the founding act of the original group that gave birth to Lotta Comunista in the first half of the 1960s. Today we are able to present a documented analysis of those first steps in our forthcoming *Lotta Comunista. The Original Group 1943-1952*: a publishing choice that takes into account the current cadre training process and the complex battles looming ahead. Those first steps were taken in wartime, in the 1943-44 strikes, then in the partisan struggles, and subsequently in the workers' post-war restructuring struggles. Its protagonists were a group of young men, mainly workers, who sought answers to the frustrated aspirations of the partisan struggle. Years later, Arrigo Cervetto would observe: "The collapse of myths interwove with frantic theoretical and political research into why this had happened and into why the world presented itself as a world of imperialist powers"[57].

A handful of men

That research took place in a difficult climate of bitter disappointment that pushed those young men towards anarchism, in an attempt to find answers in the workers' tradition of Libertarian Communism, another Communism counterposed to the prevailing Stalinism.

Thus was born the plan for the Anarchical Groups of Proletarian Action (GAAP), the result of a meeting with Pier Carlo Masini. Like Cervetto, he had spent a brief period in the PCI, but, attracted by anarchism, had then left it. The plan was basically that of drawing the best elements from the anarchical movement and to shape them into an organisation. Within the budding group there immediately sprang up an internal difference between Cervetto's point of view – he was inclined towards Marxism – and that of Masini, more attracted to the anarchical movement and with a "small group phobia".

In June 1949 the twenty-two-year-old Cervetto wrote to Masini: "Many comrades take me for a Marxist, but, instead of putting them off, they seem attracted to my way of thinking. I'm pleased about this, also because Marxism is an inexhaustible source of ideological riches for me. I'd almost be tempted to define myself as a Marxist-Anarchist. But I'm not yet certain about this: I still have a lot – but really a lot – to read, study, analyse, and criticise before adopting any fixed pattern".

A month later, Cervetto wrote: "I'm not an anarchist. [...] Need I repeat it? I'm someone who was attracted to anarchism (I was twenty years old at the time), and became enthusiastic about it. Afterwards, this someone started studying in earnest, and all his enthusiasm cooled down". And at the end of that July 1949, Cervetto wrote again in a letter to Masini: "I didn't believe that Marxism, and especially Leninism, could be such a powerful weapon. Day after day, I find food for my conceptions and studies. If I don't come out of this a fanatic, I'll come out of it a revolutionary"[58].

That confrontation did not prevent the setting up of the GAAP, but the difference in points of view deepened in subsequent years until it led to a rift in 1958. Masini, who would become an eminent historian of the anarchic movement, retreated into Nenni's PSI and then joined the Social Democrats. Speaking of the GAAP, the book recognises that they were "a handful of men" with a hard core in which "no more than 10-15 militants" were "the engine of the organisation"[59].

A disciplined passion

We now owe our presence in the real movement to that handful of men, to that group of young workers that chose to start all over again. What, at the time, pushed those men into making that choice? Revolutionary passion. Passion had pushed those youths to join the partisan struggle and thus risk their lives. And it was passion that allowed them to overcome the disappointment of that experience and to start all over again. In later life, Cervetto recalled the political baptism of his small Savona group: "Unaware of the real content of that imperialist war, and clinging to the myths that the opposition's dialectics effortlessly spawn, we were tiny leaves borne on the impetuous winds blowing over the world. With or without us, the winds would have continued on their course. But passion, even if it is a leaf, remains passion. It is part of the human race. And, if steered, is a powerful political factor. Politics is struggle and not an academic exercise, since no one risks a hair of his head for a mere political hypothesis. Passion alone pushes someone to risk his neck. In the end those who have more passion will prevail".

Passion, however, that must not remain purely instinctive, with the risk of being exploited by others, as had happened to those young men in the partisan struggles. They had risked their lives, and some of them had lost them, in their aspiration to a communism that had then turned out to be Russian imperialism in disguise. That experience had left a deep impression on those young men, Cervetto included, so much so that he swore he would never again be anyone else's tool: "As long as there are incandescent social and political struggles, passion will push the most eager youths into the dark nights and streets of a working class district in an industrial town. They will not have to find themselves at dawn wondering why the day is so different, and lose years studying in despair, as has happened in the past. Since then I have devoted my life to providing an outlet in political reason, strategy, and calculated struggle for my own passion and for that of the generations to come"[60].

Never anyone else's tool

And this was the way it was: without passion there is no struggle, but passion has to be armoured with reason, disciplined, and anchored in theory, otherwise it risks being a tool in someone else's hands. Basically, this is the key to being able to face the more complex and difficult deadlines of the struggles that await us in times to come.

Our accumulated wealth of theory, strategic analysis, experience and organisation is the guarantee of a firm anchorhold. We have never lacked passion. It is a case of transmitting passion as we know it to our supporters, sympathisers and, especially, the many young people who continue to approach us. "Steered [passion] is a powerful political factor", and even in our days "those who have more passion will prevail in the end".

The challenge facing european leninism in the next decade

Our "General Task" in the Era of European Unification*

Europe has reverted to forcing the pace towards integration. The agenda for unitary imperialism has accelerated as it becomes increasingly urgent for the EU to gain critical mass in order to participate in the division of the global spoils. The plan formulated by the highest authorities in the EU – the "four presidents" Van Rompuy, Barroso, Juncker and Draghi – outlines the objectives for a new political centralisation, and sets ten years as a target for the unification of the continent. This is a time horizon that we are forced to take into careful consideration; not to set deadlines in the development of the Party but in view of its historical delay. A deficit in party development we are attempting to rectify. We have always devoted considerable space in our analysis to the process of European unification; this has necessarily increased in recent years. Firstly, because European integration is an unprecedented phenomenon that tests Marxist theory. Secondly, because the process has ever increasing repercussions on our own activity

The spirit of militancy and the victory of science

Today we view how the trend towards integration, a process we had identified long ago, has advanced over the decades and is accelerating, exposing the crisis of national sovereignty. This is a victory for scientific analysis. A victory we proclaim in the spirit of militancy. But what do we mean by victory? We would like to explain so as to leave no room for misunderstanding. Under attack again, this time over the issue of Southern Europe's sovereign debt, European imperialism emerges nonetheless strategically strengthened by the crisis and has received new impetus. This means that our main enemy is more powerful, and today oppresses and crushes the European proletariat more than ever before. Furthermore the cost of the acceleration towards integration, which has been triggered by the crisis, is being paid by the European working class as a whole, in some cases very heavily. We are in the middle of a wage squeese, especially on the younger sections of the workforce. The attack on pensions has also been heavy and unemployment and underemployment are rampant in Europe. According to the ECB, unemployment in the European Union rose by four million units between 2008 and 2010. The European power elite, in assessing the new world order, are perfectly aware that the size of their nation-states has no chance of competing with the other continental powers. One of the leading opinion makers of the Italian left, Eugenio Scalfari, writes: "Political forces

---

* *Internationalist Bulletin S I*, October 2012

have to understand that Europe must exist as a state, otherwise the United States, China, India and Brazil will make the key decisions. The statelets of Europe are in decline [...] taken in isolation they no longer have the critical mass to negotiate on a par with the superpowers and the multinationals". Science and the struggle. The above is a fine summary of the situation as it stands today: the European establishment is aware of the dangers and is quickening its pace. Tomorrow the leaders of the EU, with the same gravity and aplomb with which they now talk about financial rigour and competitiveness, will begin to point at external enemies. They will then call the young and the workers to arms in defence of Europe, and perhaps even of its Christian roots. We have no doubt that this is how events will evolve! But why do we insist on seeing the acceleration towards European unification as confirmation of Marxist scientific analysis? The explanation is deep-rooted and is directly related to the effectiveness and incisiveness of our internationalist struggle. We have verified, on the basis of incontrovertible facts, that the instruments of Marxist analysis, together with the substantial elaboration of Arrigo Cervetto, have provided – and still provide – the tools with which to unravel what is happening in Europe. We have not been diverted in our analysis by secondary considerations and the related bickering. We do not state this merely to boast and highlight the veracity of our thesis, although this would be legitimate, but as an act in the revolutionary political struggle.

Ours is a victory for science because our strategic analysis has been shown to work in changing circumstances; it is, and always has been, focused, on essential elements. It has demonstrated its value over the long term and the ability to identify fundamental trends[61]. This has allowed our Party to lead a relentless struggle against European imperialism, to intensify the battle by focusing its attack on the key targets without wasting any of our time or efforts. This is essential for a revolutionary minority.

The short summer of François Hollande

How can we forget what François Hollande and "Hollandism" has represented in recent months? The whole of the European Left, from Paris to Athens, hoped for a shift towards a "Social Europe". Some imagined that German rigour would be tempered by the new course in France, others saw an undermining of the Franco-German axis, and yet others hoped for a softening to austerity. All were committed to entering the fray by supporting Hollande from a variety of political positions, and, in so doing, to spreading illusions and identifying false objectives. We did not waste a drop of our energy, we did not waste a single shot against false objectives. We were focused on the real target and because of our strategic analysis we were able to identify before others the real nature of the phenomenon generated by the French election.

All our energies against European imperialism

After all, this is the way our Party has got stronger through the decades. Basing itself on a strategy which has been subject to continuous review, and which has resulted in an effective revolutionary political struggle and a militant organisation. This explains our reliance on Marxist scientific analysis in interpreting the acceleration in course towards European imperialism. These reflections should also make our tactics for the next decade a little clearer. It is true that the European proletariat is being squeesed and that there are no signs of a general struggle, but there are no alternatives in this phase. However, it is equally true that forces are emerging from the ranks of the working class that can be harnessed in the fight against European imperialism. After all, our class has a conscious vanguard, an organisation that, albeit small, is on the field of battle and is in action, fighting resolutely the main enemy at home. So, instead of despairing over the dominance of the European bourgeoisie, why not see the acceleration of the integration of imperialist Europe as an opportunity for the complementary growth of the bourgeoisie's great antagonist – European Leninism? The objective conditions for such growth are all in place. Although at the present time it is only a possibility, a possibility for which it is worthwhile committing all our energies.

The "general task" of the battle of organisation

In assessing the current crisis in global relations we have considered the previous world crisis, the one caused by the restructuring of the mid-1970s. Despite its lower intensity and duration, it was seen as a "sudden change in direction" at the time, even though "it was the result of the evolution of pre-existing conditions". In the middle of this crisis, in September 1975, this newspaper published an article by Arrigo Cervetto entitled *Il compito generale* [The General Task]. It was an in-depth reflection based on Lenin's work, which looked at the consequences of this "sudden change" on the actions and tasks of our Party. There is no doubt that the crisis of recent years has led to deeper changes than that of the 1970s. The outcome of the crisis and its effect on the debt cycle are impacting the balance of power and has accelerated the move towards European union. So today, more than ever, we need to reflect on the repercussions of these changes on our party and its struggle. We need to return to *The General Task* and update it for the new objective and subjective conditions. In 1975 Cervetto noted that "it is the proletariat that pays for every crisis of capitalism" and added: "This is obvious. A phenomenon that Marxism has never ceased to highlight. What is not obvious, on the other hand, is that the revolutionary proletariat should not reap political advantage from the crisis". This must be our starting point: how can the revolutionary proletariat take advantage of this crisis today? Let us return to Cervetto: "The materialistic method of analysis [allows] a scientific prediction of the general evolution of events while, at the same time, affirming the impossibility to account for specific events and a series of contingent factors. It is because of this impossibility that materialism inevitably leads us to discard any rationalistic and doctrinal tendencies". And again: "In our time, the accumulation of historical experience can, without doubt, increase our understanding of contingencies, of crises, and complications on the world scene. This benefits the Leninist party in its in reading of specific events and their outcomes – in its specific predictions"[62].

An updated plan for the new strategic phase

The conclusions that Cervetto drew at the time are of the utmost importance in understanding the tasks that lie ahead of us: "Only systematic efforts which are based on the general trends we have identified in the evolution of events allow us to make use of all the contingencies which are part of this evolutionary process". In other parts of the text Cervetto underlines that "the party must proceed according to a plan of action that is independent of these contingencies and that is based on the determined evolutionary process"[63]. Our strategic analysis was able to predict general trends in the evolution of European imperialism and European integration. "The accumulation of historical experience" has been further enriched by additional decades of analysis and revolutionary political struggle. This is another advantage for the Party and for the "specific predictions" of our analytical framework, which allows us to identify and evaluate the acceleration in the evolution of European imperialism caused by the current crisis. It is impossible to predict all the complications that will occur on the road towards European integration. However a "plan of action" that is based on "the expected evolutionary trends" must drive our struggle today. For it to be an effective plan it cannot be a re-hash of past policies. It must take into account this new strategic phase and the subsequent acceleration of European integration. The new modified plan of action must take into consideration how our Party is to develop and the new dimensions of the internationalist struggle. *The General Task* of 1975 has been the foundation of our development during the intervening decades. A plan of action, one which has been duly modified and updated in line with today's new and unprecedented conditions, is a prerequisite for taking the struggle forward. A passionate militant commitment, analysis, the accumulation of experience and political leadership must do the rest.

Internationalist strategy in the global transformation

A World Battle*

Debate is going on about economic recovery for 2014. Christine Lagarde, the IMF Managing Director, has summed up the situation as follows: "while we are seeing some signs of recovery, global growth remains subdued". The advanced economies are in better condition than six months ago, but the emerging markets are slowing down. The slowdown of the so-called BRICS has been at the centre of attention also because the currencies of some of these countries have been devalued.

There is a basic reason for this focusing of attention on the so-called emerging economies. According to *The Economist*, from the beginning of 2010 to date China's contribution to global growth has been one third, while another 40% has come from the other emerging countries.

The crises of modernisation

It is precisely in these countries that we have seen the emergence of a cycle of what we have defined as *crises of modernisation*, the product of capitalist development with all its consequences.

This is a process in which we find different stages of development and different combinations of modernity and backwardness – a modernity that now unites Beijing and Shanghai with São Paulo and Istanbul, and even with such Arab capitals as Cairo or Tunis, but which rests on greatly different levels of backwardness. The social and political outcomes of these crises will also be different.

As regards the new imperialist powers, we also need to consider that they have to deal with the deadlines of industrial restructuring in advance.

The Shanghai offensive

These processes are now underway in China. Shanghai, where a big free trade zone (FTZ) was inaugurated at the end of September, may be taken as a symbol of Chinese restructuring. This FTZ envisages liberalisations and facilitations for investment and foreign banks. Moreover, the full convertibility of the yuan will be tested through the liberalisation of the interest rates.

The Chinese press compares this choice to the setting up of the special economic zones (SEZ), with Shenzhen in the fore. Thirty-five years ago, these led to the Chinese take-off towards full imperialist maturity. A

* *Internationalist Bulletin*, October 2013

research by the Antwerp Management School observes that, since January 2013, the Chinese have invested in 7,148 European enterprises: a 60% increase with respect to 2012. China is now the third-biggest investor in Europe after the United States and Japan. It has recently been announced that the second-biggest Chinese car-manufacturing group, Dongfeng, is negotiating a 30% stake in the French Peugeot.

These are the capital exports of Chinese imperialism. But Beijing also has to suffer all the contradictions of imperialist maturity.

The restructuring battles

We have documented in these pages the processes that are affecting China's iron and steel industry, but restructuring is much vaster than this. In July, the Ministry of Industry decreed the closure of old plants and cuts in productive capacity. This involves 1,400 companies in 19 sectors in which overproduction has led to a price war. Among the sectors affected are iron and steel, cement, ferroalloys, aluminium, copper, papermaking, glass and fibres.

A clash that challenges the state monopoly of the Three Sisters of Chinese oil, CNPC, Sinopec and CNOOC, is shaking the oil sector. PetroChina top managers have come under investigation. The separation of extraction from refining is on the agenda, and debate is going on over the unbundling of the distribution network through introducing greater competition and opening up to foreign groups.

The electricity sector is also undergoing restructuring, and here too debate is going on over separating generation from transmission. Transfer of the state-owned grid to the free market has been decreed, but the reform has not been carried out and the state-owned groups are apparently growing stronger. There is also a clash over prices – whether they have to be fixed by the state or by the market – as well as over the grid – a single national grid or various regional grids.

Then there is the chemical industry: China now accounts for one third of the global chemical market. A McKinsey report observes that the sector has been the centre of a wave of investments that, with the economic slowdown, are leading to overproduction. China's chemical industry looks as if it has now entered a new phase, since overcapacity is affecting a series of productions.

According to *China Daily*, an antitrust body for the Chinese market is about to be created. The former American Secretary of the Treasury, Henry Paulson, also mentions this in the *International Herald Tribune*. He links the antitrust body directly to the struggle to break the energy monopoly and to the clash between the state-owned groups. Battles over restructuring inevitably lead to bitter political clashes.

The Chinese political imbalance

We have already observed that these political struggles are still kept in check within the single party. The case of Bo Xilai, the powerful head of the province of Chongqing, is a good example of this. In fact, he was Xi Jinping's rival in the succession to Hu Jintao and represented a group of powerful forces.

Bo was defeated in the struggle for the succession and ended up in jail, on trial, and sentenced to life imprisonment. The *Financial Times* of October 12th relates that the net is closing in on Zhou Yongkang, a powerful Politburo member that allegedly backed Bo. Various members of his entourage have been arrested. However, it is clear that single-party pluralism is malfunctioning. Confrontations and clashes between groups and factions cannot be fought through trials and jail sentences. Imperialist democracy clearly works better and is the best political shell for mature capitalism.

It is more than evident that the Dragon is hatching a political and institutional imbalance of huge proportions. We have written that it is impossible to tell exactly when this will happen, although it is possible to imagine its social and political effects[64]. The prospects in China are anything but tranquil.

The Arab Springs

The spectrum of crises of modernisation includes the Arab Springs, in a combination of modernisation and backwardness in which the latter has greater weight. The movements that sprang from them were hailed by the media as revolts against the area's old tyrants, peoples' revolts that would decree the triumph of democracy through free elections.

The events in Egypt brought everyone back to harsh reality. The revolt against the tyrant Mubarak ended with the generals' coup and full restoration with his rehabilitation. And in Syria the Spring has ended in a long civil war. Last month, that conflict became the occasion of a harsh confrontation between great and local powers. We have dealt with this in detail in these pages[65]. Now everything is being fought out in the diplomatic arena, with a confrontation that has spread from Syria to Iranian nuclear power. In these crises, the new powers gear themselves up to fighting harder on the international markets, and the world contention grows fiercer.

This offers us initial scope for further deploying our revolutionary strategy: the autonomy of our class position needs to be guaranteed in this state of affairs.

One billion people in the transformation

There is another link between the effects of the modernisation crisis and our internationalist battle. We need to consider the fact that these processes will drag vast masses into the vortex of social transformation: in the next ten years another billion people will be involved in it. Millions of youths and workers will be involved in the struggles that these processes will generate.

Part of these youths and workers will fall prey to the social-imperialist ideologies that permeate those movements. Even the young leaders of the new powers will emerge from them. There will, however, be a minority that will not be satisfied, that will want to forge ahead in its thirst for social justice, that will seek support, and that will be inspired by the media themselves to look out to the world. In our book about our founding group we asked ourselves "what way will be chosen by the class consciousness of millions of proletarians that are now beginning their apprenticeship"[66], particularly in that immense China where the state party that they will have to fight against still wears the ideological garb of false socialism. We cannot know the answer beforehand. The course of events will reveal it.

There is one thing, however, that we do know: a *European Leninism* that is firmly entrenched in the Old Continent can set itself the aim of meeting up with those vanguards, however small they may be, and put at their disposal a theoretical, political and organisational patrimony accumulated over three or four generations. Today this possibility depends on the extent to which and when these small vanguards give themselves a political form: this is a process that we cannot influence. However, it also largely depends on the entrenchment and influence of the Leninist party in this European metropolis.

This is where, first of all and above all, we have to fight the battle to link up with the vanguards that will emerge from those millions of proletarians – we have to start from this Italian metropolis and from our entrenchment in the heart of European imperialism.

Our internationalist battle

The way forward remains that of widespread organisational work among the masses and of a vast political campaign among the new generations. The disasters of *their* politics continue to offer us space for *our* internationalist politics. This is the moment to press on, to give no respite, to draw attention to the violation of the workers' interests – all this while keeping our gaze fixed on the millions of youths that are having their first experiences in the movements of the modernisation crises. And all the more so since the thousand trickles of those movements are already part of our revolutionary battle: not so much because of the drop in the ocean that is our international presence – which in any case exists – but because of the changed nature of the European proletariat, which the workers of the emerging countries now form part of.

We meet them in our work amidst the complex wage stratifications, they are with us in the factories, they form an integral part of our supporters, they come to our workers' clubs and increasingly animate our initiatives. And in the battle that we are fighting among the young, young second-generation immigrant students are increasingly by our side. These are joined by youths from the emerging countries that come to study in European universities, the children of those countries' upper social strata and of the new middle classes, and anything but indifferent to our internationalism.

It would be absurd to think that these workers and youths should give rise in their homelands to political movements that only the course of the class struggle can generate. Nevertheless, their presence in our ranks contributes to entrenching our party in the European proletariat and may be of help tomorrow in our relationship with the minorities that will spring from the social and political struggles of the modernisation crises.

Our battle needs to be fought here, as we continue to link up our organisation with our scientific newspaper as our collective organiser. But our horizon spans the world.

Our battle in the European restructuring
The Political Energies of Working Class*

The battle in the current phase of far-reaching European restructuring has grown fiercer. From the other side of the Atlantic, and from the UK, the barrage against the policy of economic rigour which Germany has imposed on Europe has intensified. Germany's exports are the source of the problem. They will generate a surplus of 250 billion euro in 2013, a level which is comparable to that of China.

Germany's industrial might is dominating the markets. There are initial signs that Europe is on the road to recovery and there is a real fear in some quarters that a successful restructuring of the Old Continent will further enhance European imperialism's grip on the markets. In Southern Europe there are those who continue in their recriminations against Germany's rigorous line. But this merely constitutes nostalgia for the unconditional, easy terms, which were conceded to the Mediterranean countries in the past, and which are today long gone.

The burden of disequilibrium

Because restructuring has been accompanied by a relentless reduction in public debt the course of treatment for Europe has been drastic, and the medicine it has had to drink has been bitter. It is no coincidence then that recovery has been a long drawn out affair and that the signals from a variety of goods and services have pointed to the onset of deflation in recent months.

The euro has gained in value against the dollar and touched 1.38, a level that adversely affects German exports. The reaction of ECB has been immediate and interest rates have been halved. Mario Draghi has again shown that the ECB is willing to use all the arms at its disposal.

The Italian bourgeoisie has to face European restructuring with the added burden of domestic political disequilibrium. The markets have forced the issues, and industrial concentration and mergers have accelerated in Europe. At the same time, the issue of overcapacity in key sectors like steel making and automobile manufacturing have become ever more pressing. The restructuring of the banking system has been a requisite for the creation of the European banking union. There is talk in Europe of binding contracts between single member states and the Union as a solution to the problem of competitiveness and public spending that foresee financial support from Europe. These are major issues that the factions of Italy's dominant class will have to resolve.

---

* *Internationalist Bulletin*, November 2013

Yesterday's battles

The Italian bourgeoisie, which has always been subject to buffoonery and has become increasingly Mediterranean, has had to pay a high price for successive waves of restructuring through the decades. Its large industries have been decimated and in recent weeks old problems have again resurfaced – in the form of Telecom Italia, Alitalia, Ansaldo etc.

These battles were lost twenty or so years ago, during the previous cycle of restructuring, but the repercussions have been exacerbated by the current crisis. At the root of these old battles was the process of European integration which forced Rome to reorganise its state industries. Brussels put a stop to the public financing of the large industrial groups of state capitalism. The Treaty of Maastricht then forced Italy to reduce its debt and introduce a programme of privatisation. Finally, the introduction of the single currency meant that all large industries in the Eurozone (and not only the Italian ones) could no longer make use of a powerful backup option: competitive devaluation.

Romano Prodi, who had been the head of the public corporation running nationalised industries, has recently pointed out that Italy now has fewer large industries than Holland and Belgium. These are very late crocodile tears. In December 2003, we commented on the declarations that Giuseppe Guarino had made at the time. Guarino had been the minister responsible for nationalised industries in the Amato government of the early 1990s. Guarino regretted how he had missed the opportunity to introduce wide ranging privatisation ten years before by opting for the creation of two large public holding groups. At the end of 2003, Guarino observed how privatisations had helped to reduce the public debt but that this had meant that in Italy today "there are no industrial giants like in France and Germany"[67].

The pressing issue of competitiveness

At the end of September, *Affari e Finanza* pointed to the successful performance of the 56 companies (with international exposure), which are listed on the Star market of the Italian bourse. They represent the beating heart of the Italian economy and are highly prized by foreign investors. Of course, there are dynamic small to medium sized enterprises in Italy with international exposure, but these companies are those which have been hit especially hard by the global crisis.

In a report last July the Bank of Italy highlighted that Italy's GDP had fallen 7% since 2007 and how industrial production had fallen 25% since the start of the crisis. This compared with a 6% fall of the German industries and a 14% fall in a weaker France. The fall in some specific sectors was especially alarming: rubber and plastic (29%), metallurgy (28%), electrical machinery (39%), footwear (39%), electrical appliances (52%) and automobiles (51%).

These statistics point to the fall in competitiveness and the deindustrialisation which is readily associated with Europe. In its recent report on competitiveness, the European Commission ranks countries in groups. It identifies a group of highly competitive countries: Germany, Denmark, Sweden, Austria and Luxembourg, a group with above average competitiveness – Belgium, Holland, UK, Ireland, France and Spain; a third group consisting of Italy, Cyprus, Greece, Slovenia, Portugal and Malta; and a fourth group made up of the remaining East European members.

One cannot help noting the position of the Italian metropolis. The poor condition of its industries is a consequence of an old malaise: their extraordinary fragmentation. According to Eurostat 47% of all workers in Italy are employed in businesses with fewer than 10 employees. In France this figure is 25% and in Germany 19%. In this case small is not beautiful! This segment, which has been especially susceptible to the credit squeese, has been hit especially hard by the crisis.

Industrial Italy

The number of large industrial groups in Italy continues to fall. One more reason to look beyond the Alps to analyse the composition of the proletariat in the rest of Europe.

Despite everything the Italian metropolis remains an industrial power. According to the Bank of Italy there are at least 561 industrial groups with more than 500 employees. Along with them, there are 732 such companies in the private service sector (non financials). And then there are the large concentrations of workers in banking and insurance which have recently come under fire.

It is among these workers that we are fighting to establish our party. It is here that class energies are continually emerging which have in no way been weakened by events. We are talking about young workers and technicians who are ready for the struggle and are searching for direction and organisation. The trade unions have been hit by the crisis far harder than their relative weakness would have led us to believe. They increasingly seek refuge in parliamentarianism and are prone to championing issues typical of parliamentary cretinism. This is also true of the industrial trade unions which, despite the objective difficulties, could have shown more resistance.

We must face up to the fact that the class forces available can only be unified on the political level of revolutionary consciousness. It is up to us to organise these forces around our journal and create a solid network of supporters in workers' clubs, which centres of propaganda, training and organisation.

The limits of the bourgeois establishment

The Italian bourgeoisie faces tough challenges in the battles of European restructuring. The imperialist onslaught on salaries is not sufficient and its politics is not up to the task. Italian politics is too far removed from the pace of change and the actions which Europe pretends.

The centre-right is embroiled in the difficult and lengthy succession to Silvio Berlusconi. The *Partito Democratico* (PD, the "democratic party"), on the other hand, is bogged down in a surreal congressional campaign. We are in the midst of an attempt by the mayor of Florence to create a new personal party by overriding everything and everyone, and a clash between party members with bloc votes who continuously shift allegiances between one federation and the next. There are those who foresee the party having two leaders, one chosen by the party members and another chosen by the electorate. This possibility is not as far-fetched as it seems.

The deep split in the *Scelta Civica* party definitively spells the failure of Professor Monti's political designs. The other parties look idly on, and the newly elected MPs of the Five Star Movement are being sucked ever deeper into the whirlpool of rampant parliamentary cretinism.

The Letta-Alfano government, the Italian style "grand coalition", manages to stay afloat despite being tossed this way and that. It is kept afloat by a very sturdy lifebuoy – the political will of the EU and the ECB.

This stage in the struggle would require more incisive action, but the Italian bourgeoisie has what it deserves. The words of Lorenzo Parodi's eulogy upon the death of Arrigo Cervetto in 1995 readily come to mind: "in the light of the current chaos in Italian politics, a chaos Cervetto had predicted twenty five years in his thesis on Italian disequilibrium, perhaps we have overestimated the bourgeoisie leadership's capacity to give itself a political form which was up to the task"[68].

The lever of organisation

Today's political chaos, which has been exacerbated by European restructuring, offers new prospects for out internationalist battle. We see this day after day. Indeed, organisational work has become an even more powerful weapon today than it was in the past.

Through the years the people distributing our journal – *Lotta Comunista* – have been derided by some and labelled as "hawkers". Through the decades, all these people, with no exception, have been either reduced to total political irrelevancy or have changed sides. Our party has continued to develop and continues to work to funnel the energies which our class continues to express despite every difficulty.

The truth is that even in the defeat of our class, during times of crisis, there is always space to reaffirm our political autonomy. Even in the most difficult of situations for our class it is possible to strengthen the party. This is the aim of our renewed militancy.

A new generation of revolutionaries

Twenty Fruitful Years*

The global economy has started growing at pre-crisis levels, and world trade too is expanding at a healthy rate. However, the mood in the capitals of imperialism is not one of celebration, there are uncertainty and worry. The recovery is fragile and there are fears of a renewed dip. The IMF warns that the "advanced economies" face risks from stagnation and deflation.

Many see deflation as the biggest risk facing the Eurozone and the ECB. While a number of opinion leaders, including the *Financial Times*, have urged "new injections of liquidity", the ECB continues to deny the risk of deflation in Europe. At Davos, Mario Draghi asserted that the ECB was ready to use every means to avoid such an eventuality. Most concern, for the moment, is directed towards the turmoil in the "emerging countries", here the IMF sees the risk of "financial excess, especially in the form of asset bubbles".

The difficulties facing the emerging economies

This particular problem concerns a large number of countries which are experiencing a huge flight of capital, prevalently back to the dollar area. This flight of capital has led to weakness in a number of national currencies and debilitating the corresponding central banks as they were forced to intervene on the markets. In order to stem this flow, emerging countries are being forced to increase their interest rates. In some cases this increase has been sizeable, and the risk is that this will have a negative impact on their growth.

The decision by the FED to reduce purchases of government bonds, also known as tapering, is said to have triggered this exit of capital from emerging countries. Expectations of rate increases in the US and other developed economies have grown and this has attracted capital back to the advanced economies. Although tapering has become associated with the problems facing emerging countries, and has generated criticisms against the USA and other rich countries, it is not the only problem. The slowdown in China and the resulting fall in the price of raw materials also weigh heavy. Some also point to a significant increase in energy import prices resulting from currency weakness. India, Indonesia, Turkey, and South Africa have been especially affected by this phenomenon, and even the Ukraine has felt a knock-on effect. A final factor which explains the flight of capital away from emerging countries is the political instability created by these economic changes.

---

* *Internationalist Bulletin*, February 2014

Uncertainty in China

Other shadows looming over the global recovery come from the credit bubble in China. The rating agency Fitch estimates that the expansion in credit over the past five years has been without precedent "in the history of any large country". A large part of this credit is in the hands of the "shadow" banking sector, which is particularly shady in China. The fear is of widespread bankruptcies in this non-bank financial sector.

More generally, the mood in the capitals of imperialism has been soured by tensions in international relations. The temperature in Sino-Japanese relations has increased appreciably. The tones adopted are extraordinary: the Japanese press openly talks of the risk of war. Ostensibly, the question continues to centre on the disputed Senkaku/Diaoyu islands but the real issue is the new equilibrium in Asia in the context of declining US power.

China's new weight on the international scene has unsettled the Asian equilibrium. Beijing is rearming and the new doctrines of its military projection are there for all to see. Tokyo has been forced onto the defensive, but its answer is limited by the growing imbalance in Asia.

The USA and the temptation to withdraw

The temperature has never cooled in the Middle East, and now there are the massacres in Syria to contend with. The Geneva Conference on Syria is struggling to make any progress, while the temporary agreement with Iran over nuclear weapons has opened new possibilities of a rapprochement with Tehran which could unsettle the regional balance of power.

These processes are ongoing, but they have not removed the uncertainties surrounding American foreign policy and its strategic withdrawal any clearer. It is striking to hear a veteran of international politics, like Helmut Schmidt, affirm that "the United States of America will gradually withdraw from the battle for world domination".

The scramble for Africa

In Africa too there are a number of flashpoints – old and new. Arnaud de La Grange, a correspondent for *Le Figaro*, notes a renewed interest in Africa on the part of the great powers. The big change is that today it is no longer the USA and the Soviet Union that are vying for the "friendship of their African brothers"[69], but China and Japan. This may seem an exaggeration, but the fact is that Chinese capital is very active throughout the continent. And it is not only a question of raw materials, although the Chinese oil companies are present in Angola, Gabon, Nigeria, Sudan and Ethiopia: between 2005 and 2013 Beijing invested approximately 58 billion dollars in Africa and built 3,400 km of motorway and 2,200 km of railways.

Tokyo has replied with the visit of Prime Minister Abe to a number of African countries. His declared intention is to open "a new frontier in Japanese diplomacy". Undoubtedly this will be another example of cheque-book diplomacy.

The Franco-German u-turn

The Dark Continent has for long been Europe's preferred hunting ground. In recent years Europe has intervened in the form of French troops, and European policy has been accused of marching too closely to the tune of the Marseillaise. European backing for the French has never been lacking, but this has often been lukewarm – especially from Germany. Today things have changed.

At the beginning of January we saw President François Hollande's complete conversion to the Rhineland creed. After a few weeks, the Ministers of Foreign Affairs of France and Germany declared that a Franco-German brigade would be sent to Mali, and that European troops would be sent to assist French troops in the Central African Republic. Furthermore, Frank-Walter Steinmeier and Laurent Fabius announced that they would jointly visit Georgia and Moldava, followed by North Africa – the two fronts of the "European backyard".

Germany has also undergone a U-turn in defence policy. The German President has announced that Germany is ready to assume a major role in European defence. The guilt of the past, continued Joachim Gauck, should no longer be used as an excuse for Germany to play a minor role in foreign affairs. He also added that Germany is ready to participate in military missions "without the usual reservations". These themes have also been underlined by Steinmeier, the Minister of Foreign Affairs, and by Ursula von der Leyen, the Minister of Defence.

In our analysis of the recent crises in "Europe's backyard", we wrote that "European imperialism will have to take the initiative, or submit to that of others"[70]. Today European imperialism is on the move – from the Banking Union to the new Franco-German initiatives. There may be difficulties, there will be tensions, but the direction has been set. And it is the one we expected – the march towards an imperialist Europe with all the powers and attributes of a nation-state.

European restructuring in Italy

All the trends mentioned above will undoubtedly impact Italian policy. The situation in Italy continues to be critical: the expected recovery is weak – GDP growth is around 0.7%. Everyone repeats *ad nauseam* that the problem lies in competitiveness and that the only solution lies in European restructuring. There are two main pillars to this: the first is the imperialist policy against salaries – a further reduction in salaries in accordance with the German model of the Hartz laws. The second is the cut in public spending, the first step in resolving the problem of Italy's colossal debt.

It will be up to Matteo Renzi to apply the cure – further cuts in salaries and public spending and greater liberalization. Renzi is a new figure in "their politics". The mayor of Florence is a product of Catholic politics, a former boyscout and an enthusiastic participant in World Youth Day celebrations. Renzi won over the "Partito Democratico" (Democratic Party – PD) and became Prime Minister by unceremoniously dumping Enrico Letta, without even waiting for an "investiture by the people". He has the backing of the media and the large Italian industrial groups, starting with ENI.

The twenty years of Berlusconism

Renzi has shown ability and a lot of cynicism in manoeuvring his party. Now we must see how he acts on the wider stage, in the European and global contest. Europe is intrigued to see how he will fare with an unpopular policy of austerity and the testing European constraints. It is our task to spearhead the battle in defence of salaries and jobs.

We detect a general disillusionment and confusion and our ideas are finding fertile ground. We have had confirmation from the success of the sales campaign for our publications. The success of our new book, *Cronache del Berlusconismo*[71] [Chronicles of Berlusconism], merits special attention. The book contains analysis, comments and an evaluation from twenty years of political struggle in Italy. We believe the material stands the test of time.

The past twenty years have been key for European imperialism and the strengthening of its powers. We have followed the progress of European imperialism, analyzed it, and fought against it on a daily basis. The past twenty years have seen changes in the Italian political parties. The crisis of the Christian Democrats, the PSI and the smaller non-Catholic parties opened the way for Silvio Berlusconi – an impolitical Lombard businessman who has occupied centre stage for the past twenty years.

The past twenty years have also been the years of the PCI's transformist experiment, an attempt to recycle itself from the Russian party into the European party. A gradual process which transformed "the party of Togliatti, Longo and Berlinguer" first into 'Partito Democratico della Sinistra' [the Democratic Party of the Left – PDS], then 'Democratici di Sinistra' [Democrats of the Left – DS] and finally the 'Partito Democratico' [Democratic Party – PD]. The PD is today in the hands of a young Catholic with strong links to the Vatican. With the strength of the PD behind him he has now become Prime Minister. For the generation of the old leaders of the Italian Communist Party [PCI], who were the dynamic force of their time, the record of the past twenty years must make grim reading.

A collective battle

To conclude, the past twenty years have been crucial for the development and consolidation of our party. They have been trying and difficult years because of the absence of, and direct contribution from, Arrigo Cervetto. Only a huge collective effort, and the work of a united group, has put us in a position to make up for his absence – both on a theoretical level and from the political leadership. Naturally, we have been able to base our work on his theoretical writings – a huge body of work we are still in the process of ordering. Also the human resources we started with have also been selected and formed at the party school he founded.

During the past twenty years we have had to contend with the European cycle, with Berlusconism and his Northern relations – the Northern League – and transformist opportunism. Our timely understanding of the profound nature of these phenomena has meant that we have not wasted our energies. They have been very productive years for our struggle. Twenty fruitful years during which we have raised and formed a new generation of revolutionaries. In this way Marxist science, revolutionary strategy and the Leninist party are transmitted and strengthened across generations.

Our party and the new strategic phase

Tenaciousness for an Unprecedented Battle*

Along with the ongoing battle on the Stability Pact, Italy is also in the midst of a political struggle over the *jobs act.* The government's proposed reform of the labour market is a product of European restructuring and is part of the complex negotiations with Brussels.

Italy has arrived at this appointment twenty years late. The model Matteo Renzi is looking to replicate is the German model, the model championed by Gerhard Schröder at the beginning of the 2000s. It was part of the imperialist policy against salaries which, in the words of Schröder himself, became one of the most efficient low salary systems for the service sector anywhere in Europe. Although the main focus is the battle of capital and for greater industrial productivity, the onslaught on salaries is a means by which Europe – considered as an integrated power – hopes to increase its general competitiveness and face the challenge from China and the other powers. It is a choice Leninist workers have opposed from the very beginning.

Renzi and the European powers

The *Partito Democratico* [PD – Democratic Party], led by the young Catholic Renzi, is pushing through Europe's strategic line with conviction. Any internal opposition has been brushed aside and humiliated with the challenge of a no-confidence vote. Any residual opposition in the Senate has surrendered unconditionally and has voted in favour of the government.

Today the PD crucially has the support of the powers and institutions in Brussels. It also has the support of Italy's large industrial concerns, above all Sergio Marchionne's FIAT-Chrysler. This massive show of support provides Renzi's "fluid party" with confidence and solidity, so much so that it has even been claimed that the party would rather lose the elections than see the reform plan jeopardised. This departure from traditional Italian opportunism follows the lines of European social-imperialism. However, we must wait and see if the Renzi government is up to the task of tackling "the mother of all battles" – carrying out European restructuring in Italy. This will inevitably lead to drastic cuts on public spending and to aid for the impoverished South.

Two crises and the European imperialism

All the European governments are concerned by the crises unfolding in Ukraine and the Middle East. In both cases argument has turned into

* *Internationalist Bulletin*, October 2014

violence which has sown victims among the civilian population. In the Middle East today there is war. We have dealt with examples of two separate epicentres of crisis before on the pages of our journal. This time, however, they are both on Europe's front door step. European imperialism is a major protagonist in the clashes in Ukraine, and is also heavily involved (on a military level too) in the Middle East. "The main enemy is at home!" is the rallying cry of internationalism, and today that enemy is European imperialism. If Europe is involved, then our party inevitably has a role to play. This is doubly the case because a significant proportion of Europe's proletariat comes originally from these countries, and these workers are increasingly seeking direction and instructions for struggle in our Workers' club.

These crises are the clear manifestation that the world order is teetering under the pressure. The uneven development which results from imperialism alters the balance of power between the nations, creates new powers and forces others into decline.

This incessant process means that establishing an equilibrium between states is impossible and a breakdown of the world order is inevitable. Just as in past centuries, the only solution is war – the continuation of politics by other means. The only way to stop this is for the international proletariat to stop fighting on either side, to unite, and affirm its own social revolution. We already have an example of this from the past: the October revolution in Russia brought the war to an end.

The world order is teetering

Today profound forces – which are independent from the policies of nations – are acting on the global market and altering the balance of power. China has become a new and powerful imperialist power which is challenging the old powers. The United States reacts by managing its decline the best it can. Old Europe looks to the unification of its capital, its power centres and its arms as a way to meet the Asian challenge. After having lost its "empire", Russia is now intent on extending its sphere of influence to its closest neighbours. Narendra Modi's India is also emerging as a great power, while Japan is intent on resisting the rise of the Chinese giant in Asia. And in the background we have the rise of Brazil.

The world is being divided up by a handful of large continental powers. The division of the global market is at stake – a process which also involves a number of voracious local and regional powers. Negotiations are under way for the creation of two huge free trade areas which span the Atlantic and the Pacific Ocean respectively. These are means by which the old powers seek to defend their positions. America and Europe are keen to impose their rules of the game on China and the other emerging powers. On their part, China, Brazil, Russia, India and South Africa have reacted by questioning the legitimacy of the existing international institutions. The existing world order is being eroded by these profound forces and is tottering under the pressure of these new tensions. The dominant classes are concerned, this is shown by the reaction of their media and their pundits. Writing about the crisis in Ukraine, Niall Ferguson noted in the *Financial Times* in early August that: "it is dangerous to believe that the skirmish in Ukraine will not develop into a calamity [...] What about the role of globalisation in diffusing international conflict? Sorry, you could have made the same argument 100 years ago. [...] Very high levels of economic interdependence do not always inoculate countries against going to war with each other. Often I am told told that it is the existence of nuclear weapons that has reduced the probability of a world war in our time. But even if that were true, it surely does not apply here"[72].

War and the pendulum of ideologies

Herfried Münkler, a professor at the Humboldt University in Berlin and author of a recent work on the First World War, has commented on the two crises in *Focus* magazine. Münkler argues that: "military action could become politically attractive as a means of imposing a lasting change to the international order [...] both these crises could provide the sparks which destroy the existing order"[73]. Walter Russell Mead, a famous international relations expert at CFR, observes that: "one hundred years later, the world is [...] asking itself whether history could repeat. [...] Could some incident somewhere in the world spark another global war? History, perhaps unfortunately, cannot give us a clear answer to the question [...]. Our situation today is different enough from that of a century ago to make renewed great power war much less than a certainty, but there are enough troubling similarities that we cannot rule the prospect out"[74].

The pendulum of ideologies swings in line with the phases of the global struggle. For decades war was considered an impossibility – it was argued that the growth of democracy, the presence of the UN, and the fear of a nuclear holocaust, meant that there could be no world war. However, today – in the midst of the ideological crisis brought on by globalisation – distinguished thinkers argue that the breakdown of the world order and war are realistic possibilities.

In his latest book, entitled *World Order*, Henry Kissinger argues that the existing concept of world order "is in irreversible decline"[75]. However, if war is now widely considered a realistic outcome, so too should the only way of avoiding it: proletarian revolution. We are well aware that the revolution requires a communist, internationalist party to guide the masses in the face of objective contradictions. We are fighting with all the forces at our disposal to establish a Bolshevik style party in the heart of the European metropolis.

We have entered a new strategic phase and the weakened world order is teetering. We do not believe that war is imminent, but we foresee that a period of growing contradictions will continue to undermine the existing order.

A condition for the party

By the end of the year we plan to publish the second volume of the history of our party.* This will cover the period between 1953 and 1965, the year in which we published the first issue of *Lotta Comunista*. The new book includes tracts from Arrigo Cervetto which are taken from his *Quaderni 1981-1982*. In his reflections on the early 1960s, Cervetto wrote: "Thanks to Lenin I finally saw the development of capitalism in Italy as a molecular process [...] This process would create contradictions of such size and number as to enable a group which had the ability to scientifically analyse the process to form a revolutionary organization"[76]. This is what actually happened.

Thanks to the work of the founding group, and of Cervetto, we are able to analyse the development of imperialism. This process has created, and will continue to create, "contradictions of such size and number" as to facilitate the establishment of the Leninist party in this European metropolis. The growth of this party is subject to one condition: we must be able to exploit these huge contradictions in full.

In *The Difficult Question of Times*, Cervetto reminds us that "there is no irreversible crisis, there is no automatic collapse of capitalism"[77]. It is therefore useless to fix deadlines and timelines for the breakdown of the world order. Cervetto goes on to observe that, like Marx and Engels, "likewise for Lenin, the 'question of times' did not so much concern the world market and the fate of capitalism as it was linked to the assessment of the number and nature of the contradictions and to the subjective ability, i.e., his vanguard party's ability, to exploit such contradictions".

The militancy of theory

This is the issue which faces us, standing the current level of our party's development. Cervetto wrote in his *Quaderni* that: "the fundamental problem of the revolutionary movement [...] is the practical application of science. Lenin puts Marx into practice. [...] Leninism is the militancy of theory, the obstinate, tenacious, constant attempt to translate theory into practical struggle. If we fail in this, we do not solely make an intellectual error, we will be defeated"[78]. The revolutionary struggle is ruthless. This "obstinate, tenacious, constant" attempt must be applied to crises, contradictions and wars.

This is where the "militancy of theory" must act, and not in idle preaching and intellectual debate. It is the struggle to create the lever with which to topple the existing order. The "militancy of theory" – the attempt to translate theory into revolutionary action – requires great dedication to the cause and an iron will.

---

* *Lotta Comunista*: *Towards the Strategy-Party 1953-1995* [éditions Science Marxiste, 2018]

To go beyond

The following is another piece from Cervetto's *Quaderni*. This time it is from the late 1950s, during the difficult period immediately following the break with Carlo Masini. Cervetto writes: "the outlook was not particularly bright [...] the few who remained became isolated once more and were left without a newspaper. The network of militant workers we had formed in the preceding eight years had succumbed to disillusionment and confusion. The huge distances we had travelled and the many hours of meetings had come to nothing, just like their hopes. Once again life tested me, and I had to start from scratch once more. There was little cause for celebration. I was at my lowest, without the money for political activity or for survival. I have never been superstitious, but it really seemed as though I had again been the subject of an evil spell. Luckily I could make use of a resource which I could always count on and which I could ultimately rely on: my tenaciousness. This had helped me in the winter of 1944 when many around me despaired; it helped me after the war; it had also helped me when Masini himself had been discouraged"[79].

The fact we have come so far is due to both the scientific analysis and leadership of Cervetto. Above all, it is due to the tenaciousness which allowed him to rebuild the party. Today we are in better shape, our party has progressed. But, if we want to deal with the historic delay which persists, we must endeavour to transcend current dimensions. In order to do this we must be able to analyse the "quantity and quality" of the contradictions of this new phase. Furthermore, we must continue with the "obstinate, tenacious, constant" attempt to translate theory into revolutionary practice. Above all, we require the same "tenaciousness" which emerges in the fight for survival and apply it to really unprecedented tasks.

The fiftieth anniversary of our newspaper and the twentieth anniversary of Arrigo Cervetto's death
A Particular Year*

2015 is a year which is particularly significant for us: in December, our newspaper will celebrate its fiftieth anniversary, and in the last few weeks we remembered the twentieth anniversary of the death, in February 1995, of Arrigo Cervetto, the founder with Lorenzo Parodi of Lotta Comunista. To mark the occasion, the second volume of our story[80], which is partly the story of his political battle, was published.

An editorial continuity lasting for half a century is unusual in the revolutionary movement. That newspaper could have remained at its six original pages, perhaps read by few people and commented on by a circle of close friends, as has unfortunately occurred in the history of the labour movement. Instead, it has grown and spread widely among the masses, has a big number of backers and is walking on the legs of hundreds of propagators, many of them young.

Generational continuity

In all of these years, our newspaper has been the organ of our party-strategy, but at the same time a collective organiser, as Lenin wanted. In the era of the Internet, Facebook and Twitter, a revolutionary organisation modelled on the Bolshevik Party is continuing to grow.

Instead, twenty years have gone by since Cervetto's death, the span of a generation, which our party has faced without his direct presence. In these twenty years, our party has continued on its way, finding its continuity in a new generation, the third for us. We have developed and grown and our political influence has spread, which means that the foundations on which our organisation was built are solid. Having worked successfully for its multigenerational continuity is one of Cervetto's most precious results, a rare result in the history of the revolutionary movement.

Libertarian communism

Our original group was very small, a handful of workers won over to politics in the partisan struggle J131

between 1943 and 1944. That group was initially attracted to libertarian communism. At the time, there were alternatives in the revolutionary field which those youths discarded. Their initial idea was to move beyond anarchist "nihilism" and Bordigist "liquidatorism".

* *Lotta Comunista*, March 2015

Inasmuch as it was a historical expression of an authentic component of the labour movement, we have always considered the anarchist movement with sympathy: after all, Cervetto and Parodi set off from its internationalist and anti-state circles. Lenin wrote that "the similarity between Marxism and anarchism" is that they both stood for the "'smashing' of the modern state machine"[81]. The distinction came afterwards, regarding the dictatorship of the proletariat and the withering away of the state. Our original group discussed this for a long time once it had become part of the Anarchist Groups of Proletarian Action (GAAP) – a libertarian, antiparliamentary and abstentionist circle of honest and often seriously committed militants, but an absolutely ineffective circle, so much so that it was almost completely absorbed by Stalinism in the first years of the postwar period.

Amadeo Bordiga's analysis

We are in debt to Amadeo Bordiga. In the new volume of our story we report one of Cervetto's June 1956 letters regarding Bordiga's analysis of the Soviet Union's social nature. Cervetto wrote about it: "It is as valid as anything that can be found in Italy today." It is necessary "to develop Bordiga's results, but in the meantime, we'll have to anchor ourselves in these"[82]. And eight months later he would write that "Bordigism is a political reality in the revolutionary movement, a reality that also produced us"[83], adding that refusing to acknowledge this Bordigist role means denying there has been revolutionary opposition to Stalinism.

Bordigist circles were also internationalist, abstentionist and in favour of the dictatorship of the proletariat... honest and in some cases also competent, experienced militants, but entrenched in a wait-and-see position that became liquidation. In fact, they denied every possibility of intervention in the workers' struggles.

The verdict of time

At the time, however, the confrontation was between very small minorities, and the presence of anarchists and Bordigists was much more important than that of the GAAP. To demonstrate that Cervetto and Parodi's approach was more effective from the viewpoint of the revolutionary movement was therefore not at all simple.

Today, on the contrary, seventy years later, the verdict of time is unappealable. Their conception of the strategy-party and their elaboration of the development of capitalism in the world, of imperialist maturation in Italy and of unitary imperialism and power relations, were decisive. They allowed the small group of militants that published the first issue of *Lotta comunista* in 1965 to link up with a new generation of young and very young militants, coming from the workers' struggles and student protests of the end of the 1960s. The revival of the development of our party was the result of the militancy of its theory.

The new strategic phase

The trends of the uneven development identified at the time came to fruition over the decades and changed the framework of reference structurally. We are now in a "new strategic phase".

First of all, the prodigious development of Asia has produced an imperialist giant, China, from what was a backward area at the time. Secondly, there is the enormous increase in the world proletariat, especially, but not only, in Asia. And, as far as we are concerned, the formation of a vast European proletariat which has stably absorbed millions of immigrants from Asia, Africa and Latin America. Thirdly, the imperialist struggle has increasingly become a contention between big and very big powers – China, America, Europe, Russia, India and Brazil – which face each other in ever smaller spaces. The backward areas that were their hinterland no longer represent two thirds of the world population but only about one third.

The level of tensions is raised and compromises and adjustments are becoming much more complicated. The course of partial crises will be more difficult. The confrontation between China, the new forces of imperialism and the old powers is exacerbating the world contradictions. The weight and force of the Chinese or Indian state are pressing on the world balances and the world order is inevitably vacillating. The moment will arrive when they will no longer be able to guarantee the equilibrium of the world balance.

We do not believe there is any appointment with the breakdown of the world balance: setting a deadline has no political sense. However, we do have a well-defined task to carry out: to transform a quantitative and qualitative crescendo of contradictions of unitary imperialism into an advantage for the labour movement, into an acceleration of the entrenchment of our revolutionary party in the European metropolis.

The global crisis and China

The overcoming of the crisis in global relations, which broke out more than seven years ago, is following a really bumpy path. The ongoing recovery continues to be slow and weighed down by unknown factors, especially in the eurozone. Everyone hopes that fine weather will arrive again, but, while waiting for this, the ECB has finally had to throw caution to the wind and intervene by force in the markets also by purchasing sovereign bonds.

The messages sent out by imperialist China have been strong and clear: the tensions with Japan in the China Sea and then the agreement with the other BRICS (Brazil, Russia, India and South Africa) for the formation of a new development bank and a new fund. The world has read in this a threat to the World Bank and the IMF. Then we must add the agreement with Russia for a new gas pipeline and the launching of the two "Silk Roads", which are none other than two ways of imperialist expansion: one maritime, across the Indian Ocean, towards the Middle East, and the other terrestrial, in the direction of Central Asia. This is not a matter of mere words, but of the creation of a bank and fund dedicated to them. And then, units of the Chinese Navy have access to Iranian ports, and military exercises with the Russian fleet in the Mediterranean have been announced.

China demands its weight should be acknowledged and no longer accepts a Euro-Atlantic brand of world order. It wants its place at the "brigands" table.

The Middle Eastern tangle

In the Middle East, an inextricable tangle of violence against the background of a religious clash between Sunnites and Shiites continually generates clashes between states, civil wars and tribal feuds, with reactionary terrorism as an everyday weapon.

The Middle Eastern bourgeoisies, weak, powerless and incapable of unifying the area in a regional federation, have very serious responsibilities. The hypothesis of such a unification as, moreover, of a lasting truce, has by now lost all possibility of being realised. The ruling Arab classes have grown rich on the oil rent which has exasperated the divisions and ethnic-religious rivalries.

The responsibilities of the great powers are heavy, including those of the "very civilised European democracies" which divided this region up among them in the form of colonies, drawing up arbitrary borders that no longer hold up. Subsequently, its energy resources have made the Middle East the battleground between the United States, Russia, Europe and now the great Asian powers. These powers have not ceased to push factions and states one against the other in order to prevent a regional force from becoming hegemonic, thus dominating the energy supply sources.

Imperialist Europeanism

The conflagration in the South of Europe has approached the European capitals, while the war in Ukraine is still causing violence and victims on the North-eastern borders of the Union. In that region, too, the great powers – Europe, Russia and America – are on stage. What is at stake is the division of the spheres of influence and the territories that the old Yalta partition had given to Moscow.

With the implosion of its empire, Russia was obliged to yield vast territories that Power Europe has de facto annexed. Poland, the Czech Republic, Slovakia, Hungary and also Slovenia first joined the European Union. Bulgaria and Romania followed them, and in 2013 Croatia led the way for the Balkan countries. Putin's Russia resists where there are still grey areas as in Moldova, Georgia, and now in Ukraine. The compromise reached in Minsk is fragile and biased in favour of Moscow. It is the result of a Franco-

German initiative that gained the upper hand, also thanks to a kind of temporary US mandate to Angela Merkel.

These conflicts put the European Union under pressure, especially in the field of foreign policy and defence, where the surrender of state sovereignty is struggling to impose itself. The Union must also face the battle of Athens, which is calling the powers of the euro into question. European imperialism is finetuning its institutions and testing its powers. At the same time, it is preparing the ideologies of Power Europe. The ideologies of imperialist Europeanism, of "Fortress Europe", are being put to the test by widespread fears and the echo of Eurosceptical populism that is stirring up xenophobia and racial hatred. Thus the ideological weapons of tomorrow, which will support mobilisations in favour of the European power in the clash between the giants of imperialism, are being honed.

The fourth generation

This imperialist Europeanism is preparing the ventures and conflicts into which European youth will be thrown tomorrow. To stem these campaigns, we must increase our mobilisation and commitment to bringing communist internationalism to the masses and young generations. Our strategic elaboration is strong enough to grasp global contradictions and turn them in favour of the European proletariat and its vanguard, European Leninism. The way to follow is to turn, once again, to the young generations in a battle to form a new generation of young Leninists and to strengthen the ranks of our fourth generation, which is already in the arena.

Besides, that is the way we have always followed. That handful of men who resumed their journey towards the end of the 1940s were young, 18-20-year-old workers. We were able to avoid the difficulties of the early 1960s thanks to a new generation of youths, all of them about twenty years old. This was our second generation, stemming from the struggles and agitations of the end of the 1960s.

The descent into the arena of our third generation allowed our party to grow and reach its present levels. It consists of young and very young people convinced by our internationalist struggle in the years of the "handover period" between the end of the 1980s and the 1990s.

The fiercer battles of the new strategic phase will bring on stage a vast generation of young militants. We need to organise them, select them and train them. As always, it is militant commitment that is decisive.

The sign of the times and the internationalist battle

Four Generations in the Field*

The first two volumes of Arrigo Cervetto's *Opere* [Works] have been published. It is the culmination of twenty years of work, the result of the growth of our movement and of a collective plan. Every militant has contributed through their own specific activity. Publication has been made possible through scientific work and by a remarkable organisational effort. While the odd, old stalwart from the generation of our Founders is still amongst us, the *Opere* are the result of the specific contribution of our second generation – one which collaborated with Cervetto for a long period.

These comrades had to give a scientific framework to Cervetto's theoretical and political work. A major responsibility for the generation of *Lotta Comunista* which is now proudly celebrating fifty years of militancy. There is a special pride in being able to transmit the party's legacy to the third generation – one which has reached its own maturity and has, in turn, been called to assume new responsibilities. It is able to face new challenges with a richer scientific and theoretical arsenal, one which is also now available to the fourth generation which is currently in the field.

Finally, the *Opere* are the product of our concept of the party as science-strategy. Without this key concept all our work would not have been possible.

A prophetic theory

The recently published *Quaderni* on "Method and Science" contain material which has never been seen before.

In the section entitled "The Marxism of the II and III Internationals", Cervetto comments on Karl Kautsky's *The Origins of Christianity* (a work written while Kautsky was still a prominent Marxist). Cervetto annotates passages from the text, underlines the text in red and black and adds notes to the margins. Everything has been faithfully reproduced in the new volume published by our publishing house – Edizioni Lotta Comunista. In his work Kautsky reflects on the fall of the Roman Empire and the invasion of the Germanic barbarians "which takes the form of a migration of peoples". Kautsky went on to write: "the migration of peoples played a role in the ancient world which today is played by revolutions"[84]. Cervetto copies this passage, underlines its contents and adds notes to the margins entitled (in bold letters): "Notes on the role of migration and of violence-war". Apart from polemical observations with some treatment of other schools

---

* *Internationalist Bulletin*, October 2015

of thought of the time, Cervetto highlights how Marx, Engels and Lenin had analysed the objective historical role of migration and "therefore of violence-war".

As early as 1970 Cervetto was already underlining the epoch-making historical role of migrations. In that moment Cervetto had the studies of our teachers to go by. Furthermore, our founders could also analyse the internal and European migrations, which had reached their highest point in Italy during the 1960s. We see an example of this in the highly prophetic article written by Lorenzo Parodi in the September 1967 edition of *Lotta Comunista*. In his analysis of the growth of Italian capitalism, Parodi foresees: "something which is possible theoretically: an inversion of migratory movements"[85] which would transform Italy into a net importer of labour.

With these theortical instruments Cervetto had little difficulty in treating the issue of migration when Italy became a mature metropolis of capitalism. In a piece taken from 1976, which is taken from the *Opere*. Cervetto writes: "the international movement of labour is a phenomenon which is linked to the growth of capitalism. [...] Generation upon generation of proletarians – tens of millions of people – have crossed mountains, rivers, and seas, in search of bosses who would buy the labour they were unable to sell in their places of birth. Never had humanity seen such huge patterns of migration"[86].

The demographic winter of imperialism

Often alone, we have been studying demography and migration for decades. Our journal is not a prophet unarmed, our analysis has strengthened and "armed" our politics. There has been generalised shock regarding the huge size of migratory flows, the epoch-making character of this movement and the duration of the phenomenon have generated surprise, confusion and perplexity. For us it is merely a confirmation of one of our basic theories, a confirmation which strengthens our resolve. Millions of migrants are currently on the move. The growth of capitalism in Asia and Africa has set them in motion in search of bosses "that will buy their labour". Again, the growth of capitalism, and the onset of imperialist maturity, has generated the incessant struggle between the great powers for markets. This in turn generates localised outbreaks of "violence-war" which further encourage migratory flows.

Furthermore, it is the growth of capitalism, once it has reached the final phase of full maturity, which leads to a fall (which is often dramatic) in the birth rate and the onset of the demographic winter which lambasts powers old and new and leads to gaps in their labour markets. In Europe the average number of children per female is 1.57, a long way below the 2.1 which is needed to maintain a stable population. This means that while there are six hundred and seventy eight thousand births in Germany each year there are eight hundred and fifty three thousand deaths (the average of the last ten years). This leaves a deficit of one hundred and seventy five thousand people each year. Without migration the population of Germany would be in net decline; the same is true of Italy. At the same time the population is ageing, which creates further difficulties for social welfare spending. According to the *Financial Times* there is a shortfall of three hundred and fifty thousand qualified workers in Germany each year.

This process is bound to continue given the current economic and social conditions. They can continue to praise capitalism, and ignore war and crises, they can continue singing the praises of the market economy and point to the growth that it produces; but no one can that once capitalism reaches its highest phase of maturity it leads to a fall in the birth rate, and without external forces, an inexorable fall in the population. Through its development the social order of capitalism puts into question the very survival of the species. There can be only one conclusion, only communism represents the "civilisation of life"

The European imperialist policy on immigration

Karl Marx explained how the development of modes of production leads to irremediable contradictions with the relations of production. Capitalism is historically outdated and only a superior social order can resolve its fundamental contradictions. It is for this reason that we are communists. Going back to migration, it is evident that Europe needs migrants. The German magazine *Der Spiegel* writes that 32% of those asking for asylum in 2014 were under 17 years of age, and 49% were between 18 and 34. On the one hand Germany and Europe are desperate to fill the gaps in their labour markets, on the other masses of young people are "looking for bosses".

These are the objective contradictions. The subjective capacity of political leadership is needed to take full advantage of these conditions. Angela Merkel has been able to capture the "sign of the times" for European imperialism. It is no coincidence that Germany is the motor of Europe. Germany also has a long experience of migration – of its own population, of migration from Southern Europe in the 1960s, and more recently from Turkey.

In this way Germany has managed to drag France into outlining a *European imperialist policy on immigration.* A policy which will have to deal with refugees and economic migrants; issues which EU powers will have to deal with. A further cession of sovereignty is required from member states. However, this is a delicate issue – it involves national borders, and touches a number of social concerns and the welfare system.

Migrants – pawns in the war

Any European imperialist policy on immigration must take into account the migrants' countries of origin in order to control the flow, to define policy with regards to quotas and repatriation, but above all to evaluate opportunities for imperialist penetration and the delineation of spheres of influence. As far as Europe is concerned the main areas of interest are the Middle East and North Africa. Refugees and migrants are pawns and tools in a struggle between the great powers, between these powers and regional powers, between the regional powers themselves and, finally, between different ethnic and religious groups. The current war is not solely restricted to the skies above Syria and Libya, it is also being fought in the refugee camps of Turkey, Lebanon, Jordan and Libya which are on the route towards Europe.

In its strategy towards migrants Berlin has opted for a policy of accommodation. By saying "we are doing it" Merkel has taken on an increasingly vociferous opposition at home. Against the resistance to her plan from the UK and some Eastern European countries, she has used the benign face of European imperialism – an inclusive one which offers the refugees the prospects of the "European Dream".

It is obvious that Berlin and Brussels have more brutal measures – including the closure of Europe's borders – as an option, but the shortage of labour in Europe requires a policy of inclusion and integration, and the training and absorption of new salary earners. This accommodation necessarily entails restricting excessive security concerns at home, as well as the racist and xenophobic impulses which such epoch-making migration inevitably generates.

The European melting pot and the wars of tomorrow

We have not been surprised by Germany's policy of accommodating refugees. We are well aware that the most dangerous of enemies is the seductive face of imperialism. History teaches that these young migrants will be successfully integrated. These migrants are happy to have work and will produce for their new bosses. They will also be happy to have escaped war and to have "crossed mountains, rivers, and seas" unharmed. Not everyone made it, tens of thousands of migrants died in the Mediterranean and in the deserts.

The starting point of the "European dream" will be to integrate them and train them for the wars of tomorrow, to make them fight for the European Union. We can take stock from the history of the USA and the "American dream" which attracted millions of migrants. The USA became the melting pot for Irish, German, Polish and Italian immigrants and their baptism as American citizens were the first and second imperialist world wars.

A European proletariat

In the absence of an internationalist force armed with a strategy this will inevitably be repeated. Europe is playing with fire with its policy of integration because it is also strengthening the ranks of its traditional enemy – the European proletariat. Refugees and immigrants will become part of the European stratification of salaries. The vast majority will start at the lowest salary levels, indeed the Germans are counting on their rapid integration into the labour market so as to contain public spending. One study by

Deutsche Bank calls for a suspension of restrictions on part-time labour and the abolition of the minimum wage for refugees as a means of accelerating this integration into the labour market. The European imperialist policy on immigration goes hand in hand with the imperialist policy against salaries. This too does not surprise us. In Lorenzo Parodi's 1967 article[87] he quotes Nikolai Bukharin: "the levelling out of different salary levels is accomplished through migration"[88].

In this way migrants and refugees will become part of our class in Europe. They arrive with the illusions of the 'European dream'. However, it is not down to us to awaken them from this dream; the class struggle and the growing contradictions and crises of imperialism will do that. As European workers they will experience the class struggle, and the more aware amongst them will make choices which will attract them to *European Leninism* and a firmly entrenched and effective internationalism.

New Mediterranean adventures

This is why it is crucial that we extend our presence, widen our network of supporters, and attract youngsters who want to live these epoch-making events as protagonists[89].

Today, the attention of the centres of imperialism is focussed on the war in Syria – a subject we deal with elsewhere in this journal. So far this war has resulted in three hundred thousand victims, barbarous acts and vile acts of terrorism against innocent people, including women and children. This conflict which has given rise to all manner of monstrosities, including the dominant ideas. Everyone claims to be fighting terrorism, but perhaps, in reality, no one is doing so. The Americans, together with the French and the British, are bombing ISIS, but are on the same side as Bin Laden's Al Qaeda, the "tyrant" Asad, Putin's missiles and side by side with the Iranian Ayatollahs!

Despite this awful mess the calls for intervention are growing ever louder. In Rome, the prime minister Matteo Renzi is pushing for Italy to lead a military mission to Libya, oblivious to Italy's tradition of "ragamuffin imperialism" which still weighs on Italian foreign policy. We won't stand for it, our policy is internationalism. We will be in the field with our intransigent opposition to the Mediterranean adventures of European imperialism.

Chapter Three

STORMY TIMES IN THE NEW POLITICAL CYCLE

The internationalist political battle

Stormy Times*

A climate of uncertainty and anxiety is pervading the world capitals. A deeply troubled economic trend, the persistent pressure of migration flows of epic proportions, and the wars on the European borders with the threat of reactionary terrorism are fuelling these feelings. "The fog of war" has anything but dispersed.

The global recovery is feeble, slow, and subject to threats in spite of the huge amount of capital injected into the markets by the central banks. "The globalisation of uncertainty" remains a feature of the current cycle. The unexpected and unusual proportions of the ECB's quantitative easing are a confirmation of these anxieties. What is particularly frightening are the problems of the emerging countries and the slowdown of China.

Winds of war

The marked fall in the prices of raw materials, and of oil in particular, is conditioning the recovery. For the energy-giving substances, the main cause remains the excess of offer on the markets. The International Energy Agency (IEA) predicts that only from 2017 will it be possible to speak of a rebalance between supply and demand and hence of a recovery in prices that would contribute to chasing away the spectres of deflation. The fall regards all the raw materials, from metals to corn and soy, which have halved their quotations: the economies of the producing countries have been hit, even hard-hit.

In the emerging countries these difficulties are accompanied by a capital outflow that also regards Beijing, even if in the latter case the outflows also signal the capital exports of Chinese imperialism. The fact remains that China is frightening in any case: today the fears are that the Chinese slowdown and the emerging countries' difficulties will spill over onto the fragile recovery of the old metropolises, killing it off.

Meanwhile, winds of war continue to blow from the blood-stained Middle East. On the Syrian front, the "ceasefire" agreed upon by Russia and the United States is underway. The times of any possible division of Syria will not be short and the negotiations will be obstructed by the clash among the

* *Internationalist Bulletin*, April 2016

global and regional players; the Kurdish question remains unresolved and subject to being a pretext in the power game.

Meanwhile, in Libya, a conflict is already brewing: small contingents of French, British, American, and perhaps Italian special corps are allegedly already on the ground. Various pressures, some of them intrusive, have attempted to accelerate Rome's decisions. Prime Minister Renzi has stuck to his guns with a formula that aims at a Libyan government of national unity and a UN mandate, but his is a policy-mix that, in its calculated ambiguity, does not exclude military action in the future at all.

The link-up with the Angela Merkel line for a European solution to the migration crisis, in which Libya is part of the question in the same way as Turkey is, is obvious: the inner consolidation of the Union is inseparable from the projection of the influence of the European Union onto the southern shore of the Mediterranean.

Rome and Berlin

We have written that this is a "historic collision" with migratory flows of unprecedented dimensions that continue to shake the European Union[90]. Berlin was the capital most ready to devise a line with strategic depth, carried on by both the political parties of the grand coalition. It is a line upheld even at the cost of paying a price in terms of votes, as has occurred in the recent partial local elections. Apprehension and fears, widespread in Germany, too, rewarded a conservative national-liberal party (AfD), which reinforced its Eurosceptical nationalism with xenophobic undertones.

People are talking about the weakening of Angela Merkel, who, however, has reconfirmed the European line given to the migration crisis. The German position, backed by the European Commission, was fully supported by Rome and also by Paris, which, however, struggled to keep up with Berlin. France is feeling the effect of the national identity campaign triggered by the hateful attacks of reactionary terrorism; an intense campaign that has rewarded Front National, its main interpreter. And not only this: French politics are weighed down by the culture and tradition of the Republican state, which act as a brake whenever shares of national sovereignty are being debated. But now the Franco-German axis is faced with choices that will be hard to postpone.

Italy's ambitions

The agreement with London and the referendum on whether Britain should remain in the EU are sparking a de facto battle for the centralisation of the "hard core" of the innermost circle of a multilevel Europe. And in this battle the role of the Franco-German axis is essential, as it was in the past. Various people have reminded Matteo Renzi, engaged in a heated confrontation with Brussels and Berlin, of this.

The Italian prime minister's "active Europeanism" does not seem to want so much to challenge the Franco-German axis as to promote Italy's interests in Europe with greater assertiveness, claiming at the same time a role on equal terms with France and Germany. This is a very ambitious project that requires very solid credentials: Italy's huge public debt remains a burden and a serious weakness. This is why Renzi wants to play the reforms of an Italy that, according to him, has changed, on the European tables. From the Jobs Act, now being imitated in France but modelled on the German Hartz Reform, to the banking reform and even institutional reforms: the abolition of bicameralism, the strengthening of the executive and electoral reform.

It is since the 1960s that Italy's big business groups have yearned for political modernisation, an upgrade of the state and its institutions. Renzi, his Democratic Party and his government have pledged to give a solution to the unresolved thorny problems of the decades-long Italian political imbalance; this is why the prime minister has gone so far as to tie his permanence in politics to the outcome of the referendum on the constitutional reforms. In autumn, it will become Italy's main political deadline and will also inevitably take on a European significance.

Political deadlines

Turbulent times are looming ahead for European imperialism. The situation in Syria will take time to stabilise, and in any case that area will continue to unleash violence in the foreseeable future. No one can predict the consequences of another war in Libya. Iraq and Yemen remain unstable and a transition that is rich in unknowns is on the Algerian horizon. And this limits us to Europe's near abroad alone, without considering the tensions that are accumulating in Asia.

The migration flows will continue to press on the European Union and continental restructuring will continue to snap at the heels of very slow recovery; the ECB has used all its ammunition but is also experiencing its limits. A series of political deadlines that are bound to interfere with choices in Europe follow one another: in June, the British referendum, in October the Italian, in 2017 the presidential election in France and the general election in Germany, and then the Italian general election in 2018, unless it is held earlier.

The American presidential election in November and the future administration in Washington are also unknowns, so much so that the German Foreign Minister Frank-Walter Steinmeier has said he is afraid that the "politics of fear" will push America towards isolationism again.

Our battle

A tormented, if not stormy, period for European imperialism, today caught up in international chaos, with its load of populist fevers, concern about safety measures and xenophobic drives fuelled by fears and insecurities destined to increase. We will be called to a fierce internationalist battle against all of this and against all of the expressions of imperialist Europeanism; and, if and when it occurs, also to firm internationalist opposition to another war in Libya.

We come from a period of very intense activity: our organisational battle for self-financing took great steps forward with our subscription campaign in December; in January, there was unprecedented participation in the rallies for the fiftieth anniversary of our newspaper; in February, the month of our publications confirmed the attention to and interest in the books of our Marxist school and not even one title in our catalogues remained on the bookshelves. Arrigo Cervetto's *Opere* are coming out regularly – six volumes have already been published – and the work of completing the Italian edition of Karl Marx and Friedrich Engels' is proceeding on schedule.

We are offering the workers' movement precious material that our founding group did not have at its disposal at all and most of which was not even usable by our second generation. This is development of the Party in the true sense of the word, because it implies the formation of cadres, organisation and that revolutionary passion that alone can fuel continual, growing, militant commitment.

A problem solved

At the end of a meeting in Genoa in March 1981, Cervetto observed "The basic problem is whether in a situation like the Genoese it is possible to develop a party model borrowed from another historical experience that is our point of reference. This isn't a foregone conclusion. [...] We set off from the concept that it's possible. We don't have the result in our pockets; we're working on a trend"[91].

The development of these years has provided a solution to that problem. It was possible to establish that party model in Genoa, from where it spread to the rest of the peninsula and elsewhere. It was also an answer to our party's historical delay: it can be dealt with, we have dealt with it. But imperialist development has spawned a continental power such as China in Asia, while the European Union, in defining its federal and co-federal powers, has also unified the European labour force. We are bound to consider that continental space: "the main enemy [...] at home" has become European imperialism and our strategic target cannot but be the entrenchment of the Leninist Party in the European metropolis.

The European horizon

In this sense, our historical delay remains a fact, but we have an advantage with respect to the past: we now know that delay can be dealt with and we know the way. In *The Difficult Question of Times*, Cervetto considers how Lenin, in his turn, dealt with the party's historical delay by working on long times, transforming the question of times also into an organisational question: "It went from a difficult to a less-difficult question, because organizational work made it daily practice with which it was possible, by improving it, to accelerate the party's development time so that it could approach that of the productive forces"[92].

It goes without saying that, for us, this was possible only by restoring Lenin's theory and then by guaranteeing generational continuity for the elaboration and development of our science. This is what we have done; now, as we look at the European proletariat, we need to move beyond this. This is a very tiring path and it could not be otherwise, because we are dealing with growing dimensions and problems. However, we have a road map: in-depth work on that "daily practice", "improving it", in order to "accelerate the party's development time"... and doing this starting from the forthcoming battles in the stormy times looming ahead, wielding our newspaper that will have to circulate even more than in the past.

This will be an internationalist battle in the course of which a vast new generation of Leninists will have to be trained. At the end of the day, the European Establishment and its big business groups, amidst imbalances, clashes and adaptations, will find a framework of powers better suited to the world contention. At that point, they need to find themselves facing a stronger, more deeply rooted and more influential Leninist Party in Europe. We can do it.

130 years after Chicago's days of glory
The Internationalist 1st of May*

It's been 130 years since the glorious days when in Chicago the struggle for the eight-hour working day reached its peak, unleashing police attempts to frame strikers, and harsh repression. But if our now regular celebration of May Day was born from the great 1886 Chicago strikes, its roots are planted in the centuries-old struggle to reduce working hours that ended in winning the eight-hour day – a conquest that was always to be under threat.

The origins of this struggle lie in England, the cradle of world capitalism. Its first traces can be seen in the works of Thomas Moore (1478-1535) who in *Utopia* advocates a six-hour working day, considering the large proportion of the population "who are idle". Later came the Utopian socialists. Robert Owen, audacious pioneer of communism, instituted a ten-hour working day in his New Lanark factory. There followed the English Chartist movement, the manifestation of the first great industrial proletariat.

The Chicago Martyrs

It was no accident that English workers were the first to win the ten-hour working day, in 1848, and it was English workers and Chartists who, landing on the shores of new continents, brought the movement with them to Australia and America. And as Marx wrote, in America the movement would pull on "seven-league boots" and stride on to the Chicago days of 1886. Eighty thousand workers went on strike, coming together in a huge march on which police violence rained down, ending with the explosion of a police-planted bomb.

A year later, on November 11th 1887, the main organisers of that movement – anarchists, socialists and internationalists – were hanged. They were: Albert Parsons (aged 39) August Spies (31) Adolph Fischer (30) and George Engel (50). Louis Lingg (22) died two days before the date of execution. These are the Martyrs of Chicago, and this year again we honour them.

Repression did not halt the movement, which spread throughout the whole continent alongside capitalist development. May 1st was adopted by the Second International in 1889 as an international day of mobilsation for shorter working hours. It has marked over a century of the history of working-class struggle. And although the bourgeoisie and the opportunists never stop trying to distort it, attempting to transform it into some kind of jamboree complete with balloons, fireworks smoke bombs and masks,

---

* *Internationalist Bulletin*, June 2016

they cannot cancel the indelible markings of international working-class struggle from this day.

It's a story that needs to be known, spread far and wide, and studied. The catalogue of our éditions Science Marxiste includes a book well worth reading – *May Day in Working-class History*[93] which we recommend to our readers.

Marx and the working day

Karl Marx, scientist and revolutionary, produced fundamental work on the length of the working day, that crux of the exploitation of labour. In *Capital* he wrote that "The working-day is thus not a constant, but a variable quantity [...] the minimum limit is, however, not determinable [...] of course, if we make the surplus-labour = 0, we have a minimum limit, i.e., the part of the day which the labourer must necessarily work for his own maintenance". But this is impossible "on the basis of capitalist production". The maximum limit is determined "first, by the physical bounds of labour-power"[94]. Marx then considers how "Besides these purely physical limitations, the extension of the working-day encounters moral ones" and reaches the conclusion that "the determination of what is a working-day presents itself as the result of a struggle, a struggle between collective capital, i.e., the class of capitalists, and collective labour, i.e., the working-class"[95].

Within the International Workingmen's Association (IWA) Marx the revolutionary leader strove to promote the struggle for a shorter working day. As early as 1868 the IWA approved a resolution Marx had drawn up to this effect. On this issue he observed in 1871 that "every movement in which the working class comes out as a class against the ruling classes and tries to coerce them by pressure from without is a political movement". And he added that "this naturally requires a previous organisation of the working class developed up to a certain point and arising precisely from its economic struggles"[96].

Lenin and internationalism

In 1900, in the wake of the wide international spread that the movement for the eight-hour day had achieved, Lenin wrote "The demand for an eight-hour day, however, is the demand of the whole proletariat, presented not to individual employers, but to the state authorities as the representatives of the entire present-day social and political system, to the capitalist class as a whole, the owners of all the means of production. The demand for an eight-hour day has assumed special significance. It is a declaration of solidarity with the international socialist movement"[97].

Here is the meaning of the internationalist First of May, which we have stubbornly defended over decades and which inspires the May Day march of our Workers Clubs each year. A moment in the midst of concrete struggle for the working class to recall not only the concept of solidarity in struggle, but also the vision of internationalism, today so vital for preventing the proletariat becoming a tool in the hands of the big powers in the current imperialist clash. So it's also a moment in our battle within trade union movement, where we continue our work in the wake of the winning experience of the Bolshevik Party. A commitment that we continue mindful of Lenin's warning on the need for revolutionaries and communists to work in "yellow, social-chauvinist, compromising and counter-revolutionary trade unions"[98]. This holds even truer today: certainly, today's trade unions still demonstrate those divisions bequeathed by parliamentarianism, and are late in uniting, but they remain the home of the workers, and therefore our home too.

In this battle of ours we have built up nuclei of communists, of internationalists, in large concentrations of wage earners, in the big factories; an essential step in linking up with the deepest and most scattered levels of the proletariat, today largely made up of the immigrant workers who continue to arrive in their thousands.

Office workers, technicians, immigrants, labourers, temps

Certainly, it's not enough to work within the trade unions, which seem unable to organise these workers. A great deal of in-depth daily work with the masses is required, a militant commitment to organise and educate the proletariat. Only thus will it be possible to create stable links with the deep levels of the scattered wage earners, who through the revolutionary newspaper can connect with the workers of the big factories within the Workers Clubs. And this work with the masses contributes to strengthening the battle within the trade unions to give voice to internationalism, as evidenced by the speech we have here reproduced.

This militant commitment will allow us to reunite the wage strata that the labour market has inexorably divided – something that no trade union can do. These strata can be unite by revolutionary strategy and a shared internationalist battle. This has been visible even in our marches: engineering workers and technicians from big companies alongside workers from small factories, immigrants from outsourced agencies alongside the steelworkers of Ilva, those forced to work on the black market or on temporary contracts alongside those still looking for a job. What unites them is the internationalist First of May. True, the times are long, and it takes a great effort, day after day. Hard work has never frightened us, because in the course of the years, as one generation succeeds another, we have seen the growth of a party on the Bolshevik model, a party that the working class sorely needs. An unstoppable drive onwards.

WORKERS OF ALL COUNTRIES, UNITE!

We publish a summary of a speech made from the platform of the national May Day demonstration at Genoa, Italy, called by the CGIL-CISL-UIL federated trade unions, which was attended by all three national secretaries. The speaker was Comrade Armando Palombo, who works at RSU Ilva and is a member of the Genova Province Executive Committee for the FIOM trade union.

Comrades and fellow-workers

this is an important square for Genoa's working-class movement; it was here, between Piazza de Ferrari and the Carlo Felice Theatre, that in 1900 there took place the first general strike ever called in Italy, against the authorities' closure of the trade union headquarters. Here, in the days that led up to April 25th 1945, violent clashes between partisans and Nazi-Fascist forces preceded the liberation of the city and the Nazi surrender to the partisans. On June 30th 1960 this square witnessed the great working-class demonstration against the Fascists, who were once again raising their heads. And it was here, in 1979, that the workers of Genoa honoured Guido Rossa.

Today's demonstration is particularly significant because it sees all the workers here united over and beyond their trade union membership – and not before time!

And this is why I believe this is the right occasion to say that we need to make a further effort towards greater trade union unity, and to say this to the general secretaries present on this platform.

United, the workers and the unions are stronger – and never have we needed strength as much as we do now. Sadly, we need strength above all to defend ourselves, here in Genoa and in Liguria.

This is not an easy time: many are the sectors of production – big and small – where the workers are under attack: from Piaggio in Genoa and in Albenga to the employees of the outsourced AMT: from Busalla's IPLOM to the restructing in Finmeccanica: and to the continuing uncertainties for many other workers, those of the port and of the Single Company.

Then there's Ilva, "the mother of all crises" as it's been called, in great difficulty because of European restructuring, in which as usual the workers are paying for errors not theirs. For the present, at least here in Genoa, we have succeeded in defending ourselves.

We are committed to continuing this difficult battle to defend the steel industry, and on this point we call on the three general secretaries to give maximum commitment to defending the Ilva workers, and finally we also ask them for a solid and decisive attempt to build a European trade union, which today is a vital necessity. Only the European dimension can today provide a defense for the working class. But whenever we need to defend Ilva, or any other group of workers, we'll be there, ready for the struggle even under the most difficult conditions.

The First of May is a great day, when the world remembers the struggle for the eight-hour working day. For us, before being a holiday, May Day is a practical example of how strong our class can be when it fights compact and united.

May Day was born in America in 1886 with what became known as "the great uprising". There were strikes and demonstrations in all the major American cities. The biggest was in Chicago; thousands and thousands of workers of every nationality, language and religion came together with one aim: to win the eight-hour working day. A struggle that its trade union leaders paid for with their lives. Remember the Chicago martyrs!

From 1890 it was adopted as the great day the world remembers the victorious international struggle for the eight-hour working day.

And on this day we cannot but recall the hundreds of thousands of the working class, including women and children, who are on the march on the seas or by land, on boats or on foot.

All of them risking their lives. Human beings fleeing terrible conditions, wars, reactionary terrorism or 'simply' thrown off the land by violent capitalist development in the areas in which they lived. Thousands are migrating towards Europe in search of work and a life of dignity. Whatever their story, we welcome them warmly as new European workers. And we are pleased to see here with us so many of our working-class brethren from every part of the world. Welcome here too, comrades! We must unite their energy with ours. Our need for this union brings to mind the conclusion of a famous, and currently vital book – Marx and Engels' Communist Manifesto*:*

"Workers of All Countries, Unite!"
Long live the internationalist 1st May.

Our party battle in the political cycle of the new strategic phase

The New Political Data of Class Abstentionism*

Tension is high on the top floors of the powerhouses in both Europe and the United States. The economy is slowing down again and international trade is struggling as it hasn't for a long time. Chinese restructuring is imposing severe choices on both Western manufacturing and finance, especially to the struggling European banking system. Reorganisations, mergers and cuts to branches and employees are required.

Aleppo and Mosul

Meanwhile the world order continues to vacillate. The battle for Aleppo being fought by Bashar Assad's troops, backed by Russians and Iranians marks a crucial moment in the Syrian war, with the tragic sacrifice of the civilian population. UN sources put the victims at 400,000 to date. Now it is Mosul's turn in Iraq. Here the attack is led by an American-headed coalition; Turkey is demanding its share of the future division.

Signals and warnings follow hot on each other's heels in the various strategic theatres. Russia has announce further joint manoeuvres between its paratroopers and Egypt's, after programming naval manoeuvres together with China. The Chinese Deputy Foreign Minister Li Baodong has stated that the positions of Moscow and Beijing over Syria are the same, and that this is also true of Afghanistan. A joint Russo-Chinese communiqué denounces the installation of an American antimissile system in South Korea. This unusual Russo-Chinese convergence is cause for concern: the "Financial Times" has warned the West not to underestimate it. *The Wall Street Journal* is harshly critical of the gap left by America's withdrawal.

A vacillating order

In a jointly-written article, David Lipton, the IMF First Deputy Managing Director, and Ian Bremmer, the Eurasia Group president, interpret these fears. They observe that for two generations a stable global order has allowed unprecedented increases in standards of living: millions of people have moved from below the poverty line and a global middle class has been created. Today, they write the world order is being challenged and its mass support is in doubt. They see discontent growing in the old metropolises because of the damage of the crisis and the consequences of restructuring. They argue that the middle class's stagnant income and growing inequalities

* *Internationalist Bulletin*, November 2016

are eating away at the social contract, while opportunistic leaders play successfully on people's fears.

Even more important, according to Lipton and Bremmer, is that the international landscape is changing. China is shifting the balance of power in the economy and politics; the future, they say, is uncertain and they conclude: "To repeat a question famously posed early in the last century when the global order was being called into question, what is to be done?"[99] We know something about this.

Fears in Europe and America

The future is indeed uncertain on both shores of the Atlantic. There is a whole spectrum of widespread fears, frustration caused by thwarted expectations, and social resentment. All of this interweaves with the fears aroused by epochal migrations, which political schemers and demagogues associate with the devastating acts of reactionary terrorism in Europe. This climate and these social psychologies are fuelling nationalist, socio-cultural-identifying, protectionist and xenophobic ideologies that are holding vast intermediate social strata of petty bourgeois and also of wage earners in their grasp.

The marked oscillations that characterise the new political cycle stem from all of this. In Europe they are at the root of the Brexit political catastrophe, and in the United States they have brought Donald Trump, with his nationalism, protectionism and xenophobia, to the threshold of the White House.

Class abstentionism

In the latest elections these ideologies have emerged in various forms in the voting everywhere in Europe. But a phenomenon that is new for its size has arisen in these elections: very widespread abstentionism, so much so as to become the leading party everywhere. This is a phenomenon to which millions of waged workers contributed: large-scale class abstentionism that did not let itself be involved in security, nationalist and xenophobic campaigns.

The abstentionism of salaried strata has always existed in Italy. There has always been a part of the proletariat that has never had the illusion of being able to improve its condition through a ballot paper. Which is what we think, too. In the Italian general elections from 1948 to 1976 abstentionism always oscillated around 10% of those having the right to vote, from the 2.8 million of 1948 to the 3.7 of 1976, including blank ballot papers and spoiled votes. In the 1979 elections abstentionism leapt forward by about another two million, exceeding five and a half million and 13.1%.

This was a new phenomenon in Italy, which was dealt with by our analysis in this newspaper in June 1979 and in a national internal meeting in the same month.[100]

We saw in that abstention a protest against the policy of sacrifices imposed at the time by the government under pressure from the employers and accepted by the trade unions. A few years earlier, in its electoral rise, the PCI had profited from the trade-unionist surge of the wage struggles at the end of the 1960s: hence it was now a refusal of the policy of the "historic compromise" that involved the wage problem. We had fought our political battle over that in the 1970s.

It followed from this that Italian abstentionism was basically of an economic nature and did not regard either power or the state. However, if it was not revolutionary abstentionism, it was in any case class abstentionism. At the time this was a new phenomenon for Italy, which drew it nearer to the electoral behaviour of the more mature metropolises, such as the USA, where participation in elections had been much lower for some time. In this field, too, the "American script" was valid.

The battle of the 1970s

Cervetto saw an important aspect in that mass phenomenon, because it defined future behaviour. And this was in fact the case. At the time we had carried out a detailed study of the Genoese districts which revealed that vast waged strata turned their backs on 'their' politics. This defined a vast field of work for us; the phenomenon could suffer setbacks and in some cases subside, but by now the trend was set. It was a question of turning that class abstention into political maturity. The following year's regional elections exacerbated the phenomenon with another one and a half million abstentions.

We worked in depth on that mass manifestation of the irremediable crisis of parliamentarianism. We extended our detailed study to the working-class districts of Genoa, Milan and Turin. It emerged that workers, employees and pensioners were largely responsible for driving this phenomenon. Our newspaper devoted three articles to it in the three summer months. Cervetto wrote: "It is not political irony that an abstentionist newspaper should provide the first scientific analysis of the electoral trend: it is an example of the seriousness of the Marxist method applied to a sector of social statistics. This method inspires our Leninist activity, which proposes to make class abstentionism mature into strategic abstentionism"[101].

In a national meeting in that year specific indications for our work in correlating class abstentionism to our activities among the masses, to our sphere of influence, to the circulation of our newspapers and to our supporters were given.

An international phenomenon

Today we have 70 years of election statistics, which are precisely "social statistics", at our disposal. The trend towards gradual growth in abstentions is very clear. From 1948 to 1976 it was around 10%, in 1979 it rose to 13.1%, and in the 1980s it fluctuated around 16%. In 1994 it arrived at about 20%, in 2001 it stabilised at 25%, and in 2013 it arrived at 20% of the total electorate. The abstention rate has tripled with respect to the levels of the 1960s and 1970s, and this is the first political fact. In 2013 it regarded 13 million voters in Italy, it can be estimated about 10 million wage earners, and it is clearly the leading Italian party, one and a half times the weight of the PD (Democratic Party) or the Five Star Movement. In the successive local elections abstentionism would leap to 50% and over.

Even today this is not revolutionary abstentionism: it is that a growing number of workers, employees and pensioners is realising that a vote in a polling booth can do nothing in the face of the imperialist policy against wages, against the loss of one's job in company restructuring, or against the erosion of welfare.

It has been said and it is being said that this is an international rather than an Italian problem. In February we reported a detailed analysis, published by our French comrades in their newspaper *L'Internationaliste*, regarding the regional elections in France[102]. Abstentionism in the first round amounted to 50% of the electorate. In Paris and its *banlieues* abstention clearly grows with the growth of the incidence of workers and employees in the population. In its first ten districts and municipalities with the strongest working-class composition it is always more than 60%, peaking at over 70%.

In the working-class districts and *banlieues* where our comrades circulate their newspaper and have most of their supporters, the vast majority of the workers, mainly youths, did not vote.

It is obvious that there is a percentage of protest vote, a kind of "electoral abstentionism", ready to subside when a party or movement that expresses its resentment comes onto the scene. This happened in Germany, where the pro-security, anti-European and xenophobic Alternative für Deutschland (AfD) recouped the votes from the abstention in the recent local elections. In Mecklenburg, where the AfD overtook the CDU, 10 election points were recouped from abstention, almost all of them going to the xenophobic party. Even so abstention remained at 38.4%, by far the leading party with an electoral weight three times the AfD's 13%. Almost 7 electoral points were recouped from abstention in the Berlin urban vote. AfD remained below 10% of the electorate, but abstentionism was still three times as much: 33.1%. In the municipal elections around Hanover, the AfD did not get more than 4% of the vote, with abstention standing at 44.5%.

We can add the vote in Russia, which we documented in the latest issue of our newspaper[103]. People have spoken of a triumph for Putin, but the majority of the voters, 52%, abstained. What is striking is the urban vote, with abstentions reaching 65% in Moscow and 67% in St. Petersburg. And here, too, it is workers, employees and pensioners who are swelling the ranks of abstentionism.

Abstentionism was the protagonist in Hungary, where the government held a referendum against the European quotas of refugees... a clearly anti-immigrant referendum, in which abstentions reached 57%, nullifying the legal value of the referendum. This was a hard lesson for the Prime Minister Viktor Orbán, with abstentionism brandished by his parliamentary opposition. And it was also a lesson for us: abstentionism can also be wielded and used by "their" politics.

The working-class districts against "their" politics

These weeks in Italy are full of the constitutional referendum, but the stone guest of abstention will also weigh on this deadline. In the recent municipal elections, class abstentionism peaked. For the occasion we chose samples of mainly wage-earning workers' districts in Milan, Genoa and Turin. In the Lombard capital, abstentionism leapt to 46.6% as against the 24.3% of the 2013 general election. In our sample of wage-earning districts, abstention leapt to 53%. One worker out of two did not vote, indeed even more: in Rogoredo abstention reached 59%, in Corvetto 58.5%, in Giambellino 57% and in Quarto Oggiaro 56%.

In Genoa, abstention was already the leading party in the 2013 general election. Here we considered the 2015 regional elections, those of the PD catastrophe. Abstention with respect to 2013 practically doubled to 50.5%. In the working-class districts it arrived at 58.8% in Marassi, 53.3% in Cornigliano, and 52.6% in Bolzaneto. The same happened in the Turin of the success of Chiara Appendino and the Five Star Movement. Abstention in the municipality leapt to 45% in the first round, by a long chalk Turin's leading party. In this case, too, the working-class districts were decisive, with Le Vallette at 53.7%, Mirafiori Nord at 55%, and Madonna di Campagna at 51.3%.

Class abstentionism has taken on a mass dimension and regards millions of wage earners. Thinking of representing it is impossible, but we, forever abstentionists, have arguments, men and an organisation to transform its growing percentages into strategic abstentionism. "Their" politics are directed towards ever smaller circles; the wage-earning masses are looking elsewhere. It is a question of continuing our work by multiplying our militant commitment.

The party and the unknowns of the new political cycle
A Real Storm*

We had predicted "stormy times": what has arrived is a real political storm.

Donald Trump's election as President of the United States has shaken the chancelleries of the world; there is evident bewilderment, and fear for an unpredictable future.

The editorial staffs of the most important newspapers are breathing the same air. At the beginning of the year one of the *Financial Times* headlines was: "The Long and Painful Journey to World Disorder". Martin Wolf's thesis is that we are at the end of "both an economic period – that of western-led globalisation – and a geopolitical one [...] of a US-led global order". The question is whether what follows "will be an unravelling of the post-second world war era into deglobalisation and conflict, as happened in the first half of the 20th century, or a new period in which [...] especially China and India play a bigger role in sustaining a co-operative global order"[104].

Disillusionment at the 'Financial Times'

Such a clear and illuminating alternative reveals a mixture of concern and disillusionment: Let's follow Wolf again: we are living, once again, "in an era of strident nationalism and xenophobia"; "the hopes of a brave new world of progress, harmony and democracy, raised by the market opening of the 1980s and the collapse of Soviet communism between 1989 and 1991, have turned to ashes".

We recall the editorials of the time, celebrating the glories of globalisation and the end of the USSR, and we recall the promises of a new, prosperous world without inequalities, even "the end of history". And today, after the deepest crisis since the post-WWII period, while nationalism and xenophobia create difficulties for *their* politics, the same editorials have to realise that the myths and dreams have turned to "ashes". And not only this: in a future that has become uncertain, they no longer exclude major wars.

There's a really bad atmosphere. We should say that Martin Wolf is writing from London, where trouble had begun to brew after the Brexit referendum. In London, amidst a thousand contortions, they have to decide how to leave a market of 500 million people, the EU, which has the City as its financial capital. This was not the will of the British government, but the result of the outcome of the referendum gamble. Hence Britain has to get ready to limit immigration; it dreams of sailing the "open seas" of the world

* *Internationalist Bulletin*, March 2017

market, but it risks finding itself a dwarf among continental giants, in the presence of China, India, America and Europe itself.

'Their' politics in trouble

If this is the result of the referendum gamble, it is clear that something is not working in *their* politics. After a few months, a great real estate developer, but TV billionaire completely extraneous to politics, was elected to the presidency in the United States.

Trump was unpopular with the Establishment and faced the opposition of party bigwigs in the primaries, without the majority backing of the big economic groups. And yet he gradually imposed himself over the other much more highly esteemed Republican candidates and in the end prevailed over Hillary Clinton, the Democratic candidate, in the Electors' vote. With his *America First*, Trump became President of the United States with a nationalistic, protectionist, and often xenophobic rhetoric, but no one yet knows what his real politics are.

Also in the American elections it is clear that *their* politics is in trouble. The Republican Party, the majority of the big economic groups, the elites and the major newspapers all underestimated the Trump phenomenon; they were taken by surprise and did not succeed in stopping it.

The French unknown

The same problem is being in France, where the elections have a significance that goes well beyond the choice of the President of the Republic. What is being questioned in Paris is the Franco-German axis, the locomotive of the European process.

The outgoing president François Hollande did not run for president again, the Socialist Party is splitting apart, and Marine Le Pen, with her anti-Europe, nationalist and racist positions, is in the lead in the polls. Her main competitor, François Fillon, has got himself into a mess over salaries paid to family members for parliamentary collaborations that are apparently inexistent. Marine Le Pen's election to the presidency remains improbable because of the French electoral mechanism, but today no one any longer judges it to be impossible.

The mass power base of big capital

What is happening to the old powers? To a certain extent, the relationship between the fundamental groups, the big bourgeoisie, their strategic guidelines, and their traditional mass base in the petty bourgeoisie, the intermediate strata and sizeable strata of wage-earning aristocracies has fallen apart. These are the social stratifications of late imperialist maturity: they had benefited from globalisation, but today they are reacting to the drastic change triggered by China's rise and the consequences of the global crisis, which has sown the seeds of uncertainty.

We have dwelt on these social stratifications of late imperialist maturity, produced by the major restructuring of the 1980s, subsequent to the 1975 crisis, in the pages of our newspaper. At the time our Party fought a fierce battle to avoid being marginalised by the ideologies of imperialist opulence that were penetrating our class precisely through those stratifications. This is a battle we won, because our Party has established and rooted itself. Today those stratifications are reacting, affected or threatened in their conditions and even more in their expectations; this is shaping the new political cycle, so branded by the currents that seem to offer protection in nationalism or localism, or that are the receptacles of widespread resentment.

The social strata of parasitism

It cannot be said that the descending phase of social-democratisation has had a profound effect on the welfare and one thousand conditions of imperialist privilege and parasitism, but pressure to cut their expense has undoubtedly been weighing for years on these strata, and the 2007-2008 crisis further aggravated the phenomenon. The living conditions of the intermediate strata are closely tied to public expenditure; this is also true of a sizable part of multi-income, property-owning families. The new phase is being lived in uncertainty, as a kind of threat exacerbated by the crisis.

Instead, the global crisis has affected or brought into question vast strata of the petty bourgeoisie: numerous small companies are being forced to close down; and just as numerous are the *zombie firms* we deal with on another page of this newspaper[105]. According to a Confesercenti (an employers' association) report, in Italy, in the period 2007-16 the number of retail shops fell by over 91,000 units. Obviously the number of actual closedowns is much higher in comparison to the new start-ups. Generational turnover undoubtedly has its weight: the grocer's daughter has a university degree, no longer wants to stand behind the counter, and becomes a teacher. But the sweeping scythe of the crisis and the ruthless competition of supermarkets also have their weight: the drop is considerable. According to Confesercenti, a 17% drop for butcher's, perfumeries and bookshops, 20% for textile and clothes shops, and 33% for goldsmith's. If these sectors of the petty bourgeoisie are feeling resentful, other vast wage-earning strata have also been affected. Firings in industry and the services have also regarded highly-skilled sectors – various "production engineers" and other white-collar strata have been fired: we need only think of bank clerks – from now to 2019 about 20,000 redundancies are expected.

An anticipatory analysis

There are really many multi-income households involved, and vast strata of the wage-earning aristocracies see themselves at risk. It is inevitable that uncertainly about prospects, fears of standard-of-living retrocession, but, even more, disorientation about betrayed expectations in a progress that seemed limitless and is now hanging in the balance, should spread.

For those who have followed our Marxist analysis in this newspaper over the years, this is certainly not a surprise. In far-off 1994, Arrigo Cervetto wrote as follows: "The world cycle is changing, [...] the '[economic] miracle' is now leaving its mark on the Yellow River and Ganges valleys and no longer on the Po valley. The forty years that quadrupled the wealth of the first decile of the Italian population, that tripled the assets of the second and the third, and that doubled the possessions of the four central deciles are over. Masses of petty bourgeois and wage earners corrupted by the property-owning, servile and transformist spirit have not yet become aware of this and dream of a kind of Club Méditerranée world in which to continue as before"[106].

The impact of migrations

And now: with the onward march of uneven development and the crisis and its consequences, they are becoming aware of it. Among other things, that very same development is bringing with it epochal migration flows, and the intersection with the blind violence of *reactionary terrorist attacks* in Europe's cities is adding fuel to the fire; an easy game for every kind of demagogic pedlar of fear in the uncertainties exacerbated by the ageing of the population.

And this is the wind that swelled the sails of Brexit, Donald Trump, Marine Le Pen and the No to Matteo Renzi's referendum. This is again why *their* politics are hobbling.

The big economic groups, the fractions of big capital, are finding it difficult to persuade what has always been their mass power base, which had supported globalisation and opening up to the markets in the years of long expansion, to follow them.

The deep causes of these oscillations – the descending phase of social-democratisation, European restructuring, big migrations, and a world order that is teetering – are destined to remain. Hence the difficulties of *their* politics, which risk growing worse and even becoming chronic, will remain. *Our* politics, those of a revolutionary and communist Party that is developing and in good health, can and must take advantage of their difficulties and disorientation.

Class abstentionism

Both in America and in Europe, the majority of our mass power base, the wage-earning strata, have chosen abstentionism in the latest elections and referendums.

It is significant that *Le Monde* [February 17th] gave the headline *The Vote of the Increasingly Fragmented Class* to an article that examines the polls about the upcoming presidential election. Bearing in mind only those registered to vote (a restrictive figure), the first party among workers would be abstention with 42% and Le Pen would poll only 25%. Among white-collar workers abstention is also in first place, with 39% as against 21% to Front National. This is a class vote, this is class abstentionism. We are not getting our hopes up; we are very well aware that the ruling ideology is that of the ruling class: the proletariat will always be subject to bourgeois and petty-bourgeois influence in all its variations, hence also in its nationalist, identitarian and racist suggestions.

A European battle

This is a battlefield – abstentionism may grow or decrease, but that political fact is an advantage we can seize to strengthen ourselves in the new political cycle of Atlantic decline. We must do it looking concretely to our establishment in Europe.

There are many young comrades who have entered workplaces, often among white-collar workers and technicians. It is up to them, together with the generations already in factories, to work on class abstentionism by creating a solid network of supporters. That network will have to gather in the new generations of workers. In these stormy times we need to increase our efforts to address the new generations, the thousands of students, among whom there are inevitably tomorrow's workers and worker cadres. This society is unable to offer anything to the young. Our struggle for communism can offer them dignity, courage and the certainty of a struggle for a better society.

Our party in a world cycle of unprecedented tensions

A New and Difficult Challenge*

In the last few months our mobilisation for the 100th anniversary of the October Revolution has received unusual results: from the participation in the rallies of our workers' circles to the extraordinary distribution of our book *October 1917*[107], which brought back to the masses the memory of the October Revolution and its unsung heroes, and to the militant commitment in our political campaign of many youths and workers.

Our Fundraising Campaign in December also received a very positive response, and interesting signals are coming from the anti-racism campaign being conducted by our young members. Their slogan 'Hands off my friend' is a breath of fresh air amidst the xenophobic miasmas emanated by the election campaign. Among the masses we are meeting with a certain uncertainty, fears, and great disappointment in *their* politics. But also curiosity, interest and searching for a frame of reference, together with tangible, growing sympathies. To meet with this it is sufficient to go a little beyond the surface of talk shows, amidst our class in flash and blood, as we do every day. This undoubtedly requires study, militant commitment, and a revolutionary passion that no Twitter in the world is able to synthesise.

We glimpse in the positive reactions to our internationalist battle the reflection of the unprecedented and very stormy times that await us, and in which we are already fighting. In that sense these are results that may prefigure our future political battles.

War and peace

The world balance is changing under the pressure of China and Asia, and all the capitals of imperialism are involved. At the same time, the blows of extensive restructuring, accompanied by the impact of migratory flows on the old powers, are making themselves felt... powers, with Italy in the lead, that are debilitated by an ever more rigid demographic winter that is exacerbating their ageing and decay. These are the two horns of a *historic collision* that is increasingly disturbing the old world order, to the point of putting the dilemma of war and peace back on the tables of the imperialist powerhouses.

In the previous issue of this newspaper[*International Bulletin* January 2018 – *War and Peace in Asia in the Chinese Century*] we reported a judgement of Henry Kissinger's about the China-United States confrontation[108]. The former American Secretary of State did not exclude the possibility of war in the next twenty years, and invited Washington to work according to

* *Internationalist Bulletin*, February 2018

the dual perspective of a possible conflict or of possible inevitably temporary negotiations and agreements. The *Financial Times* [January 19th] reports a survey among the participants at the Davos World Economic Forum. Almost 80% believe there is a growing danger of military conflicts and that major countries may be dragged into regional wars. Here we have the nightmare of war being discussed by the world's financial and political leaders!

Fifteen years of huge tensions

We have been very explicit in these pages of ours: a concentrate of "huge, unprecedented tensions" [109] is building up. The next 15 years will be among the stormiest, with the world contention faced with two possible solutions: either a clash to the point of a major conflict, or a temporary agreement between China and the United States. The real outcome will probably be one of the intermediate gradations between the two possible solutions: the strategic "Indo-Pacific" option is being discussed in the USA... a conflict between China and India cannot be excluded tomorrow.

The hypothesis of a major Asian war was carefully examined by Arrigo Cervetto in a December 1993 article [*Il mondo multipolare* (The Multipolar World), in *Opere*, Vol. 4]. The theses of the analyst Paul Dibb, still today at the Strategic and Defence Studies Centre of the Australian National University, Canberra, about the unpredictability of the Asian balance of the time were considered. In his summing up, Cervetto observed: "According to the Australian scholar, the Pacific era may lead to a major Asian war within two or three decades" [110].

Everyone to the test

We are not faced with any mythical deadline, with any appointment with war in fifteen years' time, and not even with a hypothetical agreement. But there is one certainty in this time span: in the next 15 years the world contention will become much more bitter, much harder, and much fiercer. This is the deadline we are faced with, because ideas, political parties and individuals will be put to the test. All of them: of our class and of the ruling class.

In considering the hard times ahead we need to bear in mind that the epochal migration flows will continue. In the old metropolises the *population law of imperialist maturity* will continue to act, inexorably. The number of births will continue to fall, and the population as a whole to diminish. In 15 years' time, in Italy, over 5 million units in the 20-49 age group, the backbone of the labour force, will be missing. This is not an estimate and not even a trend, but the result of a simple arithmetical operation between age groups of people already born and resident in Italy.

The fearmongers can shout as long as they want to, but that void will be even greater, because there is an emigration of skilled labour from Italy. If the Italian bourgeoisie wants to maintain the present labour-force levels in that age group, it will have to increase the number of immigrant workers by more than 5 million. There are no alternatives: either an increase in the number of migrants or even swift decline. Far from *helping them at home*: they are indispensable to factories, hospitals, offices and as carers, in Italy as in Germany, Japan, Spain, and so on.

Italians first say our home-grown electoral peddlers, without realising that there is no longer even a sufficient number of Italians to cover the available jobs! We will continue to fight for the unity of all the workers without any distinction; for us *the proletarians will always come first.*

Eurafrica and European restructuring

Japan is thinking of importing labour from India to deal with its *demographic crisis*; Europe is looking towards Africa. This is also why *Eurafrica,* as Emmanuel Macron has called it, is one of the directions in which European imperialism is expanding, in which it is already committing men and means. Basically this forms part of that *European counteroffensive* to which Brussels is committed, starting from the big processes of industrial and financial restructuring, which have as their aim the creation of big economic groups with global dimensions.

To fight off the competition of the big global groups, first of all of the new Chinese competitors, the old national champions no longer suffice. The Alstom-Siemens merger, and in its wake the acquisition of Ilva by the iron and steel giant Arcelor-Mittal, or the Fincantieri-STX (Chantiers de l'Atlantique) merger, in this case with the aim of forming a European champion of the civil and military shipbuilding industry, are emblematic. In our class field it is on the last two fronts that our comrades are engaged in a difficult defensive battle, in a restructuring and concentration process that is a threat to jobs.

The Franco-German axis

On the European political front, the laborious attempt to form the new German government, again an expression of a CDU-CSU and SPD *grand coalition*, is drawing to a close. It is turning out to be a difficult path, which reveals how also in Germany the new forms of *proprietary populism* are causing problems for *their* politics. Although they remain in the minority, these forms, by agitating security and socio-cultural identifying themes, linked to the migration phenomena, influence the political processes and complicate the search for mass consensus for the big capital lines.

The *European counteroffensive* needs a strong Franco-German axis; this is confirmed by the importance given to the votes of the French and German parliaments regarding the renewal of the Élysée Treaty, with the image of Angela Merkel and Emmanuel Macron side by side in the

Salon Murat, where Konrad Adenauer and General de Gaulle signed the pact in 1963.

The Federal Minister for Foreign Affairs, the Social Democrat Sigmar Gabriel, took it upon himself to give the strategic meaning of the European initiative in a crucial speech at the Berliner Forum Aussenpolitik: we give an account of this further on in this newspaper[111].

The 'perpetual motion' of public spending

In the Italian election campaign *decisive world facts* are almost absent; if anything, what stands out is that, in the country with the highest debt in the West, all the political parties promise greater recourse to public spending. A reborn Silvio Berlusconi is waving the flat tax flag, a tax cut in the form of a single rate, a proposal that is drawing more attention in the North. Instead the Five Star Movement is increasingly turning to the South, as a public spending party. Here a singular economic recipe that no one had thought of before has cropped up. "Down with austerity!" their leader thunders: to reduce the public debt it is necessary... to increase spending. The extra debt that would thus be created would be paid back thanks to economic growth, and this would allow new debts to be made, paid back again by spending. They have invented *perpetual motion* in economics, a discovery that merits a Nobel prize.

Election campaigns have never been a great show: we have proof of this from our masters, Lenin's proof. In 1912, Lenin commented on the political race for the Duma and observed an "election campaign ... attended by the most brazen self-advertisement", in which all the bourgeois parties "are advertising themselves in the same way as individual capitalists advertise their goods". Even "the names of some parties, both in Europe and Russia," – he added – "are chosen with a direct eye to advertisement, and their 'programmes' are quite often written for the sole purpose of hoodwinking the public"[112].

A century has gone by, and *TV democracy* has only taken the farcical side of *their* politics to extremes. We cling to our abstentionism, thanks to which we know we can address a great number of workers. Of course we know very well that *class abstentionism* is not in itself a vaccination against the ruling ideologies, including the viruses of xenophobia and racism, but reflection and conviction can start from there.

The link of the plan-party

Returning to the years that lie ahead, those fifteen years "among the stormiest", how are we to deal with them?

The solution continues to be the one indicated by Cervetto in *Il compito generale* [The General Task – Uneven Political Development, in *Opere*, Vol. 2]: "At every moment, our organisational plan, our systematic work as the guarantee and necessary condition to be able to deal with about-turns, social explosions, and political complications, is present"[113]. This is precisely what lies ahead for us: we will need to grasp even more firmly the link of organisation, which is the link that "can be torn from us with the greatest difficulty".

In the prospect of such a complex period, there is another aspect about which Cervetto can be consulted again. There is a very pertinent note in the book *The Difficult Question of Times*. Cervetto reflects on the "erroneous conclusions" the communist movement had drawn from the crisis of capitalism starting from 1914. The crisis was conceived of as irreversible, he observes, notwithstanding Lenin's constant reprimands, and he stresses: "There is no crisis that is irreversible, there is no automatic collapse of capitalism. [...] the imperialism that triggers war, and hence crisis, spreads capitalism in the world at the same time".

Cervetto considers how, for our masters, the *question of times* regarded not so much the world market or the fate of capitalism, "as much as the evaluation of the quantity and quality of the contradictions and the subjective capacity, hence of the vanguard party, to use them"[114]. If we predict the next fifteen years as among "the stormiest", the quantitative and qualitative judgement about their contradictions is implicit. The question of our party's subjective capacities to use them remains open. That is the challenge facing us as militant revolutionaries. It is a difficult challenge, and new for our generations. It can be faced only if we stretch all our energies to the utmost.

The new cycle and our internationalist battle

The Hour is Striking for Our Politics*

The difficulty of *their* politics, of the politics of capital and its parliamentary parties, is evident in all the old powers, faced with epochal changes. The eruption of Chinese imperialism is challenging the old balances. Beijing is now openly claiming its share of the booty, a new share-out in which the old powers are called upon to make room for the new arrival on the world goods and services markets, in the financial flows of capital exports, and in the division of the spheres of influence.

The United States, Europe and Japan are thus called upon to reckon with their relative decline. China has stated it wants to become the first-ranking world power and is pressing on the old order with its economic, financial and political tools. But it is above all its great rearmament plan, *military modernisation*, that is impressing the world and challenging the other powers.

China, the USA and the "nuclear triad"

The old world order is wobbling. It had been forged with the fire and sword of the Second World War, including the atomic bombs dropped by the American air force on Hiroshima and Nagasaki. It was the order of the victorious powers with the USA, the world's leading power, at its heart... an order that has resisted for decades, even in its transformations. But now that China is demanding its assertive place among the powers that old order is struggling to hold out. The new tensions, the new global threats are re-invoking the strength of the states and their military power. Xi Jinping has asked his armed forces "to be able to win any war" and has decided to increase military expenditure in support of their modernisation.

We have already written this: Beijing is building its third aircraft carrier and is planning its fourth, which will be nuclear-powered. It will not be the last because China has planned to build one every three years. The *Global Times*, a newspaper that wants to be the Chinese answer to the *Financial Times*, denies that China is committed to a rearmament race. According to them it is simply the concentration of military expenditure on aircraft carriers, fighter jets and Cruise missiles. In addition, they write, with the development of a strategic bomber.

It is inevitable that the Pentagon should see in this a kind of rearmament challenge going so far as to realise the Chinese *nuclear triad*, the capacity to launch nuclear missiles from land, sea and air. The United States' response is a

* *Internationalist Bulletin*, May 2018

clear increase in military expenditure and the announcement of its *modernisation* regarding the nuclear deterrent. The French daily *Le Figaro* argues that the use of lower-potential nuclear warheads, also in the face of a clash with conventional weapons, is at the heart of this modernisation. According to the French newspaper, these are bombs with half the power of the one dropped on Nagasaki by the Americans in August 1945, causing 70,000 deaths. *Le Figaro* makes a sarcastic comment: "the Pentagon needs an extreme but credible weapon", i.e., this is our translation, a weapon causing 35,000 deaths. This is what is being debated in the capitals of imperialism!

The rearmament race

The other powers are not standing still: Japan has announced the transformation of a helicopter carrier into an aircraft carrier equipped with new F-35 fighter planes, armed with Cruise missiles. Furthermore Tokyo will adopt a new American antimissile system. India has announced a new aircraft carrier and here, too, *military modernisation*, in this case of its missile system. Vladimir Putin has presented to the world on TV and in grand style the Russian response to the current rearmament: a series of "ultramodern nuclear weapons" which, he asserts, "no one else in the world has or will be able to realise in a short time"... among these a Cruise super missile with an "unpredictable trajectory" able to reach "any point in the world".

In Europe, France's response was prompt: it will raise its military expenditure from the present 40 billion dollars to 60 billion in 2023. It is speaking about four nuclear submarines, frigates, drones, and Rafale, Mirage and A330 aircraft. And its Navy is pressing for a second aircraft carrier.

Europe and war

In Germany, too, albeit timidly, increasing military expenditure is in the Grand Coalition's programme. In spite of the persistence of qualms and checks due to the *past that does not pass* of the Nazi catastrophe, clearer signals of rearmament are coming from Berlin. At the beginning of March the economic daily *Handelsblatt* sported the headline: *Germany Is Rearming.* First of all it will be up to the Franco-German axis, which has resumed the initiative, to deal with the question of European rearmament. It is at one and the same time a huge and a delicate question because of the political problems that have to be overcome, as the war in Syria and the affair of the joint US-Britain-France missile attack has confirmed: if Paris is aspiring to head a European military intervention force, Berlin is struggling to break away from the post-1945 tradition of great caution in the military field. In any case the new attempt has been launched and one of the terrains will be the EU's liberation from American weapons systems.

This is how the force of the states comes back into play, and with it the call for war is by now continual. We have seen *The Economist* devote its cover to this, *The Next War.* We commented in these pages[115] on the

CSIS report that had at its beginning the photo of the attack on Pearl Harbor. In mid-April a *Financial Times* insert was headed *War or Peace?*, and presented four new books about war. The CFR president, Richard Haas, was even more explicit: "The world is in disarray. It risks returning to the time of direct wars between powers". He was echoed by the former UN Under-Secretary General Antonio Maria Costa: "The clash between the two US and China superpowers and the rhetoric that accompanies it are reaching the point of no return. Nothing is excluded, not even conflict".

Decline and its nightmares

There is nothing new in this for us Marxists: capitalism and imperialism are unable to maintain world order. Capitalism inevitably generates war. For us this is a tenet, but until a few years ago anyone who made a statement of the kind was considered a dogmatic doom-monger and out of touch with the real world. The ruling ideas excluded war between great powers: either because there was the UN, they told us, or because nuclear weapons guaranteed the balance of terror, or because democracy was now extensively widespread throughout the world. Today the spectre of a great destructive war is being continually conjured up by their media, and acts as a background to every regional tension or conflict: we only need to look at Syria.

More than ever this is the moment of internationalism; our communist battle against imperialism and its wars is impellent. The old powers are under pressure; it is precisely the spectre of their decline that is generating the worst nightmares. Evident political difficulties for the ruling groups in the United States, Europe and Japan are emerging. The wounds of a global crisis that kept them in check for ten years have not yet fully healed: this crisis affected the interests of many, but above all it shattered the dreams and expectations of "eternal welfare" for vast strata of the petty and middle bourgeoisie, vast intermediate strata, and wage-earning strata. The dissatisfaction, resentment and rancour that this generated combined with the fears triggered by intense migration flows, fears amplified by the gradual ageing of an amply capitalised population and hence sensitive to *law and order* propaganda. Moreover, the European constriction has reduced the flow of public spending, or threatens to do so, exacerbating malaise and fears.

It was easy for the fomenters of fears of every kind to turn these states of mind against the consolidated political parties and their traditional political forms. Thus anti-establishment, eccentric, xenophobic, and for the Old Continent often Eurosceptic, forms took off in all the old powers. These are phenomena that have made the necessary mass support for the general line expressed by big capital and its groups very complicated. Disorientation that we have defined as unprecedented, and "even destructive political swings", have derived from this.

Transformist wave

This is also what the general election in Italy revealed in the transformist wave of March 4th; we analysed it in detail in the previous issue of our newspaper[116]. Tax protest and securitarian instances fuelled property-owning transformism in the Centre-North, swelling the League's sails. In the South resentment over the reduction in the flows of public spending and pork-barrel welfarism fuelled a statist transformism raked in by the Five Star Movement, by now the real container of the jumble of Southern demands. Berlusconi's party, which was not able to avoid the League's cannibalism or the Southern wave, paid the price for this. The price paid by the PD [Democratic Party] was also very high, as it was, moreover, for all the Social-Democratic currents in all the old powers.

This is the crisis of a Social Democracy that has struggled over the years to respond to the social transformation of its electoral base, with the wholesale emergence of multi-income and often quite wealthy property-owning families... and which has been hit in the meantime by the reduction or less increase in the glue of public spending and welfare. In Italy it was the European constriction that undid the interclass compromise on which their politics has been based for decades, i.e. relative tax impunity in the North and public-spending-funded welfarism in the pork-barrel South.

The myth of a PD that lost because it neglected the peripheries, where there are families that cannot make ends meet, continues to circulate. If this were the case, it is not understandable why those votes did not go to the much more experienced Bersani and D'Alema, who ended up, instead, in an electoral abyss. We explain to ourselves the balsamic use of that myth, to soothe with a convenient explanation the wounds dealt at the polls, but this is not the case. It is true there are some millions of families in Italy who struggle to make ends meet and who live on the outskirts. These are families renting their homes, with only one income and dependent children, unemployed, or at the lower levels of the wage scale. But they are above all those 2-3 million families of immigrant workers, denied equal rights, including the right to vote, by the Italian Republic. This is a shameful discrimination that we do not accept. So? The election figures should be studied more carefully: where did the PD lose more votes? First of all in fat rich Emilia, then in plump Tuscany and the rest of the central Quadrilateral: a haemorrhage that may be fatal. And then in Liguria, the Triangle and the rest of the country.

Weakness of "their" politics

As for wage earners, on the other hand, many of those votes fuelled abstentions, which grew still further reaching an all-time high. And we repeat that if we really count all the workers, "in much of the North, in the productive heart of European imperialism", the majority of our class does not vote. Here is the vast space that opens up to our communist politics! *Their* politics is struggling; the new forms that are emerging have very weak ideas. What does the Five Star Movement offer to those who are venturing into politics? Let's let their founder speak: "We are a little Christian Democrat, a little right-wing, a little left-wing, a little centrist. We can adapt ourselves to anything"[117]. This is the perfect portrait of unprincipled opportunism that, precisely, adapts itself to everything, like a well-oiled weathervane that rotates with every gust of wind.

And what does Salvini offer? An old, imported sovereignism, an imitation of the French Front National, xenophobic and even racist. And then right-wing social ideas that have their roots in fascism. Is this the new politics that is marching ahead? And what does the PD offer? For today a colossal failure, for tomorrow, at the moment, even they don't know. Will the key ideas of imperialist Europeanism arrive? We will fight them relentlessly, but at the moment *their* politics are struggling in the whole of Europe.

This is the moment to strike a blow, the moment of *our* politics starting from those millions of workers and youths who do not listen to *their* politics, who do not vote. We can offer them the prospect of a conscious struggle, a strategy, solid principles, and key ideas that unite various generations... a struggle for communism that is and remains a cause for the whole of the human race.

The new generations in the new political cycle

Youths and Communism*

On May 27th the Internationalist Youth Day was held in a very crowded Sala del Porto in Genoa. We publish a synthesis of its conclusions.

This May is the 200th anniversary of Karl Marx's birth; we have commemorated it with a highly successful initiative: the diffusion of the anthology *Marx scienziato e rivoluzionario* [Marx: Scientist and Revolutionary][118]. Exactly! Marx was a great scientist of the proletariat: this is testified by the imposing legacy of his writings, the fruit also of his precious collaboration with Friedrich Engels. At the end of the year the first volumes of their "Works" will begin to appear in our editions: the best possible homage to our masters. Their basic approach regarded the possibility and the necessity of facing the political struggle scientifically, and they devoted their whole lives to that commitment.

Marx and the clowns of "their" politics

Wilhelm Liebknecht has left us some memories of this that are highly topical: "Politics was to Marx a study. Beer-politicians and barroom politics he viewed with deadly hate [...] But politics is, theoretically, the recognition of these millions and billions of factors busy at the "loom of Time", and, practically, action based on this recognition. Politics is also science and applied science".

Liebknecht continues: "Nevertheless every ass thinks himself a great politician or even a great statesman". "How wild Marx could become when speaking of those hollow skulls who arrange matters for themselves with a few cant phrases and, mistaking their more or less confused wishes and ideas for facts, direct the fate of the world at the beer-table, in newspapers or in public meetings and parliaments. Happily, the world does not take any notice of them. By those 'hollow skulls', very famous, highly celebrated "great men" were sometimes meant"[119].

The generations of Marxism

At the same time Marx was a great revolutionary in the most practical sense of the term. Engels is categorical about thus. "Now, we were by no means of the opinion that the new scientific results should be confided in large tomes exclusively to the 'learned' world. Quite the contrary. [...] It was our duty to provide a scientific foundation for our view, but it was equally

* *Internationalist Bulletin*, July 2018

important for us to win over the European and in the first place the German proletariat to our conviction"[120].

Starting from that corpus of elaborations the successive Marxist generations were gradually able to deal with the new phenomena of concentration, centralisation, capital exports, and the development of financial capital. Lenin's contribution to the study of imperialism was decisive. Other contributions to revolutionary thought came from Leon Trotsky, Rosa Luxemburg and Amadeo Bordiga.

However, it was not possible to stop at those generations of Marxism. After the catastrophe of the second imperialist war, the thread of Marxist theory had to be knotted together again and commitment on the front of the development of Marxist science had to continue. One confirmation of this is to be found in the works of Arrigo Cervetto, the founder of Lotta Comunista, which we are publishing. These are the result of a lifetime of study and struggle which has allowed our party to develop and grow until today. It is necessary to continue: the study of the new phenomena of late imperialist maturity is up to us. Woe betide us if we had stopped at the 1848 *Manifesto of the Communist Party*; woe betide us if we had not set off from the "Manifesto".

The "Manifesto" and the world order

Let's look at the world of today, at a world order that is struggling. What is happening? For an answer we return precisely to Marx's 'Manifesto': "Modern industry has established the world market, for which the discovery of America paved the way. This market has given an immense development to commerce, to navigation, to communication by land. This development has, in its turn, reacted on the extension of industry; [...] In place of the old local and national seclusion and self-sufficiency, we have intercourse in every direction, universal inter-dependence of nations".

This is exactly what has been happening in the one and a half centuries behind us and especially in the decades following the catastrophe of the Second World War. "How does the bourgeoisie get over these crises?" Marx and Engels ask themselves. "On the one hand by enforced destruction of a mass of productive forces; on the other, by the conquest of new markets, and by the more thorough exploitation of the old ones"[121].

The destruction of productive forces was evident in the war; the conquest of new markets has characterised the post-WWII decades.

Fifty million migrants

Whirlwind industrialisation and a highly intense capitalist development that has lasted until the new century and that has involved Asia, Africa, and Latin America. Capitalist development in these continents has gradually led to the rapid depopulation of the countryside, with huge flows of migrants to the towns.

Let's return to the "Manifesto" again: "The bourgeoisie has subjected the country to the rule of the towns. It has created enormous cities, has greatly increased the urban population as compared with the rural". This is what has happened first of all in Asia, with enormous cities like Shanghai with more than 18 million inhabitants, Karachi with more than 16 million, Beijing and Mumbai with more than 12 million, Delhi and Guangzhou with more than 11, Jakarta with 10 million, and Tokyo with over nine. And in Africa, with the more than twelve million inhabitants of Lagos, the eleven of Kinshasa, and the nine of Cairo.

Today most of the world's population lives in towns. And these are at the root of the huge flows of migrants that cross those continents. They are estimated at about 50 million individuals a year, roughly 30 million in Asia and 10 million in Africa. Only a small part of these flows – perhaps 10% – spills over into the West. Even less in Europe, where they are estimated at about one million a year, to which refugees from Syria and the Middle East – another million or less – have added themselves recently. Hence the flows of migrants to Europe can be estimated at about two million individuals a year, compared with demographic dimensions of over half a billion. In other words: the so-called "invasion" amounts to 4 per thousand of the population!

Ageing and fearful societies

There is another important, crucial fact: these migrants arrive in a continent that is demographically ailing, where births have plummeted and the population is diminishing. What is happening? The fact is that capital is voracious; it has stocked up on female labour and has called more and more women to become wage workers. In the last few decades millions have entered the labour market... undoubtedly a positive process for us communists, because it has increased the ranks of the proletariat in all the old metropolises. But the more "developed" bourgeois society, that of "women's rights" and "gender equality", is also a greedy, cynical society. It has made ample recourse to female labour, often at lower wages and by blackmailing working mothers, but then it has left women alone in the face of such a delicate, demanding, and essential task as that of maternity.

The late maturity of imperialism means senile, inward-looking societies. Worrying gaps are being created in the old powers' labour market that only immigrants will be able to fill in. But foreign workers arouse fears in an increasingly ageing and amply capitalised population. These are fears that interweave with the disappointments and insecurity left by the 2008-2014 *global crisis*, and with the more general uncertainty of an existence in a world shaken by restructuring, clashes, violence, and wars.

Government of fear

And those fears are brandished by fear-mongers, unscrupulous rascals who stir up people's feelings against foreigners for a few more votes or seats in parliament. They do not hesitate to agitate xenophobic, racist themes in a country like Italy, which was a country of migrants; in a country that experienced the race laws passed 80 years ago by Fascism against Italian citizens of Jewish faith. At the time *Italians first* did not count; what counted was discrimination and segregation. We know the abomination those laws contributed to: concentration camps, forced labour, and extermination.

Furthermore these unscrupulous adventurists agitate xenophobic, racist themes in a country that could not keep going without foreign workers. Let's leave science aside for a moment: if by magic all the immigrants were to go back home overnight, Italy would collapse. The morning after many of the factories would be closed, activity in the building industry would be suspended, fruit and tomatoes would be left to rot on trees and plants, much of the services and transport would be at a standstill, and millions of elderly people would be left to their own devices without any more carers.

We have conducted an intense campaign among the younger generations against racism: thousands of youths were involved. Our internationalist commitment remains firm and determined: we say this in the face of the Salvini-Di Maio government that looks like taking shape, a government that will be held together by only one thing, fear – a gloomy, *ragged Europeanism* prospect.

Proletarians first!

They continue to tell us they represent the majority of Italians. This is a lie, because the League and M5S together represent 35% of the Italians with the right to vote. They are the government of a minority, little more than one third of the Italians. The first party is by far that of abstentionism; among workers and wage earners non-voters exceed 40%. Millions of youths and workers do not listen to them at all.

Therefore we strongly reiterate that our motto is *proletarians first*. Migrants are our class brothers and we want to fight with them in order to bring internationalist consciousness to a European proletariat that already can be none other multiethnic.

Let's return to the "Manifesto" and the whirlwind capitalist development that has given birth, apart from the big flows of migrants, to great new powers, with China first of all. Today Chinese imperialism is heading for global heights and is shaking the old balances of power. China is demanding from the old powers new spaces on the markets, in financial flows, and in the spheres of influence. The world contention is growing fiercer; the force of States that have committed themselves to a real arms race is coming back into play.

The tension among the great powers is increasing; their newspapers and think tanks continue to believe a war between great powers is possible and even probable. These are prospects we can in no way exclude; they are the abyss towards which the ruling classes are taking us. There is great confusion in Europe (and much more in Italy, left in its "poor man's imperialism" as always). Transformism and amateurishness are spreading, ignorance is lording it, and in *their* politics they are more and more often groping their way. This is why this is more than ever the hour of *our* politics, which for us remains "science and applied science". It requires study, in-depth investigation and a militant commitment that becomes a lifestyle choice. It allows us to raise our eyes to the world, in a battle that is undoubtedly daily, but that looks towards the future, the future of Communism.

Rebuilding internationalism is possible

It Can be Done*

The growth rates of the world cycle are far from negligible, even though strong concern is spreading: a slump in the global economy is feared. In general, it is the huge debt, which has grown by 60% with respect to 2007, which is causing this concern. This, in its turn, is fuelled by Donald Trump's protectionist stance and duties and the crises among the emerging powers, such as in Argentina and Turkey, made fragile by the strengthening of the dollar.

Having said this, American pressure on China is strong: Beijing has matched it blow-for-blow, but its power is being put to the test. The direction being taken by the *Silk Road* is beginning to provoke reactions in Asia: some projects have been annulled, others reviewed, and for the contracting countries are arising debt problems that are hard to face. For the moment, the biggest clash between Washington and Beijing is limited to trade disputes, but neither of them has renounced parading ships, aircraft, missiles and submarines in every kind of exercise. CNN has announced there will soon be a big American naval exercise in the South China Sea and Taiwan Strait, in an escalation that is increasing tension in Asia.

Global tensions

There is no part of the world theatre that is not facing stormy times. Latin America is seeing times of fierce contradictions approaching. Maduro's Venezuela is continuing to collapse, in spite of loans from China with which Beijing is wedging itself into the area, and Argentina has been forced to ask for IMF intervention. Now there is Brazil in the midst of election turmoil: Jair Bolsonaro, of the Brazilian far right, has polled an unexpected number of votes; no one knows where this huge mass transformism will lead to. The slings and arrows of Donald Trump's "America First" policy have reached Europe: negotiations over customs duties are going on, but transatlantic relations are being poisoned by the contrast over the Iranian nuclear programme, with the USA abandoning the 5+1 Treaty and Washington threatening retaliation against enterprises and companies that continue to do business with Iran. The Europeans have reacted: Brussels is attempting to fine-tune a system of defence for the groups that continue to deal with Iran, but no one knows how effective this will be. Agonising negotiations over Brexit, caught up in the British impasse caused by the divisions that are lacerating the Tories, are always underway; a transitory solution that would defer a definitive agreement seems to be emerging. One thing is certain: the

* *Internationalist Bulletin*, November 2018

new turbulent phase in the contention has highlighted a European delay with respect to the challenges that have arisen.

European imbalance, Italian imbalance

The efficacy of the European powers, with their institutions and ideologies, no longer corresponds to the requirements imposed by the *second half* of the *new strategic phase*. This is a feature of the new political cycle in the European Union's political imbalance that necessarily also involves Rome. This is an unprecedented change, which adds itself to a long-term non-correspondence in Italy; Italy is the only major country in the EU that has populist, sovereignist and racist forces in its government.

Here, too, as elsewhere, we saw mass transformism at work in the polls, but with a peculiarity of its own. In the North and Centre of the country, vast strata of the petty bourgeoisie, intermediate strata, and also part of the wage earners, affected by the crisis, disappointed in their expectations, and worried about the prospect of a decline, abandoned the old political parties. They mainly turned to the League, attracted above all by its promises of tax cuts or impunity. Matteo Salvini's securitarian and racist approach did the rest. In the South, strata that are historically more closely tied to statism turned to the Five Star Movement, convinced it could obtain more transfers of money to the South and open up to many the way of a job in the public sector.

North and south overdrawn

This brings us to the impact of European restructuring on a weakness that the Italian bourgeoisie, thanks to its own ineptitude, has never succeeded in overcoming: the dualism between North and South. Moreover, the cloud of property-owning fear, which weighs on social strata that are both ageing and laden with assets, is hovering over the whole country. Now Salvini and Di Maio, united in the government, should guarantee a compromise that would allow the property-owning transformism of the North to hold together with the statist transformism of the South: this is possible only by incurring debt.

The clash with the European Union and market pressure will leave their mark on the next few months; a further increase in the spread could easily trigger a crisis in some banks. If, then, doubt about the solvability of the Italian State were to spread, a catastrophic crisis could occur. There are possibilities of a European compromise: Mario Draghi's statements and some of Angela Merkel's and even Pierre Moscovici's hints suggest a certain willingness in Europe to offer the umpteenth "Mediterranean discount".

In the government they are convinced that Italy is "too big to be allowed to fail", and they have cunningly chosen to push the blackmail of their weakness to extremes: an attitude at one and the same time adventurist and typical of "poor peoples's imperialism". It goes without saying that a compromise with Brussels would calm the markets; otherwise, we wrote in May referring to Salvini, "before or together with a catastrophic Italian crisis there will be the crisis of his government"[122].

An internationalist campaign

Even if it is seeking a propagandistic distraction, the government, however, has meanwhile chosen to spread the poisons of xenophobia and racism, stirring up property-owning fears. We have always fought against every discrimination, but the action of the government of fear and racism has required an extraordinary commitment. In the last few weeks our workers' groups committed themselves to an intense political campaign, concluded everywhere by public initiatives; in Genoa, Milan and Turin three parades crossed the city centres and ended with internationalist rallies.

These are initiatives that merit reflection, undoubtedly because of the unprecedented participation in them, but above all because of their political significance. In the North, in the Industrial Triangle, our internationalist banners have always been present in the streets and squares on the occasion of May Day. However, those demonstrations are historically the trade unions' prerogative, as it rightly should be: that, then, the trade unions have abandoned that tradition in many situations is another matter. However, we need to ask ourselves how many years have gone by since unequivocally internationalist parades and rallies, with slogans denouncing the government without any ambiguity and claiming class unity, have been missing from those streets and squares.

Milan 1925

Well, the last time in Milan was in 1925, ninety-three years ago. It was a demonstration organised in the afternoon and evening of Sunday March 22nd 1925, well attended and spreading, as the newspapers reported, to the nearby streets. The official orator was Amadeo Bordiga, already at odds with the Communist Party of Italy's executive and the International. It was an internationalist demonstration against the government and hence against Fascism. At the same time, it was also a fierce denunciation of the by then rising Stalinist counterrevolution: subsequent to that initiative, the PCd'I Executive dissolved the Milan Committee; proof of this is to be found in the volume of our editions in memory of Bruno Fortichiari[123].

To see the authentic banners of internationalism – and not the falsifications of Stalinism or the left-wing interventionism of Third Worldist myths –, in the streets and squares of Milan again it was necessary to wait until the afternoon of Sunday September 30th 2018, this time in Piazza della Scala. Precisely 93 years had gone by.

Turin 1922, Genoa and Savona 1920

In Turin, the *Ordine Nuovo* of October 15th 1922 reported a "parade of more than 400 communists and sympathizers" that was singing the praises of

Soviet Russia and the Third International in the Barriera di Nizza working-class district. Ninety-seven years have gone by since then. There would then be the attempted Communist rally, held by Ruggero Grieco in 1924 in Piazza Statuto, but the demonstration was routed by Fascist squads.

At that time, Genoa was smaller: all of today's districts in the industrial Ponente (West) were independent municipalities, and Genoa was a reformist centre. The Genoese Communists had their centre of reference in Savona. It was there that the last significant internationalist demonstration took place on May Day 1920. The chronicles of the time speak of a trainload of one thousand dockworkers from Genoa and an impressive demonstration in which, according to the reporter, 10,000 people took part. Errico Malatesta, surrounded, according to reporters, by "about one hundred Anarchist Communists", brought the rally to an end.

Well then: at the end of September, after almost one century, internationalist flags, waved by thousands of workers of the most diverse nationalities and by wage earners of the most diverse trades, returned to the heart of Milan, Turin and Genoa. Almost one century of the absence of internationalism from those streets and squares speaks to us clearly of the depth of the defeat of the labour movement in the 1920s and of the historic delay accumulated by our revolutionary party. At the same time, our parades clearly announce that that delay can be made up for. There is still a long way to go: we proceed without any triumphalist claim, according to Leon Trotsky's maxim, "neither to cry nor to laugh". However, one fact is demonstrated: rebuilding internationalism is possible; it is really possible to entrench a party based on the Bolshevik model in the heart of Europe. It is for this that we are fighting.

At the same time as our demonstrations two other initiatives took place: a PD rally in Rome and a kind of happening in Milan's Arengario, promoted by the Milanese orange Left, which had voted for Pisapia to become Mayor.

The centres of their politics

One centre, in Milan, evidently wanted to liaise with the PD centre in Rome, and perhaps also to weigh in its congressional debate. For what it is worth, as regards numbers, participation in the two centres of opportunism and in our class demonstrations was altogether similar. However, their composition was different: immigrant workers were almost absent in Rome, and completely absent from the orange left-wing happening in Milan. We suspect that in their incurable parliamentarism they are anything but enthusiastic about letting themselves be seen arm in arm with "blacks", who, moreover, cannot vote: they are afraid of frightening people and of losing votes, and some of them, under their breath, did not make a mystery of this. If anything, what is hard to understand is the attitude of the leaders of a CGIL which, moreover, is fast losing members: where do they think they can breathe new life into ageing organisations if not also by turning to the immigrant labour that is destined to account for more than one third of the whole in the North?

Woe to those, however, who forget there are other centres, hence other forces, with which confrontation is harder. There is the centre of Salvini's League. We have known Beppe Grillo's circuses, half carnivals and half rallies: they, too, were crowded. There is then a fifth potential centre, the Roman Catholic, which, if it were to ring bells and church bells would undoubtedly be the most impressive. All of them are centres of *their* politics, the centres of parliamentarism, the only centres the media and social media see: this is their world, where they attempt to condition, to influence, to shift some votes, sometimes even on command.

But we have demonstrated that, since there are other politics, there is another centre that does not look at votes, but at the world. A centre that does not fight for the confused and contradictory rights of mass individualism, but for the unity and autonomy of all the working class, no matter what its colour, ethnic group, or religion.

An internationalist centre, whose banner is *first the proletariat*; a centre that fights for equal wages, for social security for everyone, and for equality of working conditions for immigrant workers. This is our internationalist political battle: it has to contribute to the entrenchment of a party based on the Bolshevik model in the European metropolis.

Our battle in the new political cycle

Crisis in "Their" Politics*

The Economist is one of the international bourgeoisie's most prestigious magazines. British by birth, founded in 1843 in support of free trade and against the protectionism of the time, it extended the circle of its readers to the other shore of the Atlantic. Incidentally, from 2015 Exor, the Agnelli family's strongbox, has become the majority shareholder. Stressing the need to guarantee the scientific nature of our newspaper, Arrigo Cervetto told us that *Lotta Comunista*, from the viewpoint of authoritativeness, had to become "*The Economist* of the labour movement".

This is why it was so striking to see, on *The Economist* cover at the end of January, a big photo, torn, of Westminster, the seat of the British parliament, with the words "The Mother of All Messes" superimposed.

The seriousness of the magazine and the austere prestige of the first bourgeois parliament say a great deal about the depth of the crisis in their politics. It is not only a question of the United Kingdom and Brexit but, as our analysis demonstrates, of a cycle that regards all the old powers. Big capital is reeling in the face of the electoral insubordination, and not only that, of vast strata of what has always been its traditional mass power base. The petty bourgeoisie, together with vast intermediate strata, has begun to swing electorally and ideologically under the blows of the big *historical collisions* of globalisation.

A new political cycle that needs to be investigated and studied has begun. This is the moment for theory and study. It is worth repeating this in a political situation that has something of the tragicomic in Italy. Farcical characters and hooligans from the outskirts, blown up by TV channels and the Internet, make ignorance, amateurishness and adventurism a title of merit. It is necessary to return to Lenin: "Without revolutionary theory there can be no revolutionary movement."[124] It is necessary to take books in our hands and to deal with politics using the tough tools of science: this knocks *Twitter*, *YouTube* videos or posts on *Facebook* into a cocked hat!

Reactionary interclassism

At the root of social oscillations and political confusion are the blows of the 2008 crisis, the stranglehold of debt, and welfare that is reduced or no longer growing at the old rhythms, with an ageing and property-owning population that is intersecting with epochal migration flows. What weighs even more is the fizzling out of expectations of a continually improving standard of living, the old myth of progressivism. Deep uncertainty,

---

* *Internationalism*, April 2019

resentment and rancour accompanying fears and real dread have spread in the petty bourgeoisie and the intermediate strata. These social strata "are revolting" against those governing in the powers of the Old World, reviving old mythologies of the *people versus the state* that are taking on the nature of a petty-bourgeois *jacquerie* and the red-brown hue of xenophobic and racist ideologies.

The old capitals of imperialism are shaken and the forms of imperialist democracy are struggling to regain a connection with their traditional mass power base. The emphasis of the new political cycle is shifting to the conservation of what has been acquired; attention inevitably focuses on reassuring property-owners and security matters, paving the way for fearmongers and interclass movements that leave the way open to xenophobic and racist demands. Even the old ideological garbage of *national socialism*, including anti-Semitism, is being dredged up.

The affair of the "gilets jaunes" in France is exemplary: the interclass deception in which the wage earners' interests have been mixed up with those of vast parasitical strata has ended up in fearful conservatism and even in anti-Semitism. The responsibilities of those who have indicated that movement to workers and the younger generations as a field of political action are heavy. We have nothing in common with that reactionary interclassism; indeed, it is a matter of fighting to the bitter end against the wily red-brown ambiguities that wink at the defence of the workers and the protection of welfare, but then avoid really raising the question of wage disadvantage in the dust cloud of small businesses.

National sovereignism and European sovereignism

It will not be simple for the big bourgeoisie, or for European imperialist democracy, "to assimilate or neutralize" the new populist and sovereignist uprisings, since they find themselves with the lever of welfare weakened. It will be a complex task for the ruling class, and will take time in a deeply contradictory process: here, too, there may be advantages to grasp for our battle to entrench the Bolshevik party model in Europe, providing we analyse and get to know the situation. In these months, we have seen with our own eyes the new spaces that have opened up. In order to make full use of them, we have written it is necessary to make our way in the "unknown sea of the new political cycle"[125]. We have pointed to the compass of the autonomy of our class, in an unrelenting struggle against any kind of interclassism. A *people versus the elites* does not exist. What exists are two classes: the proletariat, the wage earners, in constant struggle against the bourgeoisie and its fractions.

TV channels and the *Internet*, which threaten to become a problem for *their* politics, are amplifying a petty-bourgeois *jacquerie* that is dragging with it vast intermediate strata and relaunching reactionary myths, which somehow or other will have to be brought back to the basic current of the ruling ideology. Not by chance, in the Old Continent the ideologies of *national sovereignism* are already demonstrating they are soluble in *European sovereignism*: a European Power to keep it up with competition from the USA and China.

Lenin and our class autonomy

Hence it is not a matter of facing a resurgent fascism, which does not exist, but of fighting a wide-ranging battle to bar the way to the petty-bourgeois reactionary conceptions which, through the interclass deception of the *people* are attempting to involve wage-earning strata in their "uprisings". Hence struggle for our class autonomy means struggle to prevent the viruses of property-owning populism infecting the labour movement.

The question of the relationship between the proletariat and the petty bourgeoisie is an old one. The modern class of wage earners was born in the workshops of the petty bourgeoisie or among the immense peasant masses of the time. There has always been a reactionary socialism of petty-bourgeois origin, and the representatives of the petty bourgeoisie have always tried to influence and use strata of the proletariat in the continual attempt to increase their weight.

In 1908 Lenin returned to the question in *Marxism and Revisionism*, in which he draws up a concise balance sheet of the battles Marxism had had to fight in the first fifty years of its life. Then he dwells on the last battle fought at the beginning of the "second half-century", i.e. the struggle against revisionism. This was a struggle, he wrote, against "a trend hostile to Marxism within Marxism itself", which had now become an "international phenomenon". Lenin asked himself what "makes revisionism inevitable", why it is "more profound than the differences of national peculiarities and of degrees of capitalist development". His answer is clear: "Because in every capitalist country, side by side with the proletariat, there are always broad strata of the petty bourgeoisie, small proprietors." And it is capitalism itself, Lenin observed, that, in its development, continually casts again "new small producers" into the ranks of the proletariat. Therefore it is "quite natural that the petty-bourgeois world-outlook should again and again crop up in the ranks of the broad workers' parties"[126].

This phenomenon is still present today, albeit with its weight and metabolism transformed with respect to then. The relationship and commingling between the petty bourgeoisie and the wage-earning strata has changed considerably in the course of the century of imperialism. The big processes of concentration have reduced the weight of the traditional petty bourgeoisie, albeit to a lesser extent in Italy than in the other metropolises.

The virus of "property-owning populism"

The social changes subsequent to the restructuring crisis in the mid-1970s and that characterised the final decades of the last century had a notable impact. At that time there was a massive transfer of vast petty-bourgeois strata to local and state bureaucratic jobs. Cervetto dealt with this phenomenon in his book *Forze e forme del mutamento italiano* [1997]. He set off from one of Lenin's considerations: as early as his own time Lenin saw "the agrarian, artisanal and commercial bourgeoisie attracted to the side of the big bourgeoisie with bureaucratic jobs"[127]. Starting from the 1980s the transfer of strata of the petty bourgeoisie to the public sector was dramatic, favoured by the generational turnover.

The considerable increase in scholastic education and the huge increase in women's employment in the services and the public administration meant that the sons and daughters of shopkeepers and craftsmen, with degrees and diplomas paid for by the state, ended up swelling the ranks of a bloated, parasitical public sector. They moved into the world of wage labour bringing with them traditions, customs and ideologies of the class they came from. And this was not all. That process contributed to the expansion into various kinds of intermediate strata, formed by family units with at least two independent incomes: the *multi-income family*.

These strata, whether wage earners in the new form of the *wage-earning aristocracy*, or only formally wage earners, or a mixed combination with incomes and annuities of different kinds, ended up reaching living, consumption and property-owning standards similar in every way to those of the petty bourgeoisie. It is inevitable that they should fully assume petty-bourgeois lifestyle and ideologies and now also its uncertainties, disillusions, resentments and fears. It is thus that the petty-bourgeois conceptions of *property-owning populism* can infect, via interclassism, the variegated world of wage stratifications. It is on this front that we have to fight our battle for the autonomy of our class, with intransigence and without any concession to senseless grassroots political activism.

But this battle of ours to influence effectively, to make our mark, has to become an organisational battle among the wage-earning masses, starting from a struggle to the bitter end against the xenophobic and racist drives that are circulating today... a struggle that cannot stop at propaganda. It is necessary to put our workers' circles in touch with the deeper strata of the proletariat, with the lowest steps of the wage scale. Aware of the friability of that terrain, we need to link the upper strata of the proletariat with those workers, whether legal or not. This is, basically, the only way to give practical expression to our struggle against racism and for the autonomy of our class that can find fulfilment only in revolutionary strategy.

Employees and technicians and immigrants

This battle must be part of an overall battle plan, of an organisational plan able to embrace all wage earners... an organisational plan able to link the more sensitive members of our class to our newspaper and communist militancy, openly... hence a militancy that cannot be carried out in night sittings in an armchair, in front of a computer between *chats*, *Facebook* and

Twitter, covered pusillanimously by the anonymity of the Net. Ours is a militancy that requires direct action, in collective work in front of schools and lecture halls, on the shop floor and at factory gates, and doorway after doorway and staircase after staircase in working-class districts.

Over the years, thanks to that militant commitment, we have built up a broad sphere of influence for our internationalist positions that can act as a barrier to the viruses of the petty-bourgeois reactionary conceptions. *Their* politics is clearly struggling: we can and must exploit this to a greater extent.

Organising the new generations

We need to work more vigorously with the younger generations, numbers of whom continue to come to our circles. In the old metropolises, more than 80% of youths between the ages of 16 and 24 are to be found in schools and universities. This is a labour force in training; they are the wage earners who will face the stormy battles of the epochal restructuring of the automotive, electricity and telecommunications sectors that are already on the calendar. These are the youths from whom the Leninist militants of the next decade who will have to provide the legwork for a party on the Bolshevik model in Europe will come. We have recently written that "it can be done". We can only add that if it can be done, it must be done.

Our political battle in the new generations

Young Leninists in Europe*

The world contention is growing fiercer and the clash between the United States and China over protective tariffs has risen to the level of the American blacklisting of Huawei, a big Chinese group. The Dragon's extraordinary growth rates have ended up rocking the old order and the world contention is becoming tougher.

The Chinese dragon

In ten years, from 2008 to 2017, Beijing doubled its production of electrical energy. Today the Chinese have 25% of the world's production as against the 18% of the Americans and the 13% of the Europeans. Another example is the automotive market. In 2005, almost six million vehicles were sold in China as against the roughly 17.5 million of the American and European markets. In 2017, Europe and the USA were still at the 17.5 million level, while sales in China had risen to 29 million, 5 times their 2005 level. And this is not all: the Chinese power produces its own electrical components, is very active in new technologies, makes its own high-speed trains and builds its own aircraft carriers. Furthermore, it exports goods and capital all over the world, invests on foreign markets and has taken over important European groups. One need only think of Pirelli, the Swiss group Syngenta, Volvo, the port of Piraeus, and shares in Ansaldo, Peugeot and Deutsche Bank. The list is very long.

The world and Europe are also concerned because the so-called Silk Road is increasing Chinese pressure. In the Old Continent, some issue warnings while others, instead, are dazzled by Chinese capital. Attempts to react are being seen: the attempt, which subsequently failed, at a merger between the FCA and Renault with the contribution of the Japanese Nissan is one example. And all this will only exacerbate attrition and tension. Spaces on the markets are increasingly contended for, competition is growing fiercer and the international political struggle is intensifying.

Petty-bourgeois insubordination

We are indeed in the stormy times we were speaking about: ongoing rearmament is also looming over them. Stockholm's SIPRI reports that, in 2018, military spending rose to 1,820 billion dollars, the highest level since the end of the Cold War. This is almost 50 billion dollars more than in 2017, and 50% is US and Chinese military spending. Washington increased it by 4.6% and Beijing by 5%.

---

* *Internationalism*, July 2019

The big bourgeoisie is under pressure in all the old powers, In Europe, it is at grips with the protests and insubordination of its petty bourgeoisie and its intermediate strata, with their sovereigntist drive and their racist populism. At the same time, the big European groups are being clobbered by the more intense competition on the markets and an ever fiercer world contention. There is an aspect of the petty-bourgeois *jacqueries* that merits consideration: the diffusion of xenophobic and even racist ideologies. Huge migrations are going on in Asia, Africa and Latin America. A small part of these migrations is flowing into Europe, where it meets with an ageing population that has accumulated a few assets and is afraid of every leaf that rustles.

Adventurers of their politics

Various adventurers of vote-based politics and parliamentarism use these fears as a lever. In order to rake in votes they stir up fears to the point of inciting racial hatred. Let's make two considerations about this phenomenon. The first regards the huge failure of reformists and progressives of every stripe... from the French Socialist Party to the British Labour Party and from German Social Democracy to the Democratic Party in Italy. They have been totally unable to oppose the diffusion of racist positions. There is an unsaid kernel of truth in this failure that is a disease of parliamentarism. They fear they will lose votes if they clearly side with migrants and so they waver, "Let's welcome them, but not indiscriminately...": in Italy, they boast they have blocked the flows from Libya. Everyone knows this has meant building detention camps in frightful conditions, where migrants end up in structures run by soldiers, mercenaries, where violence and every abuse of power is an everyday reality.

The second observation regards the big bourgeoisie. European companies desperately need huge numbers of immigrants to plug the gaps the collapse in the birth rate has made. Big capital urgently needs immigrant labour: it is calculated that 270,000 arrivals a year are needed in Germany and just under 200,000 in Italy. And the Italian government closes Italy's ports to the cry of "Italians first", who are not enough simply because they have not been born. Their political representatives oppose an absolutely necessary immigration, and they do this with exclusively electoral motivations which, moreover, pay off, as we have seen. In this case, the failure belongs to the big-bourgeois and, at root, it is also the confession of the failure of this mode of production.

Capitalism at its highest level of development, in late imperialist maturity and burdened by huge parasitism, goes so far as to oppose the development of the species, triggering a considerable contraction in the birth rate. Thus, the whole of society ages and withers, while the contention is inflamed by young, new, great powers. Our opposition to xenophobia and racism is unshakable. As convinced abstentionists, we do not need anyone's vote and we openly state we are in favour of welcoming and integrating into the world of work those who arrive into our towns. This is not a moral precept for us, a "love thy neighbour as thyself" as preached by Roman Catholics, whom, moreover, we respect. We undoubtedly challenge the role played in religion by the ideology of resignation and social conservation, but this has not prevented us from often finding ourselves side by side in the concrete defence of migrant workers.

Genoa and the capital smugglers

In any case, for us it is a class, better a class unity, issue. With the new energies they bring, migrants strengthen our class and our class struggle against exploitation. This is why we fight every discrimination against them: it is even a question of historical memory. We recalled this a few weeks ago in our "Internationalist Youth Meeting", held in what is known as the "sala chiamata" of the port of Genoa. Four million Italian migrants set off for "the Americas" from those quays between the end of the 19th century and the 1920s... not only from Genoa, but also from Trieste, Naples, Brindisi, Messina and Catania, although Genoa was the main port of embarkation.

For years, the Ligurian capital was flooded with flows of emigrants who accounted for 15-25% of its population. *Il Caffaro*, the city newspaper of the time, tells us that these migrants were crowded "into dark, stinking, insanitary rooms, with inexpressibly filthy beds". A 1903 memo of the city's health police reads as follows: "50 emigrants were sleeping, most of them on the floor, amidst faeces and urine, at the back of this store in two dirty, airless, damp and stinking rooms." Italians First!! This is really true: it was Italians who first passed through the calvary of emigration. And there was no lack of harassment on the part of gendarmes who submitted the emigrants to humiliating inspections to the cry of "Forward the filthy!".

And even then there were people smugglers who grew rich from this traffic. They were the shipowning groups of the Genoese bourgeoisie of the time. Giorgio Doria writes in his *Investimenti e sviluppo economico a Genova alla vigilia della Prima guerra mondiale* [Investment and Economic Development in Genoa on the Eve of the First World War] (Ed. Pantarei, 2008): "An ever increasing opportunity to cash in freight rates with the transport of emigrants has to be added to this. These are sure charter fees that do not suffer from notable economic downturns: takings are fixed and tend to grow year by year." Further on he adds that "some ship-owners subsequently destined to grow considerably [...] like Piaggio, Danovaro, Frassinetti, Lavarello, Musso and Montebruno, Pratolongo and Vignolo, etc."[128] devoted themselves to that transport.

Staircase by staircase

This historical memory, consigned to books that, however, should be read, cannot but boost our commitment to preventing xenophobia and racism from getting a foothold among wage earners. This is an urgent battle, to be fought bearing in mind that the most effective barrier to the penetration of petty-bourgeois, reactionary and racist ideologies is an increasingly extensive network of supporters of our newspaper in the various districts.

More choices of militant commitment, more activists up and down the stairways with *our newspaper* in their hands are needed. This is the battle to be fought among the deep masses, in direct contact and face to face with people, refusing the deadly practice of tweets, Facebook and TV dramas, which only exacerbate the crisis of *their* politics.

The bottom of the barrel

Europe's big bourgeoisie has quite a struggle on its hands to choose a political staff able to cope with the world contention. Mediocre personalities, the bottom of the barrel of politics as a show, are coming to the fore. On the other hand, the big European groups are attempting to deal with the problems caused by *their* politics; the *European party* is gathering in *grands commis* and key men of the institutions: the magic formula is the "Europe that protects" of the Macrons, Merkels, Draghis and Mattarellas...

The *European elections* could not provide the solution: we know that elections do not determine anything. At the most they can pick up trends on which the big groups can work. Something has emerged from the ballot boxes: on the whole, the lines of imperialist Europeanism have been rewarded, with countertrends, however, that can weigh on the European process. This is the case with sovereigntist and nationalist successes in France and Italy. We have spoken of our intransigent opposition to xenophobic and racist populism. Just as intransigent is our internationalist battle against all the gradations of imperialist Europeanism. Our struggle to entrench an internationalist party on Bolshevik lines in Europe has the precise aim of opposing imperialist Europeanism.

Ecological scam

Europe's ruling classes may succeed in exiting the crisis of *their* politics and may find a political staff that is able to cope. But we should bear in mind that they will have to turn increasingly to the younger generations. They are attempting to do this with an ecological campaign that has left its mark on the European elections. "Let's save the planet": a big scam, because a huge energy reconversion in which billions and billions of dollars, yuan and euros are being invested is marching behind that banner... a major restructuring, an industrial, financial and social earthquake that has its epicentre in China and as its emblem the electric car[129].

We, too, need to look even more to the youths that *their* politics is attempting to manipulate. We must exploit even more an objective advantage that is growing, the fruit of *their* contradictions. The big bourgeoisie undoubtedly needs to import labour to plug the gaps created in the lower levels of the wage scale, but at the same time it increasingly needs highly-skilled labour: the big energy restructuring will increase this need even more. It will then have to invest in raising the high school and university schooling rates that are already high in the old powers. And it will therefore have to concentrate tens of thousands of youths in the big cities, the seats of big technical institutes and university campuses. Such a concentration of youths in a few big centres is an unprecedented phenomenon. Sizeable concentrations of students, budding labour force, quickly pouring into wage labour markets, year after year, are growing in Europe's big cities.

Technicians, engineers and qualified personnel for the ruling class will come out of them. At the same time revolutionary militants to throw into the struggle among the masses and to introduce into factories and offices in order to strengthen our internationalist presence may also emerge. As we are finding out all over Europe, the soil is very fertile and interest in our party is growing. The task of making the most of these advantages is up to us.

Chapter Four

OUR LENINIST PARTY IN THE CRISIS OF THE PANDEMIC OF THE CENTURY

Twenty Fertile Years*

This has been a very troubling decade for unitary imperialism, shaken to its core by the emergence of Chinese imperialism, the new competitor for the world division inducing fear in its rival. A decade marred by the consequences of the 2007-08 crisis in global relations and by a manifest crisis in *their politics*: segments of the petty bourgeoisie and vast intermediate strata have fallen prey to resentful uncertainty and fear for a future perceived as insecure and threatening.

Global disorder has increased in a concatenation of convulsions, social protests, crises and wars. The conflagration in the Middle East, where the floor has been given to public disturbances, missiles and drones, from Lebanon to Syria, passing through Iraq, Iran and Libya, has flared up again.

Stormy times

These are *stormy times*, which were easy for us to foresee. In the traditional end of year reviews in the mass media, behind the doom and gloom of the commentators, the political difficulties of the ruling class shone through, in a depressing appraisal often covering the full twenty years of this century.

A *La Stampa* editorial argues, for example, that the first twenty years of the new century "have had the crisis of the liberal state as their protagonist"; the next decade begins with the "question of the potential surrender of democratic institutions". This crisis springs from the "impact of globalisation". The removal of barriers "makes the citizens of the advanced economies perceive they are less secure and prosperous", because of the increase in migration flows and inequalities. It is this process that has led "to a collapse in trust in the institutions of the liberal state, in representative democracy".

The crisis in the liberal order

We have devoted many pages of our newspaper to the problems regarding the state, to the *powers* of what, for us, is *imperialist democracy*, and to the crisis in that *liberal order* about which we have always boasted. This is one of the fronts of the struggle to which we, as a party, have been committed for a long time. It is a matter of theoretical struggle: here the Marxist

* *Internationalism*, February 2020

school can score several points today. We can and we must tread hard on the heels of our historical antagonist, the bourgeoisie, in the face of the manifest fragility demonstrated by its ideological bases.

A fragility that is, as we have said, theoretical, political and social. A fragility that has revealed itself very clearly in the main capitals of the powers of the old order: in Donald Trump's Washington and in the cradle of parliamentary democracy, London, in the grip of the Brexit convulsions for such a long time. A fragility that is rooted in an irreversible structural change that has left its mark on these decades: China's imposition as an imperialist power. In that *"tectonic shift"*, we have written, lies the basic reason for the "political and ideological crisis in the old powers".

Everywhere, in the capitals of the *old order*, the big bourgeoisie is frantically trying to make the petty-bourgeois and intermediate strata see reason, a strategically-based reason. Those strata are disappointed, full of resentment and in the grip of fear. Everywhere there are adventurers and fomenters of those fears, who offer the poisoned refuge of sovereignism, of nationalist and securitarian positions, and of xenophobic and racist ideologies. Paradoxically, all of this makes the social field where we are fighting our battle much more fertile for the entrenchment of our Leninist party. We must work in depth, with all of our energy, to take the greatest advantage of the crisis in *their politics* and of the stormy times characterising the new political cycle. We need to make the most of our development in these years, more attentively, working against the current in the disorientation and confusion, to extend our sphere of influence. Particular attention needs to be paid to the younger generations, tossed about by the crisis in *their politics*, and to the many who seek a prospect and a new certainty for the future. It is a matter of giving "scientific order" to the convulsive facts of such troubled times. Our internationalism can be a firm frame of reference that many are looking for.

The Greater Middle East in the contention

The world contention has heated up. "At the heart of the contention among powers, the Greater Middle East, from North Africa to Afghanistan, has been and will long remain an area generating and exporting violence"[130].Yet again, this is the case with those tormented lands, where the abundance of oil and gas in the subsoil has, paradoxically, become a curse.

It is not here that we shall deal with the succession and interweaving of the crises and conflicts in Syria, Iran, Iraq and Libya, or in the Sahel strip, to which we devote other pages of this newspaper. We focus our attention on how the American forces eliminated General Qasem Soleimani with a targeted and spectacular action using drones and missiles, while he was driven away from Baghdad airport[131]. Soleimani was not a mere general, but a prominent personality in the Iranian regime and the probable heir apparent of Ayatollah Khamenei, a candidate to the Iranian presidency in 2021. Under his command, the Quds Force, made up of about twenty thousand men, was the "spearhead" of the local Shiite militias amounting to about 200,000 forces in various countries. US sources hold the general responsible for the killing of about 600 American soldiers in Iraq; the snipers who fired on demonstrators in the streets of Baghdad were under his command.

In the international press, much has been written about the targeted assassination of General Soleimani: some approved of it unconditionally; some saw it as a necessary act in the situation as it was; some criticised it as an unmeditated impulsive act on the part of the American presidency; and some rejected it as an act that tramples on every rule of international convention and which could cost the United States' strategy in the area very dear in the future.

A primitive tool

There have been numerous responses, but they have merely scratched the surface of a crucial question that regards the ideology of violence and its use by a great democratic state in the form of political assassination. In his *Quaderni 1981-82* [Notebooks 1981-82], contained in the last volume of his *Opere* [Collected Works], soon to be printed, Arrigo Cervetto retraced a reflection on the assassination of the American President John Fitzgerald Kennedy. The note is dated April 28th 1982: "The news reached us that they had killed J. F. Kennedy. It was November 22nd 1963. For months the newspapers spoke about that fact which brought back to the political columns the method of political assassination, obsolete for some decades, but booming for long historical periods. Politics has often been prevalently assassination. Even more often and abundantly, it has also been political assassination. When I began to take an interest in politics, the fascists were killing us and we were killing them. I became a Marxist also because I sought to find a science for the political passion that animated me; I sought to understand if there was rationality in the emotional behaviour that drives action. The materialist conception of history and the materialist conception of politics demonstrated to me that political action can be studied as a science. Politics can therefore be science. Finding this truth in Marxism was, for me, to become a political man as well as a political animal, to give passion a brain. Political assassination can be a calculation, but very often it is only and exclusively passion and simple political inability to resolve the problems posed by reality. It is a primitive use of a primitive tool. It is like solving the problems of economics via bartering. I have always seen in Stalinism and the Stalinist way of thinking a primitivism that is the negation of the scientific rationality of Marx, Engels and Lenin. I have always believed that the widespread diffusion of this way of thinking was a hindrance to the emancipation of the proletariat in general, and to the formation of a party that had mastered the science of revolution in particular.

I found in Marxism the rejection of the ideology of violence, together with the rejection of all ideologies. It is not the rejection springing from moral ideology, which is none other than the other face of the ideology of violence, expressions as they are of a common subjectivism. On the contrary, it is the scientific rejection of a prejudice. Thanks to it, Marxism places itself in the condition of being able to make rational use of the violence that a class-based society unleashes just as the sea unleashes storms"[132].

Marxist theory and imperialist democracy

Cervetto was writing in the early 1980s, still amidst the wave of petty-bourgeois intellectual terrorism in Italy, which have gone down in history as the "years of lead". He concluded from this that "political assassination [had] become a part of history and [was] now rooted in it", and that we Leninists would have done everything possible to prevent that "primitive phenomenon" from hindering our battle to entrench our revolutionary party.

This is why, if we are not surprised at Soleimani's assassination, we cannot but observe that "primitive use of a primitive tool" on the part of the world's leading power. We shall not discuss here the efficacy or not of that choice, but we observe that the greatest liberal democracy in the world, the one with the strongest individual rights, accepts and vindicates the use of political assassination. It is a sign of the times in the new political cycle: what we teach the younger generations is the *Marxist theory of violence*; *imperialist democracy* is a fierce contention that has no scruples in exalting the primitivism of political assassination.

Cervetto's Collected Works

We have spoken about the pessimism characterising the mass media's summaries about the first two decades of this century. On the contrary, they have been twenty fertile years for us, in which we have extended the boundaries of our work and seen our sphere of influence grow... years in which a sizeable flow of young people has allowed us to strengthen our workers' clubs and our presence in the factories and workplaces.

We can look to the future with confidence, well aware of the long journey we still have to make. These are years in which we have been able to complete a monumental work we began in far off 1996, a result that will remain in the history of our party, and not there alone. The last volume of Arrigo Cervetto's *Collected Works,* finally collected in thirty volumes with more than 26,000 pages, will soon be printed in Italian. This is a result that is the product of a collective work made up of study, research and the checking of myriad sources, not to mention the typing, photocopying, correction of drafts and layout, or the payment of steep bills, which only the organised contribution of thousands of supporters and subscribers has allowed us to face.

Every militant in Lotta Comunista can be proud of this result, one of the more tangible examples of the efficacy of our party's "Bolshevik model".

Our Marxist school has been enriched by a considerable amount of elaboration that is now at the disposal of the real movement and the future generations of Marxism. The *Opere* [Collected Works, Italian Edition] have been completed twenty-five years after Cervetto's death, which occurred on February 23rd 1995. There is no better way to pay him homage.

A new generation against the cynicism and hypocrisy of "their politics"
Politics of Science and Passion*

The Internationalist Youth Day conference was held in Milan on February 1st, in piazza San Babila's New Theatre. Below we report a synthesis of the conclusions drawn at the conference.

The heightening tensions among the powers of imperialism and exacerbating social contradictions around the world have been two unmistakable facets marking the first two decades of this century. In the last few months social protest has animated the streets and squares of various regions on the world stage, in Latin America, the Middle East, Hong Kong, India and France.

Albeit with their specific features, both protests and demands for better living and working conditions resounded everywhere. Essentially, those streets and squares reconfirm a well-known passage from Marx and Engels' *Manifesto* – "The modern bourgeois society [...] has not done away with class antagonisms" – confirming that society "is more and more splitting up [...] into two great classes directly facing each other"[133].

Those streets and squares tell us that "the modern bourgeois society" has changed enormously since 1848 and now embraces the whole planet. Consequently, the forces of the proletariat have grown, both in the number and concentration of wage earners. In the face of these streets and squares we must choose a side. For some time now we have chosen to side with the wage earners: the worker, the nurse, the shop assistant, the engineer, the dockworker, the clerk, the bricklayer... This is a variegated world, but one that, if united in revolutionary strategy, can, when the conditions of the bourgeois crisis assert themselves, overturn the present relations of production.

One and a half million victims

Weapons – bombs, drones and missiles – have spoken to us in these months of heightening tensions among the powers of imperialism. They have done this on our very threshold, in the Middle Eastern area that has always *generated and exported violence*... an area rich in oil and gas, the nerve centre of energy flows, where weapons have never fallen silent... an area where whole generations have been born and grown up amid falling bombs and the ruins of warfare and where the price paid by the population has been very high. These are undoubtedly local wars, but in these two

* *Internationalism*, March 2020

decades there have been more than *one million* victims, almost half of them helpless civilians.

In the same period the wars in Africa have killed *half a million*, mainly civilians. And then other conflicts: more than 13,000 victims in Ukraine… All in all, in this beginning of the century, official figures estimate more than *one and a half million* victims in the major conflicts, about 950,000 of them civilians. And these have been twenty years of "peace"!

What do these horrific figures tell us? This mode of production is unable to maintain world order. Capitalism lives in a perennial struggle for the conquest of markets and spheres of influence that fuels the clash among the states… a clash that continually results in local conflicts and has already broken the world order twice, in two world wars with tens of millions of victims.

Imperialism and marxist science

In *Imperialism*, Lenin writes: "The enormous growth of industry and the remarkably rapid concentration of production in ever-larger enterprises are one of the most characteristic features of capitalism"[134]. Today that characteristic feature is exaggerated: Sinopec, the Chinese petrochemical industry, has 667,000 employees, Volkswagen 642,000, the American General Electric 313,000 and the Korean Samsung 307,000. Capitalism has changed over time and Lenin analysed that change.

For our Marxist school, imperialism is neither an invective nor a policy: it is a scientific definition that characterises a stage in the development of capitalism, its "highest stage"… the stage in which the concentration of production and capital reaches very high levels and finance capital is fully developed, with capital exports at their height. And with the division of the markets, writes Lenin, there is the complete "division of the world among the Great Powers", and "they divide it 'in proportion to capital', 'in proportion to strength'". That is imperialism: it is our world of today that needs to be studied in depth in its continual transformation.

China, the new contender

These are the problems dealt with by Arrigo Cervetto in his theoretical and analytical work, an immense body on the verge of publication in its full form by our party. The force that regulates the division of the world, says Lenin, "varies with the degree of economic and political development". And that is why the tensions among the powers have heightened in this new century.

A new, great power has fully emerged: China. In its centuries-old development it has reached such a force that it can demand a growing share of the markets and a vaster sphere of influence. The old threatened powers are reacting: the United States and the European Union, but also Japan and

Russia... They are resisting, trying to counteract the erosion of their weight and their power. As a result, power relations worsen and tensions, clashes and local wars increase. We have seen the result: more than one and a half million victims in these first twenty years of the century. And who protests about this horrible massacre? How many "Fridays for Future" have been organised for this multitude of innocent victims?

They turn the other way, pretend nothing has happened and talk about something else. Thus emerges all the hypocrisy and all the cynicism with which the ideas of the ruling class are imbued and which pervade the whole of society. People despair over the koala bears, victims of the wildfires in Australia – for goodness' sake, poor animals – but nothing is said about what is a real massacre of helpless, innocent, human beings. In essence, that is the price paid by the whole human race for *their* world contention for the division of markets and the allocation of *their* spheres of influence. This is why we fight imperialism; these are the reasons for our internationalist battle, to which we need to increase our commitment and which requires new energies.

Hypocrisy and cynicism

The struggle against climate change has become a kind of religion: everyone is worried about it. World powers discuss it at the UN and the establishment deals with it in the Davos forum. Everybody praises the commitment of the young, a Friday every now and then, provided they all return to school tranquilly on Monday. Continual media campaigns about glaciers that are melting, animal species dying out, hurricanes, flowers and plants at risk.

Here, too, hypocrisy and cynicism: their own international organisms, the World Health Organisation and UNICEF, in their accurate publications, tell us that in 2017, even though the infant mortality rates are falling, six million three hundred thousand children below the age of 15 died in the world. The vast majority of them do not reach the age of five: every day in the world 15,000 of them die below that threshold.

These are well-known and available figures. Why does no one protest? Let's get it quite clear: there are doctors, volunteers and nuns who help those children in Asia and Africa and they have our full respect. But however hard they work, they will never succeed in affecting the deep-rooted causes of those deaths that are the product of the present social system. And then, in comparison with glaciers, forests, plants and animals, we say: first of all, children! What kind of society is this that, in spite of all the progress made by the food industry, medical science and pharmacology, does not succeed in nourishing, in taking care of, its children?

The green Europe of capital

And there's more: the European Commission has launched a "Green New Deal", a big plan with huge investments for a green Europe that will protect both the environment and its borders from immigration. In Austria, the Greens, with a similar programme and in government with the populists, have replaced the xenophobic far right. From Central Europe, many are looking at the Austrian model.

As regards accepting migrants, it is necessary to be vigilant: there are various nuances that conceal hypocrisy and cynicism; the various Captain Fracasses are not the only ones to be faced. Matteo Salvini is undoubtedly a champion of bourgeois cynicism. For a handful of votes, which he subsequently did not get, he reached the point of getting caught on camera while he was buzzing a Tunisian family, accusing it of drug dealing: a shameful act, indicating a target, mistaken moreover, which instigates lynching, whether moral or material.

1893: the Aigues Mortes massacre

This had already happened to Italians many years before, in France in Aigues Mortes, a small village in the Camargue, where sea salt was produced from salt flats that are still active today. Some hundreds of Italian workers, most of them seasonal workers recruited by the recruiters of day labourers among the migrant peasants of Northwest Italy as far as Tuscany, were employed in that work. The Compagnie des Salins du Midi did not even know their names: they had a time card with a number and the name of their recruiter. The piecework gathering of the salt, which burnt the skin, accompanied by raging malaria, was a devil of a job.

The election campaign was going on in that August 1893 in France. The reactionary press presented the Italian migrants as delinquents who were stealing work from the French, prone to stabbing and disease carriers, and demanded the defence of the French identity. On August 17th, the totally false news spread that in a brawl "*les italiens*" had killed some Frenchmen. Today we would say this was fake news, but even though there were no mobile phones, the news spread rapidly. There was a punitive expedition and ten Italian workers were killed. First Italians, this is true Honourable Salvini, but in the sense that first it happened to Italians: xenophobia is a terrible thing; it is hard to hold it at bay. This is why we fight, every day, against every discrimination, also of citizenship, against those who were born and work here in Italy and in Europe.

Neither votes nor social media

We do not seek votes in our battle: a prospect – the electoral kind – that has been closed for us for a very long time. We are, and we remain, wholeheartedly abstentionists, strategically abstentionists. What we need are not votes, but men and women, militants, young communists totally devoted to our cause for a better society, communism.

We do not seek consensus in a ballot box, hidden behind a curtain in a cabin as we vote, and not even on the social media. We seek consensus among the masses in factories, in workplaces, door to door in the districts with our newspaper in our hands, in schools and universities. We ask for a concrete consensus, in the light of day, for support for our publications, the consensus of subscriptions and of active participation in the work of our clubs, by now entrenched in the European continent. We continue to find that consensus, but in order to face the stormy times of unitary imperialism it is necessary to expand and consolidate it.

Generations of communism

This is a task that is up to the new generations first of all. In January 1982, Cervetto reflected on the entry into the fray of his own generation, at about the age of twenty, as has been the case with the three successive generations of Lotta Comunista. Except that they entered the political struggle in the midst of the imperialist war and the armed struggle against Nazi-fascism. This passage is in the *Quaderni* [Notebooks], which form part of the last volume of his *Opere* [Collected Works]. We let Cervetto speak:

"Unaware of the real content of that imperialist war, [...] we were little leaves in the impetuous winds blowing over the world. With us or without us the winds would have continued on their way. But passion, even if it is a leaf, remains passion. It is part of a man. Directed, it is a powerful political factor. Politics is struggle and not an academic exercise, since no one risks a hair for a mere political hypothesis. Passion alone drives people to risk their necks. In the end those who have more passion will prevail. [...] Since then I have devoted my life to giving my passion and that of the generations to come an outlet in political reason, strategy and calculated struggle"[135].

A battle in the deep strata of the proletariat for the unity of our class

Leninists' Tasks in the Crisis of the Pandemic of the Century*

The ongoing *pandemic of the century* is an extraordinary event, and certainly unpredictable as to how long it will last. But as a biological-natural manifestation it is also an event that is in no way unforeseen or unexpected.

The international scientific community had sounded the alarm about a probable pandemic some time ago. It had been discussed at the beginning of the century, on the occasion of the SARS epidemic, and more recently it was mentioned in the health crisis triggered by the Ebola virus. In October 2014 we dealt with this in these pages. In the article *The Ebola Virus and 21st Century Pandemics* we wrote: "Man's battle against pathogenic microorganisms is never won once and for all [...] pandemics are destined to repeat themselves". This is why WHO, the World Health Organization, recommended that its member states prepare emergency plans.

Science and the limits of capital

Nevertheless, the capitals of imperialism were taken by surprise by *Covid-19* which spread all over the world, with a death toll sadly all too well known. In Italy – but elsewhere too – personal protective equipment, intensive care facilities and dedicated hospital beds were lacking. We wrote about the "Virus of improvidence" which has certainly aggravated a toll of human lives that could have been much lower.

We are aware, as we have already written, that the ultimate causes of great natural catastrophes remain outside of the human species' powers of intervention. We added, however, that the development of science and of productive forces has put at our disposal the means with which to intervene in the effects of those events "by preventing or mitigating their consequences". But science and productive forces are subjugated by the relations of production, market chaos and the logic of profit. There were no facemasks, we were told, because no one in Europe produced them any more: it wasn't worthwhile, they didn't pay. They were part of the production outsourced to the Asian countries with lower wages and this is not a question of public or private healthcare.

The pandemic as a weapon in the contention

In all powers huge state intervention in the economy is underway in order to limit the disastrous effects of the pandemic on the economic cycle.

---

* *Internationalism*, June 2020

If the ranks of the statists have consequently grown, even with bizarre conscriptions, this is not – and we stress this – a question of public or private healthcare. It is a question of a healthcare system able to face a *pandemic of the century*... a challenge which requires the unitary mobilisation of the entire world's healthcare systems in a plan of cooperation against a virus that by now has spread to 212 countries. But this clashes with a system of states continually in conflict with each other, each defending the particular interests of their respective bourgeoisies.

Not only is there no unitary response, but the pandemic itself is also becoming a weapon in the clash among the great powers, at the level of medical aid and of "facemask diplomacy". The same holds true for vaccines, in the search for which dozens of research centres are engaged, but which, instead of acting together according to a plan, effectively work in competition with each other: a race for a vaccine over which the shadow of the pharmaceutical multinationals looms. If ever international alliances and collaborations are established, these will also be subject to the power logic; the violence of the pandemic lays bare the violence of the contention and the irremediable contradictions of capitalism.

Class fragmentation

At the beginning of April, the French newspaper *L'Opinion* wrote: "Who can still speak of class struggle? The coronavirus crisis unites wage earners and their bosses in fear"... a particular version of the *union sacrée* that the French and European bourgeoisie is propagandising; a particular version, because interclass national unity could be held together by fear. Fear exists and needs to be carefully considered, but fear has not prevented, indeed if anything it has spurred on, strikes for safe working conditions in various European factories. The working class is paying a double price for the pandemic: at the health level, with the risk of contagion, and then at the employment level, greatly jeopardised by the consequent economic crisis. *Le Figaro* reports the opinion of Jérôme Fourquet, a French IFOP political analyst, who argues that the pandemic is a test revealing "the pre-existing fractures in the French archipelago". It is "in the world of work that these fractures are most visible".

Fourquet divides French wage earners into five groups, based on the increase in the risk of contagion. This is a pertinent observation, which does not only hold true for France; in effect, the pandemic objectively has a divisive effect on the wage-earning stratifications, an aspect that needs to be weighed up attentively. There are sectors of our class that are in the front line in the struggle against the virus. It is the healthcare workers who are the most exposed to risk and who are paying a very heavy price. And then, workers in the large-scale retail trade, logistics and transport, not to mention workers and technicians in manufacturing, as well as sectors of the civil service, are very much exposed. Then there are the many employees teleworking from home. Diverse situations, together with which we always need to bear in mind undocumented workers without a contract or any protection at all, at the mercy of the waves caused by the pandemic. According to recent ILO estimates, as many as 60% of workers worldwide belong to the "informal" sector, i.e. two billion people.

"Informal" workers and the elderly

After we have stressed this, in order to be able to work in safety in various big European factories it was necessary to recur to strikes; this happened in Genoa's ArcelorMittal, and we are speaking about a site of the world's leading iron and steel industry group. Everywhere, Leninist workers were at the head of this activity, of the struggle for safe condition at work against the pandemic... without ever forgetting, as trade union leaders too often do, the many small and medium-sized companies, where people didn't stop working and where inspections are scarce and the level of safety is often inadequate. Not to mention the two billion informal workers. In India, a biblical exodus of internal migrants, who are abandoning the big urban centres, is taking place. Employed in the most varied activities, without contracts, taken on at daily wages, with the shutdowns and lockdowns due to the pandemic, they have remained without any income at all and have attempted to return to their villages. *The Times of India* estimates there are 50 million workers on the march with their families, in desperate conditions.

Returning to the West, on the two shores of the Atlantic, it is impossible not to speak about the massacre of elderly people in retirement homes. According to *The Telegraph*, reporting WHO sources, about 50% of the Covid victims in Europe are residents in old people's homes. In the Old Continent, but in America too, in the most technologically advanced modern cities, whose inhabitants have the greatest rights and freedoms in the world, the elderly are often forgotten and abandoned. Whoever no longer produces is no longer a source of surplus value in this social organisation, and risks ending up in structures which are often run-down and with which no healthcare reform has ever concerned itself. The virus has struck these places hard; another reason for this is the incompetence of local politics and hospital managers.

Unity in our internationalist battle

We know that material conditions in the wage-earning strata as a whole are very diverse. The pandemic tends to increase differences and divisions: this is an objective fact on which the ruling classes function. Our communist politics embraces the whole wage-earning world. The wage-earning workers' unification can occur only in the strategic perspective of our internationalist battle. In the past few weeks, our workers' clubs have offered a small demonstration of this. Covid-19 has brought us face to face with a historically unprecedented situation for our work among the masses. The health regulations, the rules about mobility, the schools closed, the factories on layoff, the staggered reopenings, the ban on gatherings, and the empty streets and squares: a very complicated situation. But no objective condition, however difficult, can make a revolutionary party "stay at home". And, fully respecting the health and hygiene regulations, we have not stopped for an instant.

We anticipated the publication of our March issue, while both our April and May issues have come out promptly. It is essential in these moments not to fail to give the masses our point of view. And our newspaper, perhaps accompanied by a carton of milk or a prescription, has arrived in all the working-class districts of the big Italian and other cities.

This has been an important moment in the struggle over spheres of influence. The pandemic has fuelled a fog of confusion and disorientation by exploiting people's fear. Our work has gone in the direction to clear that fog. Failing to make our internationalist voice heard among the masses would have meant inevitably leaving room for self-serving appeals to national unity and harmony, and to an imperialist Europeanism that is flexing its muscles in the ideological myth of the *Europe that protects*.

The theoretical battlefront

Consequently, we have also not stopped our work of political development. The pandemic crisis raises problems of in-depth investigation of the theory of the state, its powers, the forms of imperialist democracy, and the emergency legislations applied in different countries. Likewise, the analysis of the economic crisis now underway, "the worst crisis since 1945", needs to be dealt with rigorously... just as it is also necessary to delve into the strategic consequences of the pandemic, which affect power relations. The same considerations hold true for its social consequences and the inevitable repercussions on political ideologies and forms: our newspaper is providing a considerable quantity of formative, but also of informative, material on all of this.

Everyone has repeatedly spoken about the importance of information in the present situation. The government has done this, leaving printshops, newsagents and editorial offices open for this purpose. The opposition has done this too, with publishers' associations and journalists, asking for the greatest freedom of information as an antidote to the limitations of the social lockdown. We take them at their word; we, too, are in favour of the widest circulation of newspapers and, obviously and above all, of the largest circulation of our newspaper, which we know very well cannot remain "an ivory tower read by few", but has to be "circulated among the masses", "science that translates into militancy, that becomes struggle"[136]. So we have not stopped our work among the masses for even a moment; a party along the 'Bolshevik model' cannot live without continual, daily relations with our class; otherwise it falls into nihilism and political irrelevance. The unprecedented conditions have posed problems for our organisational work that the pandemic has damaged.

Our organisation's "general task"

We have faced the difficulties basing ourselves on our patrimony of theoretical elaboration and organisation. First of all, we took "Our General Task" as our starting point, one of Arrigo Cervetto's September 1975 editorials and a milestone for waging the battle for the entrenchment of our party. And then we appealed to our clubs and the supporters of our newspaper in the various districts, the fruit of decades of slow work in educating and organising the proletariat. Lenin wrote in his *What Is to Be Done?*: "Every question 'runs in a vicious circle' because political life as a whole is an endless chain consisting of an infinite number of links. The whole art of politics lies in finding and taking as firm a grip as we can of the link that is least likely to be struck from our hands"[137]. Lenin concluded that this is the one that most of all guarantees its possessor the possession of the whole chain.

In *Our General Task*, Cervetto sets off from this concept and identifies that link in organisational work: "an organisational plan, systematic work as the guarantee and necessary condition for dealing with about-turns, social explosions and political complications"[138]. There is no doubt that the *pandemic of the century* is an unexpected about-turn, with which we have dealt precisely through "systematic work" among our supporters. Many turned to our clubs to ask for help, people who were in difficulty or afraid to go out... and not only the elderly, as we have written about, but also many working mothers alone with their children, people suffering illness, people in quarantine and people who had to assist a member of the family.

On the basis of a ceaseless militant activity, our clubs were a point of reference and also, let's say it, of *humanity* among the tower blocks of the working-class districts. They did it in simple ways: shopping, medicines, and paying bills that had fallen due... simple, but very important acts for those who find themselves in precarious conditions, in difficulty, and with no way out in a fear-laden atmosphere. What amazes us is the media hype: these, for us, were simple acts of a class solidarity that is part of our history and of an authentically working-class tradition. We need only recall the workers' Mutual Aid Societies or the International Workers' Aid created by the Communist International in 1921, based on the power of the Soviets, which we deal with in the box.

A formative experience

Our clubs' initiatives of class solidarity called on consistent voluntary work on the part of factories and districts. Workers in big factories, employees and technicians, students, workers on unemployment benefits and carers, not to mention dockworkers, immigrant workers and many other employees from the traffic policeman to the check-out assistant: a moment of unity of all wage earners. This voluntary work continues to grow beyond all expectations; a phenomenon on which we need to reflect deeply because it reveals the energies that may be concealed in our class. Our workers' clubs responded with great commitment and passion. We did not meet other parties going up and down stairs or, unfortunately, representatives of the trade unions: only members of part of the Roman Catholic associations and the associations organised by the Civil Protection.

The new volunteers who continue to flock to us are integrating themselves into the traditional communist work that animates our clubs. The path before us in the struggle against the effects of the pandemic is still long and full of obstacles. But the path for the development and social entrenchment of our Leninist Party has been mapped out. We are having an experience that will turn out to be useful, but it is not only a question of one experience among many. Cervetto concluded his editorial *The Dialectics of the Political Crisis* (October 1988) quoting Lenin: "The experience of the war, like the experience of any crisis in history, of any great calamity and any sudden turn in human life, stuns and breaks some people, but enlightens and tempers others". Cervetto remarks: "Sometimes too little attention has been devoted to the fact that the events which stun and break some political tendencies can strengthen and temper others. It is a lesson of the materialist conception of politics"[139].

We treasure this for the months and years ahead, in the new period that is opening marked by the crisis and the social earthquake triggered by the pandemic of the century.

INTERNATIONAL WORKERS' AID

On July 15th 1921, three days after its conclusion, the Third Communist International (CI) Congress created the Workers' International Committee for Russian Relief, subsequently formalised [June 1923] as *Workers International Relief* (WIR) (*Mezhrabpom* in Russian). Its main task was to carry out campaigns for assistance to striking workers or those hit by crises and natural calamities. This body should not be confused with the other, called *International Red Aid* (IRA - MOPR); already in embryo from 1922 but formally constituted on July 14th-16th, right after the Fourth Congress of the International, this, on the contrary, had the aim of legally helping comrades hit by capitalist repression in every country and of supporting the families of political prisoners.

The famine and Lenin's appeal

From the very beginning, the constituting WIR was put to the test. It was the "Appeal to the International Proletariat", launched by Lenin in the pages of *Pravda* on August 6th, a call to action.

"Several gubernias in Russia have been hit by [serious] famine.

It is the painful aftermath of Russia's backwardness and of seven years of war, first, the imperialist, and then, the Civil War, which was forced upon the workers and peasants by the landowners and capitalists of all countries.

We need help. The Soviet Republic of workers and peasants expects this help from the working people, the industrial workers and the small farmers.

The mass of both the former and the latter are themselves oppressed by capitalism and imperialism everywhere, but we are convinced that they will respond to our appeal, despite their own hard condition caused by unemployment and the rising cost of living.

Those who have suffered from capitalist oppression all their lives will understand the position of the workers and peasants of Russia, they will grasp or, guided by the instinct of working and exploited people, will sense the need of helping the Soviet Republic, whose lot it was to be the first to undertake the hard but gratifying task of overthrowing capitalism".

A loan for Soviet Russia

As early as August 10th, an Italian section of the Committee, which was forming in Berlin, responded to the appeal with its "Proposal for an International Pro-Russia Loan".

The organisers wrote that it seemed to them the initiative "might find favour with the workers and peasants of Europe and America and allow the Soviet Republic to dispose immediately of an important sum for purchasing wheat, medicines and the lorries needed to take aid to the area hit by drought and the epidemic. [...] The placement of this loan, which is of a truly proletarian and popular nature, would be done exclusively by workers who would withdraw the international paper money more as a memento than as a credit instrument" [*Studi Storici*, 1-1970].

Earthquake in Japan

The proposal immediately attracted a great deal of attention. In fact, shortly after its constitution in September, various writers and scientists offered the Pro-Russia Committee their support. The aid collected in the campaign for the starving Volga region was invaluable. Between the autumn of 1921 and July 1922, it amounted to 100 million in gold marks, 100 steamships with foodstuffs, 1,638,000 tons of seed corn and 17,204,290 rations for children and adults [*Studi Storici*, op. cit.]. As time went by and the urgent reasons for its creation declined, the Committee's tasks changed, leading it to expand its range of action outside of Soviet Russia. It was now the proletariat of all countries that became the object of its solidarity. Always headed by the German communist Willi Münzenberg (1884-1936), who, from 1925, represented the CI in the WIR Central Committee and the latter's CC in the former, a new stage of wide-ranging international aid now began after the campaign for the famine in the Volga region. The first initiatives, as early as 1923, regarded Japan and the German regions of Saxony and Thuringia. The WIR collected 200,000 dollars in a short time in favour of Japan, hit by a major earthquake that caused chaos in the Kanto region, devastating Tokyo, the port of Yokohama and the neighbouring prefectures and causing the deaths of 100-140,000 people. Instead, the populations of Saxony and Thuringia were shaken by the serious economic crisis and unemployment caused by the Weimar Republic's inability to cope with the oppressive peace clauses imposed in Versailles. In their favour, alongside the distribution of foodstuffs and other aid to the population, the WIR also organised hospitality for German children in the homes of its workers or sympathisers in other nations such as France and England. The aid provided for Irish peasants in 1925 was always of this kind. The following year, the WIR organised a subscription that collected 25,000,000 gold marks in support of the English miners' strikes. In the same way, it helped the French and English textile workers in 1931, also taking action, in the course of the same year, to help the victims of the earthquake in Bulgaria.

The Shanghai workers

However, it was not only a question of economic aid, but of action that very soon acquired a specific political connotation; as early as 1925, when the big international anti-imperialist campaign was organised around the watchword "Hands off China" ... a campaign originating from the numerous dead and wounded who fell during a workers' demonstration in Shanghai, on which English troops had opened fire.

The associations created by the WIR against imperialism and colonialism first and then against fascism, Nazism and Francoism thus ended up multiplying out of all proportion and leading to various world congresses. Always to that end, various publishing houses, which began to publish innumerable newspapers in various languages, were also founded in different countries, and film companies specialising in the production and distribution of films, such as Mezhrabpom-Film and Prometheus, were also organised. The latter sector was directed by Francesco Misiano himself from 1924 on: within a few years it was producing and distributing about four hundred films and documentaries and, in 1926-27, it acquainted Paris, Brussels and Berlin with Eisenstein's film "Battleship Potemkin".

The Stalinist persecution

After Hitler came to power, the WIR headquarters was moved from Berlin to Paris and then to Moscow. There, however, it began to suffer persecution at the hands of the Stalinist ruling group which "took on the form of xenophobia", since its main leaders were not Russian [*Studi Storici*, 4-1996]. So, shortly afterwards, at the dawn of the first Moscow Show Trials (1936), the organisation practically ceased to exist, even if the decision to dissolve it formally was not made public.

In a way, the same fate also befell those who had been its greatest inspirers, interpreters and leaders. Münzenberg, accused of "Trotskyism", was expelled from the KPD in October 1937 and his appeal against this measure was rejected by the CI Executive Committee in February 1939. He then continued his battle against Nazism and especially against Stalinism, creating his umpteenth newspaper *Die Zukunft* [The Future] and his last committee, "Friends of the Future". This before being interned in a France in a camp for foreigners on the outbreak of the Second World War; after his escape, his corpse – tortured to death – would be found in a wood in October 1940.

Misiano, too, in the climate of persecution established with the assassination of Sergei Kirov, ended up being accused of political deviations and deprived of all his positions in August 1935. Accused particularly by Paolo Robotti, Palmiro Togliatti's brother-in-law, he and his wife were ostracised by the Italian section of the International Club of Political Émigrés. It was then that, although he was seriously ill, he asked to be used by the PCI in its propaganda sector, or, in the case of war, to be sent to Abyssinia to carry on antimilitarist and antifascist propaganda. The PCI's refusal, however, caused this last proposal to be fruitless, while the flareup of his illness ended up taking him to his tomb in August 1936.

Neither did their creature, the WIR, have a second opportunity. However, the spirit and practice of that organisation, which had best embodied Karl Marx's favourite maxim, *nihil humani a me alienum puto* (Nothing human is alien to me), have always remained present and alive in the ideal patrimony of every communist.

Glossary of Acronyms

AFD	Alternative für Deutschland (Alternative for Germany)
ALDE	Alliance of Liberals and Democrats for Europe
AMT	Azienda Mobilità e Trasporti (Mobility and Transport Company, Genoa)
BNP	Banque Nationale de Paris
BRICS	Brazil, Russia, India, China, South Africa
BTP	Bâtiments et travaux publics (Public buildings and works sector)
CC	Central Committee
CCP	Chinese Communist Party
CDU	Christlich Demokratische Union Deutschlands (Christian Democratic Union of Germany)
CEI	Conferenza Episcopale Italiana (Italian Episcopal Conference)
CFR	Council on Foreign Relations
CGIL	Confederazione Generale Italiana del Lavoro (Italian General Confederation of Labour)
CI	Communist International
CIC	China Investment Corporation
CIR	Compagnie Industriali Riunite
CISL	Confederazione Italiana Sindacati Lavoratori (Italian Confederation of Workers' Unions)
CNN	Cable News Network
CNOOC	China National Offshore Oil Corporation
CNCP	China National Petroleum Corporation
CNR	China North Locomotive and Rolling Stock
CSIS	Center for Strategic and International Studies
CSR	China South Locomotive and Rolling Stock
CSU	Christlich-Sozial Union in Bayern (Christian Social Union in Bavaria)
DC	Democrazia Cristiana (Christian Democracy, Italy)
DS	Democratici di Sinistra (Democrats of the Left, Italy)
ECB	European Central Bank
ENI	Ente Nazionale Idrocarburi (National Hydrocarbons Authority, Italy)
EPP	European People's Party
ESM	European Stability Mechanism
EU	European Union
FCA	Fiat Chrysler Automobiles
FDP	Freie Demokratische Parte (Liberal Democratic Party, Germany)
FED	Federal Reserve System (The United States' Central Bank)

FGCI	Federazione Giovanile Comunista Italiana (Italian Communist Youth Federation)
FIAT	Fabbrica Italiana Automobili Torino
FIOM	Federazione Impiegati Operai Metallurgici (Federation of Metallurgical Workers and Staff)
FLI	Futuro e Libertà per l'Italia (Future and Freedom for Italy)
FTC	Fixed-term contract
FTZ	Free Trade Zone
G20	Group of Twenty
G7	Group of Seven
GAAP	Gruppi Anarchici d'Azione Proletaria (Anarchist Groups of Proletarian Action)
GDP	Gross Domestic Product
IEA	International Energy Agency
IFOP	Institut français d'opinion publique (French Institute of Public Opinion)
IFRI	Institut français des relations internationales (French Institute of International Relations)
ILO	International Labour Organization
IMF	International Monetary Fund
INSEE	Institut nationale de la statistique et des études économiques (National Institute of Statistics and Economic Studies)
IPLOM	Industria Piemontese Lavorazione Oli Minerali
IRA	International Red Aid
IRI	Istituto per la Ricostruzione Industriale (Institute for Industrial Reconstruction, Italy)
ISIS	Islamic State of Iraq and Syria
ISTAT	Istituto Nazionale di Statistica (Italian National Institute of Statistics)
IWA	International Workingmen's Association
KPD	Kommunistische Partei Deutschlands (Communist Party of Germany)
LR	Les Républicains (The Republicans, France)
M5S	Movimento 5 Stelle (Five Star Movement, Italy)
MOPR	Mezhdunarodnaia Organizatsiia Pomoshchi Revoliutsioneram (International Organisation for Aid to Revolutionaries)
NATO	North Atlantic Treaty Organization
NPR	Nuclear Posture Review
OECD	Organisation for international Co-operation and Development
PCd'I	Partito Comunista d'Italia (Communist Party of Italy)
PCI	Partito Comunista Italiano (Italian Communist Party)
PD	Partito Democratico (Democratic Party, Italy)
PdL	Popolo della Libertà (People of Freedom, Italy)
PDS	Partito Democratico della Sinistra (Left Democratic Party, Italy)
PP	Partido Popular (People's Party, Spain)
PSA	Peugeot Société Anonyme
PS	Parti Socialiste (Socialist Party, France)

PSI	Partito Socialista Italiano (Italian Socialist Party)
PSOE	Partido Socialista Obrero Español (Spanish Socialist Workers' Party)
RSU	Rappresentanza Sindacale Unitaria (Unitary Workplace Union Structure)
S&D	Progressive Alliance of Socialists and Democrats
SARS	Severe Acute Respiratory Syndrome
SASAC	State-owned Assets Supervision and Administration Commission of the State Council (China)
SIPRI	Stockholm International Peace Research Institute
SMIC	Salaire Minimum Interprofessionnel de Croissance (Interprofessional Minimum Growth Salary)
SPD	Sozialdemokratische Partei Deutschlands (Social Democratic Party of Germany)
THAAD	Terminal High Altitude Area Defence
UBS	Union de Banques Suisses (Union Bank of Switzerland)
UIL	Unione Italiana del Lavoro (Italian Labour Union)
UMP	Union pour un Mouvement Populaire (Union for a Popular Movement, France)
UN	United Nations Organization
USA	United States of America
USSR	Union of Soviet Socialist Republics
VAT	Value-added Tax
WHO	World Health Organisation
WIR	Workers International Relief

Bibliography

[1] G. La Barbera, *L'Europa e la Guerra*, Edizioni Lotta Comunista, Milan, 2003.

[2] G. La Barbera, *L'Europa e lo Stato*, Edizioni Lotta Comunista, Milan, 2006.

[3] A. Cervetto, *La contesa mondiale,* Edizioni Lotta Comunista, Milan, 1990.

[4] A. Cervetto, *Forze e forme del mutamento italiano*, Edizioni Lotta Comunista, Milan, 1997.

[5] A. Cervetto, *La contesa mondiale, op. cit.*

[6] G. La Barbera, *L'Europa e lo Stato, op. cit.*

[7] R. Pastorino, *The Unprecedented Task*, Éditions Science Marxiste, Montreuil, 2012.

[8] Lenin, "Our Immediate Task", end of 1899, in *Lenin Collected Works*, Progress Publishers, Moscow, Vol. 4.

[9] A. Cervetto, *Il mondo multipolare 1990-1995*, Edizioni Lotta Comunista, Milan, 1996.

[10] G. La Barbera, *L'Europa e lo Stato, op. cit.*

[11] G. La Barbera, *L'Europa e lo Stato, op. cit.*

[12] A. Cervetto, *The Difficult Question of Times*, Éditions Science Marxiste, Montreuil, 2003.

[13] A. Cervetto, *The Political Shell*, Éditions Science Marxiste, Montreuil, 2006.

[14] K. Marx, *A Contribution to the Critique of Political Economy, in Marx & Engels Collected Works*, Vol. 16, 1859.

[15] K. Marx, *The Manuscripts of 1857-1858* known as *Grundrisse, in Marx & Engels Collected Works*, Vol. 29, 1859.

[16] G. La Barbera, *L'Europa, l'Asia e la crisi*, Edizioni Lotta Comunista, Milan, 2008.

[17] K. Marx, Introduction to the *Critique of Hegel's Philosophy of Law*, in *A Contribution to the Critique of Hegel's Philosophy of Law, Marx & Engels Collected Works*, Vol. 3, 1843.

[18] Lenin, "The Attitude of the Workers' Party to Religion", in *Lenin Collected Works, op. cit.,* Vol. 15.

[19] K. Marx, F. Engels, "Part 1: Feuerbach", *The German Ideology*, Progress Publishers, Moscow, 1968 [1845].

[20] F. Engels, letter to JosephBloch, 21-22 September 1890, in *Marx & Engels Collected Works*, Vol. 49.

[21] F. Engels, *The Origin of the Family, Private Property and the State*, in *Marx & Engels Collected Works*, Vol. 26.

[22] Lenin, *Marxism and Revisionism*, 1908, in *Lenin Collected Works, op. cit.* Vol. 15.

[23] A. Cervetto, *The Difficult Question of Times, op. cit.*

[24] G. La Barbera, *L'Europa, l'Asia e la crisi, op. cit.*

[25] A. Cervetto, L.Parodi, *Theses on Imperialist Development, the Duration of the Counterrevolutionary Phase, and the Development of the Class Party, 1957*, in *Unitary Imperialism*, Vol. I, Éditions Science Marxiste, Montreuil, 2014.

[26] G. La Barbera, *L'Europa, l'Asia e la crisi, op. cit.*
[27] A. Cervetto, *L'ineguale sviluppo politico*, Edizioni Lotta Comunista, Milan, 1991.
[28] S. Motosi, *Scritti. Indagine scientifica e passione rivoluzionaria*, Edizioni Lotta Comunista, Milan, 2003.
[29] A. Cervetto, *Forze e forme del mutamento italiano, op. cit.*
[30] *Ibid.*
[31] G. La Barbera, *Crisi globale e ristrutturazione europea*, Edizioni Lotta Comunista, Milan, 2013.
[32] A. Cervetto, *The Political Shell, op. cit.*
[33] A. Cervetto, "Il Compito Generale", *Lotta Comunista,* September 1975; in English: "Our General Task", *Internationalist Bulletin, July-August 2006,* and in G. Cavicchioli (ed.) *October 1917 100 Years, 100 Militants of the Revolution*, Éditions Science Marxiste, Montreuil, 2017.
[34] A. Cervetto, *Forze e forme del mutamento italiano, op. cit.*
[35] A. Cervetto, *The Political Shell, op. cit.*
[36] Lenin, letter to TCH., 2 August 1902, in *Lenin Collected Works, op. cit.,* Vol. 34.
[37] A. Cervetto, *The Political Shell, op. cit.*
[38] G. La Barbera, *L'Europa, l'Asia e la crisi, op. cit.*
[39] G. La Barbera, *Crisi globale e ristrutturazione europea, op. cit.*
[40] F. Engels, *Anti-Dühring & The Role of Force in History*, Éditions Science Marxiste, Montreuil, 2013, [1878].
[41] P. Rivetti, *I sindacati nella ristrutturazione europea (2008-2015)*, Edizioni Lotta Comunista, Milan, 2015.
[42] F. Engels, letter to A.Bebel, 20 June 1873 in *Marx & Engels Collected Works*, Vol. 44.
[43] N. Capelluto, *The Crisis in Global Relations*, Éditions Science Marxiste, Montreuil, 2011.
[44] A. Cervetto, *Unitary Imperialism*, Vol. II, Éditions Science Marxiste, Montreuil, 2016.
[45] A. Cervetto, *La contesa mondiale, op. cit.*
[46] L. Parodi, "ArrigoCervetto e le nostre scelte strategiche", *Lotta Comunista*, March 1995 – partly available in English in G. La Barbera, *Lotta Comunista, The Bolshevik Model, 1965-1995*, Éditions Science Marxiste, Montreuil, 2019.
[47] G. La Barbera, "Duplice riarmo in Est Asia e nel Golfo Persico", *Lotta Comunista*, September 2010 – "Double Rearmament in East Asia and the Persian Gulf", *Internationalist Bulletin*, October 2010.
[48] A. Cervetto, *L'ineguale sviluppo politico 1968-1979, op. cit.*
[49] *Ibid.*
[50] G. La Barbera, *Crisi globale e ristrutturazione europea, op. cit.*
[51] A. Cervetto, *Il mondo multipolare 1990-1995, op. cit.*
[52] *Ibid.*
[53] A. Cervetto, *Forze e forme del mutamento italiano, op. cit.*
[54] G. La Barbera, *Crisi globale e ristrutturazione europea, op. cit.*
[55] A. Cervetto, *Unitary Imperialism*, Vol. II, *op. cit.*
[56] G. La Barbera, *L'Europa, l'Asia e la crisi, op. cit.*
[57] G. La Barbera, *Lotta Comunista: The Origins 1943-1952*, Éditions Science Marxiste, Montreuil, 2015.
[58] *Ibid.*

[59] *Ibid.*

[60] *Ibid.*

[61] G. La Barbera, *Crisi globale e ristrutturazione europea*, *op. cit.*

[62] A. Cervetto, "Il Compito Generale", *op. cit.*

[63] *Ibid.*

[64] G. La Barbera, *The New Strategic Phase*, Éditions Science Marxiste, Montreuil, 2015.

[65] See:
- F. Dalvit, *Europe in the European Collisions*, Éditions Science Marxiste, Montreuil, 2019.
- G. De Simone, *Grande Medio Oriente. Crisi e guerre della nuova fase strategica*, Edizioni Lotta Comunista, Milan, 2016.
- G. La Barbera, *The New Strategic Phase*, *op. cit.*

[66] G. La Barbera, *Lotta Comunista: The Origins 1943-1952*, *op. cit.*

[67] G. Conti, "Rimpianti per una ristrutturazione subita", *Lotta Comunista,* December 2003.

[68] L. Parodi, "ArrigoCervetto e le nostre scelte strategiche", *op. cit.*

[69] Arnaud de La Grange, "Le Japon à l'assaut de la 'Chinafrique'", *Le Figaro*, January 20th 2014.

[70] G. La Barbera, "Ucraina, Medio Oriente e Africa mettono alla prova le UE nel 'vicinato europeo'", *Lotta Comunista*, January 2014 – "Ukraine, the Middle East and Africa Put the EU to the Test in Its Own Backyard", *Internationalist Bulletin*, January 2014.

[71] G. Conti, *Cronache del berlusconismo*, Edizioni Lotta Comunista, Milan, 2014.

[72] N. Ferguson, "War: In History's Shadow", *Financial Times*, August 1st 2014.

[73] H. Münkler, "Die jüngsten Kriege sind bedrohlich" [The Recent Wars are Threatening], *Focus*, September 8th 2014.

[74] W. R. Mead, "The Return of Geopolitics. The Revenge of the Revisionist Powers", *Foreign Affairs*, May-June 2014.

[75] H. Kissinger, *World Order*, Penguin Books Limited, London, 2014.

[76] A. Cervetto, "Quaderni 1981-82", *Cronologia della vita e delle opere. Taccuini e Quaderni. Indici, Opere, op. cit.* – partly available in English in G. La Barbera, *Lotta Comunista. Towards the Strategy Party, 1953-1965*, Éditions Science Marxiste, Montreuil, 2018.

[77] A. Cervetto, *The Difficult Question of Times, op. cit.*

[78] A. Cervetto, "Quaderni 1981-82", *op. cit.* – in G. La Barbera, *Lotta Comunista. Towards the Strategy Party, 1953-1965, op. cit.*

[79] *Ibid*,

[80] G. La Barbera, *Lotta Comunista. Towards the Strategy Party, 1953-1965, op. cit.*

[81] Lenin, *The State and Revolution,* Éditions Science Marxiste, Montreuil, 2017.

[82] G. La Barbera, *Lotta Comunista. Towards the Strategy Party, 1953-1965, op. cit.*

[83] *Ibid.*

[84] A. Cervetto, "Il marxismo della II Internazionale. K.Kautsky", *Opere*, Vol. 6, *op. cit.*

[85] L. Parodi, "Il capitalismo italiano e l'esportazione della forza-lavoro nel MEC", *Lotta Comunista,* September-October 1967.

[86] A. Cervetto, "Immigrati come riserva", *Lotta Comunista*, December 1976

[87] L. Parodi, "Il capitalismo italiano e l'esportazione della forza-lavoro nel MEC", *op. cit.*

[88] N. Bukharin, *Imperialism and World Economy.* International Publishers 1929.
[89] See.
– G. De Simone, *Grande Medio Oriente. Crisi e guerre della nuova fase strategica, op. cit.*
– G. La Barbera, "The 'Fog of War' in the Multipolar Contention", ***Internationalist Bulletin***, October 2015.
[90] G. La Barbera, "A Historic Collision", ***Internationalist Bulletin***, March 2016.
[91] A. Cervetto, "Conclusioni al Comitato Provinciale di Genova", March 13th 1981, *Opere, op. cit.*, Vol. 19.
[92] A. Cervetto, *The Difficult Question of Times, op. cit.*
[93] Anthologies, *May Day in Working-Class History,* Éditions Science Marxiste, Montreuil, 2013.
[94] K. Marx, *Capital*, Volume I, in *Marx & Engels Collected Works*, Vol. 35 [1867].
[95] *Ibid.*
[96] K. Marx, letter to F. Bolte, 23 November 1871, in *Marx & Engels Collected Works*, Vol. 44, *op. cit.*
[97] Lenin, Preface to the Pamphlet, *May Days in Kharkov*, in *Lenin Collected Works, op. cit.,* Vol. 4.
[98] Lenin, *"Left-Wing" Communism, an Infantile Disorder*, Éditions Science Marxiste, Montreuil, 2020/ [1920].
[99] I. Bremmer, D. Lipton, "Building Collaboration Without Crisis", *IMFBlog*, September 30th 2016.
[100] A. Cervetto, "Centro Nazionale Allargato", June 22nd 1979, *Opere, op. cit.,* Vol. 17, *op. cit.*
[101] A. Cervetto, "Il crescente astensionismo di classe", *Lotta Comunista*, July 1980.
[102] "Abstentionnisme de classe aux régionales", *L'Internationaliste*, February 2016 – "Class Abstention in the French Regional Elections", ***Internationalist Bulletin***, March 2016.
[103] D. Bianchi, "I decenni perduti della modernizzazione russa", *Lotta Comunista*, September 2016 – "The Lost Decades of Russian Modernisation", ***Internationalist Bulletin***, October 2016.
[104] M. Wolf, "The Long and Painful Journey to World Disorder", *Financial Times*, January 5th 2017.
[105] "Incubo imprese zombie per la ristrutturazione europea", *Lotta Comunista*, February 2017 – "'Zombie Firm' Nightmare for European Restructuring", ***Internationalist Bulletin***, March 2017.
[106] A. Cervetto, "I sindacati sono contagiati dal trasformismo", *Lotta Comunista*, January 1994.
[107] G. Cavicchioli (ed.) *October 1917 100 Years, 100 Militants of the Revolution, op. cit.*
[108] G. La Barbera, "Guerra e pace in Asia nel secolo cinese", *Lotta Comunista*, December 2017 – "War and Peace in Asia in the Chinese Century", ***Internationalist Bulletin***, January 2018.
[109] G. La Barbera, "Nuovo ciclo di riarmo e di inedite tensioni", *Lotta Comunista*, November 2017 – "New Cycle of Rearmament and Unprecedented Tensions", ***Internationalist Bulletin***, December 2017.
[110] A. Cervetto, *Il mondo multipolare, op. cit.*

[111] G. La Barbera, "L'Europa sfidata dal secolo cinese", *Lotta Comunista*, January 2018 – "Europe Challenged by the Chinese Century", ***Internationalist Bulletin***, February 2018.

[112] Lenin, "Political Parties in Russia", in *Lenin Collected Works*, *op. cit.*, Vol. 18.

[113] A. Cervetto, "Il Compito Generale", *op. cit.*

[114] A. Cervetto, *The Difficult Question of Times, op. cit.*

[115] G. La Barbera, "L'autonomia strategica UE a un nuovo combattimento", *Lotta Comunista*, February 2018 – "EU Strategic Autonomy Faced with Another Battle", ***Internationalist Bulletin***, March 2018.

[116] D. Bianchi, "Trasformismo proprietario e statalista", *Lotta Comunista*, March 2018.

[117] B. Grillo, interview with the daily *la Repubblica*, March 19th 2018.

[118] Anthology,*Marx. Scienziato e rivoluzionario*, Edizioni Lotta Comunista, Milan 1983, 1994, 2009.

[119] W. Liebknecht, *KarlMarx: Biographical Memoirs*, Progress Publishers, Moscow, 1896.

[120] F. Engels, "On the History of the Communist League", *Marx & Engels Selected Works*, Volume 3, Progress Publishers, Moscow 1970 [1885].

[121] K. Marx, F.Engels, *Manifesto of the Communist Party*, *Marx & Engels Collected Works*, Vol. 6.

[122] G. La Barbera, "Governo della paura proprietaria e statalista", *Lotta Comunista*, May 2018.

[123] Anthology, *Bruno Fortichiari. In memoria di uno dei fondatori del PCd'I*, Edizioni Lotta Comunista, Milan, 2006.

[124] Lenin, *What Is to Be Done?*, in Éditions Science Marxiste, Montreuil, 2020.

[125] G. La Barbera, "La crisi francese nel nuovo ciclo politico", *Lotta Comunista*, December 2018 – "The French Crisis in the New Political Cycle", *Internationalism,* January 2019.

[126] Lenin, *Marxism and Revisionism*, 1908, in *Lenin Collected Works, op. cit.* Vol. 15.

[127] A. Cervetto, *Forze e forme del mutamento italiano, Opere, op. cit.*, Vol. 2.

[128] G. Doria, *Investimenti e sviluppo economico a Genova alla vigilia della Prima Guerra Mondiale, Le premesse (1815-1882)*, Vol. I, Edizioni Pantarei, Milan, 2008.

[129] F. Palumberi, "La sfida delle piattaforme elettriche", *Lotta Comunista*, June 2019.

[130] G. De Simone, *Grande Medio Oriente. Crisi e guerre della nuova fase strategica, op. cit.*

[131] G. De Simone, "Trattative armate tra Golfo e Mediterraneo", *Lotta Comunista*, January 2020 – "Armed Negotiations between the Gulf and the Mediterranean", *Internationalism*, February 2020.

[132] A. Cervetto, "Quaderni 1981-82", *Cronologia della vita e delle opere. Taccuini e Quaderni. Indici, Opere, op. cit.* – partly available in English in G. La Barbera, *Lotta Comunista. Towards the Strategy Party, 1953-1965,* Éditions Science Marxiste, Montreuil, 2018.

[133] K. Marx, F.Engels, *Manifesto of the Communist Party, op. cit.*

[134] Lenin, *Imperialism, the Highest Stage of Capitalism*, Éditions Science Marxiste, Montreuil, 2016.

[135] A. Cervetto, "Quaderni 1981-82", *Cronologia della vita e delle opere. Taccuini e Quaderni. Indici, Opere, op. cit.* – partly available in English in G. La Barbera, *Lotta Comunista: The Origins 1943-1952, op. cit.*
[136] R. Pastorino, *The Unprecedented Task, op. cit.*
[137] Lenin, *What Is to Be Done?, op. cit.*
[138] A. Cervetto, "Il Compito Generale", *op. cit.*
[139] A. Cervetto, *The Political Shell, op. cit.*

Chronology

2007

January 1st – European Union. With the adhesion of Romania and Bulgaria, the EU now has 27 members.

January 10th – United States. President George W. Bush announces an increase of more than 21,500 soldiers in Iraq, to be concentrated mainly in Baghdad.

February 16th – United States. President George W. Bush's plan to increase the troops in Iraq is turned down by the House of Representatives; the following day the Senate does not reach the minimum threshold of three fifths of the votes needed to express a position.

March 10th – Iraq. An international conference for the stabilisation of the country begins in Baghdad. Neighbouring countries and the five member states of the UN Security Council participate in it.

March 25th – European Union. Informal summit to try to unblock the constitutional impasse: the German chancellor Angel Merkel sets the goal of establishing an agenda for the ratification of a new Treaty by June.

May 6th – France. Nicolas Sarkozy (UMP) wins the presidential election.

June 12th-14th – Palestine. In the conflict with the Palestinian faction Fatah, which began in December 2006, Hamas succeeds in taking control of the Gaza Strip.

August 7th – United States. Subprime mortgages collapse. The *crisis in global relations* begins.

August 9th – European Union. The ECB intervenes in the crisis and distributes 211 billion euros to banks in four days.

August 10th – The subprime-mortgage crisis causes the collapse of all the stock exchanges in the world.

September 13th – United Kingdom. The Northern Rock bank, specialised in mortgages, obtains an emergency loan from the Bank of England: the following day, there is a run on the bank as people queue up to withdraw their deposits. Four days later, the government announces a guarantee on the Northern's deposits.

October 14th – Italy. With Walter Veltroni's victory at the left-wing primaries, the Democratic Party, a merger between the DS and the Margherita (the Daisy), is officially born.

November 1st – Italy. The death of a woman, attacked two evenings before by a Romanian immigrant on the outskirts of Rome, leads to a campaign by the mayor, Walter Veltroni, against immigration from Romania. The government issues a decree to facilitate expulsions.

November 30th – Church. Benedict XVI publishes the encyclical *Spe salvi*, in which the Enlightenment and Marxism are criticised.

December 12th – Financial crisis. Coordinated intervention of the central banks of the USA, Europe, England, Switzerland, Canada, Japan and Sweden to offer liquidity to the credit market.

December 13th – European Union. The heads of state and government sign the new institutional treaty in Lisbon.

2008

January 19th – United States. President George W. Bush announces an economic stimulus plan that envisages over 160 billion dollars in tax cuts.

January 22nd – United States-European Union. The Fed cuts interest rates by 75 basis points in order to relaunch the economy. The ECB does not follow it and stresses the priority of fighting inflation.

January 24th – Italy. The government is outvoted in the Senate; Romano Prodi's immediate resignation opens a government crisis.

February 8th – Italy. In view of the general election, Silvio Berlusconi and Gianfranco Fini create the Popolo della Libertà (People of Freedom) list.

March 14th – United States. Public bailout of the Bear Stearns merchant bank.

April 2nd-4th – United States-European Union. The Bucharest NATO summit suspends the decision about the membership of Ukraine and Georgia. Berlin and Paris resist US pressure and initiatives that may compromise relations with Moscow.

April 13th-14th – Italy. The coalition between Popolo della Libertà and Lega Nord (Northern League) prevails in the general election. The fourth Berlusconi government takes up office on May 8th.

August 8th – Russia. The Russian army enters Georgia, after the intensification of clashes between the Georgian army and South Ossetian separatists, backed by Moscow.

September 7th – United States. Public bailout of the two home mortgage giants Fannie Mae and Freddie Mac in order to avoid their bankruptcy.

September 15th – United States. Bankruptcy of Lehman Brothers, the fourth US investment bank.

September 29th – United States. The plan of the Treasury Secretary Henry Paulson, which envisages 700 billion dollars to overhaul the banking system and emergency powers for the Treasury Department, is rejected in the House of Representatives. The plan, with part of its emergency powers amended, will be approved on October 3rd.

October 16th – China. The sovereign fund China Investment Corporation (CIC) increases its share in the American Blackstone fund to 12.5%; the financial crisis increases the presence of sovereign funds in the main Western banks.

November 4th – United States. BarackObama (Democratic Party) prevails in the presidential election. He becomes the first Afro-American president.

2009

February 24th – United States. President Barack Obama's first speech to Congress. He presents a budget envisaging a 1,750-billion-dollar or 12.3%-of-GDP deficit in 2009, with the aim of reducing it to 3% in 2013.

March 27th-29th – Italy. The founding congress of the party Popolo della Libertà (PdL) is held in Rome. Its chairman is Silvio Berlusconi and the Forza Italia and Alleanza Nazionale parties join it.

June 1st – United States. Bankruptcy of General Motors; the government takes over 60% of its capital.

June 4th-7th – European Union. In the European elections the parties affiliated with the European People's Party (EPP) advance (267 seats), while all the variants of continental socialism fall, with 159 seats for the European Socialist Party; abstention increases (56.7% as against the 54.6 of 2004).

– France. Success of the UMP (about 28% of the votes); the PS falls to 16.8%, losing more than ten percentage points with respect to 2004.

– Germany. The SPD falls to 20.8%, its all-time low. The real winner is the FDP, which polls 1.3 million more votes than in 2004.

– United Kingdom. Labour plummets to 15.7%, its lowest result since the First World War.

– Italy. Slight drop for the PdL and clear drop for the PD; the Northern League and Italia dei Valori (Italy of Values) advance. The contemporary local elections register the clear success of the majority parties, PdL and Northern League, which conquer 25 provinces in the first ballot.

– Spain. José Luis Zapatero's Socialist Party (PSOE) polls 38.5% of the votes as against the PP's 42.2%.

June 10th – Car industry. Agreement of Sergio Marchionne's Fiat with the American Chrysler.

June 17th – United States. President Obama presents the reform of the regulation of the financial system, which envisages the strengthening of the Fed's powers and the creation of new control and consumer protection authorities.

September 3rd – Italy. The editor of the Roman Catholic newspaper *Avvenire*, Dino Boffo, resigns after the attack of the daily *Il Giornale*. A campaign of the press close to Prime Minister Silvio Berlusconi had previously attacked famous names of the Italian economic panorama, from Carlo De Benedetti to Gianni Agnelli.

September 24th- 25th – G20 meeting in Pittsburgh (USA): it is decided that the meetings will become permanent and will be devoted to economic themes; the emerging economies obtain more space in the IMF and the stimuli to the economy are maintained, postponing the beginning of "exit strategies".

October 3rd – Ireland. The "yeas" prevail in the referendum on the Lisbon Treaty with 67% of the votes.

– Italy. Silvio Berlusconi's holding company Fininvest is sentenced to paying almost 750 million euros in compensation to Carlo De Benedetti's CIR Group, for its conduct during the struggle to take over the Mondadori publishing house.

October 4th – Greece. The socialist party Pasok wins the general election. A few weeks after his installation in office, the new prime minister, George Papandreou, announces that the country's deficit/GDP ratio is 12.7%, twice what the previous government had declared.

October 10th – Summit in Beijing between the leaders of China, Japan and South Korea for the creation of an East Asian economic area.

November 19th – European Union. The summit of the heads of state and government appoints the Belgian prime minister, Herman Van Rompuy, as the first permanent President of the European Council and the British Catherine Ashton as the High Representative of the Union for Foreign Affairs and Security Policy.

December 1st – European Union. The Lisbon Treaty comes into force.

2010

March 21st – United States. The House of Representatives votes definitively in favour of the healthcare reform proposed by President Barack Obama.

March 28th – Car industry. Geely, the first Chinese private automotive group, buys Volvo from the American Ford for 1.8 billion dollars.

May 2nd – European Union. An extraordinary Eurogroup summit decides to grant a loan of 80 billion euros in three years to Greece, to which 30 billion from the IMF will be added. A few days later, Athens approves a 30-billion-euro austerity plan, as the condition for obtaining the European loan.

May 17th – June 4th – China. Strike at the Foshan Honda factory in the province of Guangdong: a 24-33% pay rise is obtained. In the following days, the workers of other parts production factories working for Honda and Toyota go on strike and the movement spreads all over China.

June 15th – Italy. An agreement is signed at the Fiat plant in Pomigliano d'Arco, with the opposition of the FIOM trade union alone. This agreement envisages longer shifts and overtime, a reduction in sick leave and rest breaks, and limits to the right to go on strike, with disciplinary action for those who do not respect this. A similar agreement will be reached at the Mirafiori plant at the end of December.

June 30th – Italy. After months of clashes, 33 deputies and 10 senators who are loyal to the President of the Chamber of Deputies, Gianfranco Fini, leave the PdL and found the new parliamentary group Futuro e Libertà per l'Italia (FLI). On November 15th, the FLI ministers and undersecretaries will leave the Berlusconi government.

September 7th – European Union. Ecofin gives the green light to the introduction of the "European semester", a time of discussion between the Commission, Council and single governments for the coordination of the financial laws of the EU countries from 2011.

September 12th – United States-China. During a visit to China, the governor of California, Arnold Schwarzenegger, expresses the hope that China may invest in the construction of a high-speed train railway network in his state.

October 14th – Italy. The government approves the Stability Act (formerly the Budget) for the 2011-13 three-year period.

October 20th – United States. The Department of Defence formalises to Congress the sale of weapons to Saudi Arabia to the tune of over 60 billion dollars, the biggest in American history.

November 19th – Italy. The Stability Act is approved in the Chamber of Deputies. It will be approved in the Senate on December 7th.

November 21st – European Union. The Eurogroup approves the 85-billion-euro bailout plan for Ireland, tying it to precise disciplinary measures of its public accounts.

December 14th – The vote of no confidence in the Berlusconi government presented by the oppositions is rejected by the Chamber and the Senate.

December 16th 17th – European Union. – The European Council reaches agreement for the modification of the Lisbon Treaty and the creation of a permanent anti-crisis intervention mechanism in favour of the states of the Union: the ESM (European Stability Mechanism), which is expected to come into force from 2013.

2011

January 3rd – Algeria. Clashes in Oran and Algiers over the increase in food prices; similar revolts are also going on in Tunisia and are spreading to the whole of North Africa: these movements will be called "Arab Springs".

January 14th – Italy. Silvio Berlusconi is officially investigated for malfeasance and underage prostitution; all the newspapers publish the tapping of the prime minister's conversations. In the following months, the attack on Berlusconi's private behaviour will intensify and the media campaign will extend to the international press.

February 11th – Egypt. After weeks of street protests, President Hosni Mubarak resigns.

March 15th – Syria. The first demonstrations against President Bashar al-Assad: what will become a long and bloody civil war begins.

March 19th – Libya. France, Britain and the United States begin the military intervention against the regime of Muammar Ghaddafi, who will be killed on October 20th.

May 23rd – Italy. The Fincantieri Group announces a restructuring plan envisaging more than 2,500 redundancies and the closing down of three shipyards. At the end of the summer, the shipyard-by-shipyard negotiations cause problems for the trade unions.

July 7th – Italy. The spreads on government bonds reach their highest level since the introduction of the euro, overtaking 220 basic points; in November they will hit the record figure of 574 points.

August 5th – The ECB president Jean-Claude Trichet and his designated successor Mario Draghi send the Italian government a "confidential" letter in which they prescribe a series of urgent measures for economic growth and the consolidation of public finances, including the anticipation of a balanced budget.

August 7th – European Union. The ECB gives the green light to the buying of Eurozone government bonds on the stock exchange.

September 14th – Italy. After a difficult course lasting almost one month, the Chamber of Deputies approves a budget package of just under sixty billion euros, which anticipates the balanced budget to 2013.

October 3rd – Italy. The Fiat-Chrysler CEO Sergio Marchionne announces the group will leave the Confederation of Italian Industry (Confindustria) on January 1st 2012.

October 4th-7th – Italy. After Standard & Poor's, the rating agencies Moody's and Fitch also downgrade Italy's public debt. In the international press, Silvio Berlusconi becomes the emblem of Rome's unreliability in the international context.

October 16th – Italy. Cardinal Angelo Bagnasco holds a national seminar in Todi on the role and weight of Roman Catholics in the future Italian political landscape.

October 31st – Greece. Prime Minister George Papandreou announces a referendum on the new austerity and aid plan agreed upon with the European Union, but on November 3rd, after the suspension of aid to Athens and a meeting with Union leaders, the proposal is withdrawn. On November 10th Papandreou resigns and is succeeded by a new national unity government led by Lucas Papademos.

November 1st – European Union. Mario Draghi takes over as the ECB president from Jean-Claude Trichet.

November 12th – Italy. After the approval of the Stability Law, Silvio Berlusconi resigns as prime minister; he is succeeded by Mario Monti on the 16th.

December 4th – Italy. The Monti government presents the "Save Italy" manoeuvre which will correct the budget by 20 billion euros a year in the three years to come.

December 8th-9th – European Union. At the European Council summit, agreement is reached among 26 states (all of them except the United Kingdom) over the fiscal compact, which envisages the inclusion of the principle of a balanced budget in the national constitutions. The ESM (European Stability Mechanism) is strengthened and anticipated to July 2012.

December 15th – Iraq. A lowering of the American flag ceremony in Baghdad formally marks the end of the US military presence in the country, as announced by President Barack Obama on October 21st.

2012

January 5th – United States. President Barack Obama presents to the Pentagon America's new military strategy, which envisages a roughly 450-billion-dollar reduction in military expenditure in ten years, renouncing the possibility of fighting two wars simultaneously and special attention to the Asian region of the Pacific.

January 20th – Italy. The Monti government approves the decree-law on liberalisations.

January 26th – France. The socialist candidate to the presidential election, François Hollande, presents his electoral programme, which also envisages commitment to renegotiating the fiscal compact.

January 29th – France. President Nicolas Sarkozy announces a 1.6% increase in VAT and a tax on financial transactions, with the aim of reducing companies' social security contributions and relaunching the economy.

January 30th – European Union. The European Council summit approves the fiscal compact and the ESM "save-the-states" fund, with the sole opposition of the United Kingdom and the Czech Republic.

April 17th – Italy. The Senate definitively approves (with 235 votes in favour and 11 against) the bill introducing the obligation of a balanced budget into the constitution.

May 6th – France. François Hollande (PS) is elected President of the Republic with 51.6% of the votes, beating Nicolas Sarkozy (UMP).

June 16th-17th – Egypt. The Muslim Brotherhood candidate Mohammed Morsi wins the presidential election.

June 28th-29th – European Union. At the European Council summit, a plan elaborated by the four highest European authorities – the "four presidents" Van Rompuy, Barroso, Juncker and Draghi – is approved. It sets out aims and times of the continent's new political centralisation.

July 19th – Italy. The Chamber of Deputies approves the fiscal compact and the ESM.

July 26th – European Union. The ECB president Mario Draghi, speaking at the Global Investment Conference in London, says he is ready to do "whatever it takes" to save the euro.

October 9th – France. The National Assembly ratifies the fiscal compact by a very large majority. Only 32 deputies of the majority (20 socialists and 12 environmentalists) vote against it.

December 13th-14th - European Union. The European Council summit launches the Banking Union, which envisages only one supervisory body of EU banks, centralised in the ECB.

December 21st – Italy. After the approval of the Stability Law, the prime minister Mario Monti resigns.

2013

January 1st – European Union. The fiscal compact comes into force.

February 24th-25th – Italy. The Five Star Movement is the first party in the general election; the PD just hangs onto its majority in the Chamber of Deputies, but Silvio Berlusconi's coalition keeps its dominant position in the North and prevents the centre-left from obtaining the majority in the Senate. Mario Monti's Scelta Civica (Civic Choice) polls about 10% of the votes.

April 20th – Italy. After many unsuccessful attempts to reach an agreement among the political forces over the election of the new President of the Republic, which falls to both Chambers of Parliament in Italy, Giorgio Napolitano accepts his election to a second mandate, even though he had previously stated he was not available.

April 28th – Italy. The grand coalition government headed by Enrico Letta (PD) takes up office; the PdL Secretary Angelino Alfano is Deputy Prime Minister and Minister of the Interior.

May 28th – Turkey. A street protest in Istanbul against the construction of a shopping centre in Gezi Park turns into a contestation of Recep Tayyip Erdogan's government and spreads throughout the country.

June 17th – Brazil. Protests against increases in bus, train and underground prices which started in São Paulo, spread to the whole country.

July 1st – European Union. Croatia becomes the 28th member state of the EU.

July 3rd – Egypt. Military coup d'état; President Morsi is arrested together with his collaborators. Repression of the Muslim Brotherhood will cause about a thousand deaths.

August 21st – Syria. An attack on the outskirts of Damascus causes more than 500 deaths and Bashar al-Assad is accused of having used chemical weapons. President Barack Obama announces an American attack, backed by France and Britain. On the 29th, the British parliament rejects the Cameron government's motion to support an intervention in Syria. On the 31st, Obama announces he will ask Congress to authorise raids on Damascus.

September 1st – China. Jiang Jiemin, the director of SASAC (the State-owned Assets Supervision and Administration Commission of the State Council) as well as of CNCP (China National Petroleum Corporation) until the end of March, is accused of corruption and arrested together with another four high-level managers of the oil sector.

September 14th – Syria. The American Secretary of State John Kerry and the Russian Minister of Foreign Affairs Sergei Lavrov reach an agreement about the Syrian crisis.

September 21st – China. Bo Xilai, the former head of the province of Chongqing and Xi Jinping's competitor for the presidency, in jail since 2012, is convicted of corruption and sentenced to life imprisonment. Various exponents of the entourage of Zhou Yongkang, a powerful Politburo member who had backed Bo, had been arrested in previous weeks.

September 25th – European Union. The European Commission publishes its report on industrial competitiveness in its member countries; Italy is in the third category, with medium-low competitiveness, together with Cyprus, Greece, Slovenia, Portugal and Malta.

September 29th - China. A big Free Trade Zone is inaugurated in Shanghai.

October 17th – Italy. Mario Monti resigns from the chairmanship of Scelta Civica, a party founded by him on January 4th.

November 6th – European Union. The European Central Bank cuts its interest rates by 25 basis points, bringing them to 0.5-0.25%, an all-time low.

November 16th – Italy. Silvio Berlusconi leaves the PdL and the government. He relaunches Forza Italia (Forward Italy!).

November 23rd – China-Japan. Beijing announces it has formed an Air Defence Identification Zone in the skies above the East China Sea. The contention over the contested Senkaku-Diaoyu Islands opens up again with Tokyo.

November 24th – Iran. Agreement in Geneva over Iranian nuclear power between Tehran and the states of the 5+1 Group (USA, Russia, China, Great Britain, France – the permanent members of the UN Security Council – plus Germany).

December 8th – Italy. The mayor of Florence, Matteo Renzi, is elected as Secretary in the Democratic Party elections.

2014

January 6th-14th – China-Japan. Both the Japanese prime minister Shinzo Abe and the Chinese Foreign Minister Wang Yi, on a state visit to various African countries, undertake to increase investment in the region.

January 19th – Car industry. Dongfeng, China's second automotive group, enters the capital of PSA Peugeot Citroën with 14%.

January 20th-21st – France-Germany. The Foreign Ministers Laurent Fabius and Frank-Walter Steinmeier announce the sending of the Franco-German brigade to Mali and of European troops to the Central African Republic, as well as a joint visit first to Georgia and Moldova and then to North Africa.

January 29th – United States. The Fed decides to continue the reduction of its purchases of Treasury bonds, known as *tapering*. The expected increase in American interest rates will lead to an outflow of capital from the emerging countries with the consequent devaluation of their currencies: India, Indonesia, Turkey and South Africa are particularly hard hit.

January 31st-February 1st – Germany. At the Munich Security Conference, the President of the Republic Joachim Gauck announces that Berlin is ready to play a leading role in European defence. Official speeches of the same kind are made by the Minister for Foreign Affairs Frank-Walter Steinmeier and the Minister of Defence Ursula von der Leyen.

February 13th – Italy. The PD national leadership asks Enrico Letta to resign as prime minister in order to give life to a new executive headed by Matteo Renzi, which takes up office on February 22nd.

February 14th – Syria. The Peace Conference organised by the UN on the Syrian civil war ends in Geneva without any agreement.

February 22nd – Ukraine. Pro-Europe demonstrators occupy parliament in Kiev; the pro-Russia president Viktor Yanukovych is removed from office and leaves the capital.

March 16th – Russia-Ukraine. The referendum in Crimea, a region of Ukraine, is a plebiscite in favour of reunification with Russia. On the 18th, Russian President Vladimir Putin signs the agreement for the entry of the peninsula into the Russian Federation with Crimea's political leaders.

March 25th – Guinea's Health Minister informs the World Health Organisation of the rapid evolution of the epidemic of Ebola haemorrhagic fever. The epidemic will subsequently spread to Liberia, Sierra Leone and Nigeria and will cause more than 10,000 deaths. In the West, the risk of the epidemic spreading will trigger media alarm and a wave of apprehension, also becoming one of the arguments of the American election campaign.

May 21st – Russia-China. Agreement for a new gas pipeline between the Russian group Gazprom and the Chinese oil company CNPC.

June 10th – Iraq. ISIS takes control of Mosul, the country's second most important city; meanwhile the Kurdish regional government takes over control of Kirkuk, a national symbol and an important oil centre. On the 29th, ISIS will proclaim the restoration of the Islamic Caliphate in the territories that have fallen under its control.

July 14th-16th – BRICS. Summit in Fortaleza: agreement of the five member countries (Brazil, Russia, India, China and South Africa) for the founding of a development bank and a joint fund.

August 8th – Iraq-Syria. American President Barack Obama authorises air raids against ISIS; in September, France and Britain join the United States.

September 22nd – China. For the first time, two ships of the Chinese navy carry out joint naval exercises with Iran in the Persian Gulf.

September 29th – Italy. The PD national leadership approves Matteo Renzi's document on the reform of the labour market (Jobs Act) and the abolition of article 18 of the Workers' Statute, regarding indemnification for unlawful dismissals.

November 18th – Russia-China. Joint naval exercises in the Mediterranean Sea are announced for the spring of 2015.

November 29th – China. At the Central Conference on Work Relating to Foreign Affairs, President Xi Jinping launches a double Silk Road, one maritime towards the Indian Ocean and the Middle East, and the other terrestrial towards Central Asia, with a special bank and fund of their own.

2015

January 22nd – European Union. The European Central Bank adopts quantitative easing. Opposed to the launching of the plan, but not to its legitimacy, the Bundesbank finds itself in the minority with its opposition to the purchasing of sovereign bonds.

January 25th – Greece. In the general election, the radical left-wing party Syriza almost obtains the absolute majority. The following day, its leader Alexis Tsipras allies himself with the xenophobic and nationalist right-wing Independent Greeks in order to find an alliance against the memorandum of the troika (EU, IMF and ECB).

January 31st – Italy. Sergio Mattarella is elected as President of the Republic.

February 12th – Ukraine. In Minsk, Belarus, the Trilateral Contact Group on Ukraine reaches an agreement for a ceasefire with a document that is summed up in a statement made by four heads of state and government: the Russian Vladimir Putin, the Ukrainian Petro Poroshenko and the leading exponents of the Franco German axis, Angela Merkel and François Hollande.

March 22nd – Italy. The Chinese state-owned group ChemChina, with a complex operation, takes control of the Pirelli company.

April 18th-19th – Immigration. Between 700 and 900 migrants are drowned when their boat sinks in the Strait of Sicily during the night; this is one of the most serious tragedies of this kind in the Mediterranean.

July 5th – Greece. The referendum promoted by Prime Minister Alexis Tsipras rejects the plan of Greece's creditors by 61.3% of the votes and a 65% turnout.

July 13th – European Union. After seventeen hours of difficult negotiations, in which the German Minister of Finance Wolfgang Schäuble hypothesises Greece's temporary exit from the single currency, the Eurogroup decides unanimously to start negotiations to agree on a third aid plan for Greece.

July 14th – Iran. Agreement on the Iran nuclear deal is reached in Vienna between Tehran and the G5+1 (the permanent members of the UN Security Council, the United States, Russia, China, France and Great Britain, plus Germany).

July 15th – Greece. Parliament approves the austerity measures demanded by its creditors with 229 votes in favour, 64 against and 6 abstentions.

August 11th – Media. Exor, the Agnelli family's financial holding company, becomes the main shareholder of The Economist Group.

August 25th – Germany. Chancellor Angela Merkel announces that Berlin will take in all the refugees from Syria, suspending the Dublin Regulation, according to which a refugee can be hosted only in the first European country that receives him.

September 9th – European Union. The President of the European Commission Jean-Claude Juncker proposes a permanent mechanism of quotas for sharing out refugees, in tune with the Franco-German viewpoint.

September 30th – Syria. Russia's air raids in support of President Bashar al-Assad begin.

November 13th – France. A series of terrorist attacks in Paris, for which ISIS claimed responsibility, kill about 130 people, 89 of them in the Bataclan theatre alone. President François Hollande proclaims the state of emergency to the deputies and senators gathered in congress in Versailles.

December 6th – France. In the first round of the regional elections, Front National, with 28% of the votes, is the leading party. Abstentionism is about 50%.

2016

January 4th – Sharp fall in the world's stock exchanges due to fears of a slowdown in the Chinese economy.

January 4th-5th – Libya. ISIS launches an attack, which is repelled, on the oil ports of Sidra and Ras Lanuf. In the following months those in favour of a military intervention against ISIS will become more and more insistent, putting pressure on Matteo Renzi's Italian government.

February 3rd – China. The ChemChina Group offers 43 billion dollars for the Swiss agrochemical company Syngenta; this will be the biggest foreign purchase by a Chinese state-owned company.

February 10th – The price of oil falls to 27 dollars a barrel, the lowest point since April 2004.

February 12th – Syria. The Russian and American foreign ministers announce an agreement on a ceasefire in Syria within one week.

February 18th-19th – United Kingdom. At the European Council summit an agreement on relations between the EU and London is reached. The following day, Prime Minister David Cameron announces a referendum on June 23rd on the United Kingdom staying in the European Union.

March 10th – European Union. The ECB cuts the rates on bank reserves from 0.30 to 0.40%, increases its monthly purchases of bonds on the markets from 60 to 80 billion euros, at least until March 2017, and launches other quantitative easing measures.

March 13th – Germany. The national-liberal conservative party Alternative für Deutschland (AFD) comes first in the local elections in Baden-Württemberg, Rhineland-Palatinate and Saxony-Anhalt. In its election campaign it reinforced its Eurosceptical nationalism with xenophobic overtones.

March 17th-18th – European Union-Turkey. An agreement is reached with Ankara in the European Council over the management of the flows of refugees and immigrants.

March 30th – Libya. Fayez al-Serraj, the prime minister appointed by the UNO, lands in Tripoli and forms a government of national unity.

April 12th – Italy. Parliament definitively approves the constitutional reform put forward by the Renzi government. This envisages the abolition of bicameralism, the strengthening of the executive and a new electoral law; the reform will be put to a referendum, probably to be held in autumn.

May 26th – United States. Donald Trump officially wins the Republican primaries, obtaining the necessary number of authorisations to become the White House candidate.

June 5th – Italy. Surge in class abstentionism in the first round of the local elections. On the 19th, in the run-off elections, the two Five Star Movement candidates in Rome and Turin, Virginia Raggi and Chiara Appendino, are elected as mayors, while the centre-left candidate Giuseppe Sala prevails in Milan.

June 23rd – United Kingdom. In the referendum on Brexit, the "leave" vote, in favour of leaving the European Union, stands at 51.9%, as against the "remain" vote of 48.1%; there is a 72.2% turnout. The following day, Prime Minister David Cameron announces his resignation; Theresa May succeeds him on July 13th.

July 8th – South Korea-United States. Washington and Seoul officially announce their agreement for the deployment of the THAAD anti-missile system. China and Russia, in a joint communiqué, will express their opposition.

July 14th – France. A terrorist attack in Nice claimed by ISIS kills 87 people.

September 4th-18th – Germany. Regional elections: in Mecklenburg-Pomerania, the AFD overtakes the CDU and is second behind the SPD, but the 38.4% abstention rate is by far the first party; in Lower Saxony, the AFD does not exceed 4% of the electorate, with abstention standing at 44.5%; in Berlin, the AFD remains below 10% of the electorate and abstentionism stands at 33.1%.

September 12th-19th – China-Russia. Joint naval exercises of Beijing and Moscow in the South China Sea.

September 18th – Russia. Vladimir Putin's party, United Russia, wins in the elections to the Duma. Abstention stands at 52%, with Moscow and St. Petersburg at 65%-67%.

October 2nd – Hungary. The referendum against European quotas of refugees, promoted by Prime Minister Viktor Orbán, with a 57% abstention rate, does not reach a quorum, invalidating the legal value of the consultation.

October 9th – China. The Deputy Foreign Minister Li Baodong states that the positions of Russia and Moscow over Syria and Afghanistan match.

October 15th-26th – Russia-Egypt. Joint military exercises of Russian and Egyptian paratroopers in El Alamein.

October 16th – Iraq. The Iraqi army, with various Shiite militias and Kurdish Peshmergas, backed by the Western coalition, launch operations to reconquer Mosul, which has been under ISIS control since June 2014.

November 8th – United States. Donald Trump, the Republican Party candidate, wins in the presidential election.

December 1st – France. President François Hollande announces he will not stand as a candidate for a second mandate; this is the first time for an incumbent president during the Fifth Republic.

December 4th – Italy. The referendum rejects the constitutional reform of the Renzi government. Renzi announces his resignation as prime minister. He is succeeded by the Minister for Foreign Affairs Paolo Gentiloni.

December 22nd – Syria. The troops of Bashar al-Assad, backed by the Russians and Iranians, announce the reconquest of Aleppo, the country's second most important metropolis.

2017

January 25th – France. François Fillon, the Gaullist and Roman Catholic presidential candidate of Les Républicains, is caught up in a scandal involving his wife and children, who allegedly benefited from fictitious jobs and public money.

March 29th – United Kingdom. Brexit is formally launched with a letter signed by Prime Minister Theresa May and delivered to the President of the European Council, Donald Tusk.

April 23rd – France. First round of the presidential election: Emmanuel Macron (En Marche!) polls 24% of the votes, Marine Le Pen (Front National) 21.3%. They are followed by François Fillon (LR, 20%), Jean-Luc Mélenchon (France insoumise, 19.6%) and Benoît Hamon (PS, 6.3%). For the first time in the Fifth Republic, the two big parties of the Republican alternation are both excluded from the second round.

April 26th – China. Beijing launches its second aircraft carrier, the first one built completely in China, in Dalian and confirms the building of a third one in Shanghai. The prospect of arriving at five or six aircraft carriers in a few years is real and a political debate begins about their use.

May 7th – France. In the second round of the presidential election, Emmanuel Macron prevails over Marine Le Pen with 66% of the votes.

May 19th – Italy-France. The agreement is signed for the acquisition on the part of the Italian Fincantieri Group of STX France, which controls the Saint-Nazaire shipyards, the cradle of French civil and military shipbuilding.

June 5th – Italy. The Ilva Group is acquired by a group headed by the Euro Indian giant ArcelorMittel, the world's top iron and steel group. The following months will witness difficult negotiations between the workers and the new owners to limit the more than 4,000 expected redundancies.

September 24th – Germany. In the federal elections, the CDU-CSU Union headed by Angela Merkel is confirmed as the first party with 32.9% of the votes; the SPD is second with 20.5%; AFD arrives third (12.6%) and enters the Bundestag with more than 90 deputies.

September 26th – France-Germany. An agreement is signed between the French company Alstom and the German Siemens for the merger of their railway activities. In February 2019, the European Commission will veto this merger.

October 18th-24th – China. At the 19th CCP Congress, Chairman Xi Jinping speaks of a "new era" which will take place in three stages: in 2020, China will be a "moderately prosperous society"; in 2035, "military modernization" with a "world-class" military presence will be completed; and in 2050, China will be a "modern" country which "will rise to first place in the world".

2018

January 21st – France-Germany. In the Salon Murat where Konrad Adenauer and Charles de Gaulle signed the *Élysée Treaty in 1963,* President Emmanuel Macron and Chancellor Angela Merkel make a joint statement to further strengthen Franco-German cooperation. The following day, the French and German parliaments vote to renew the Treaty.

February 2nd – United States. The Pentagon announces the updating of its doctrine on nuclear deterrence, the Nuclear Posture Review (NPP). The core of this modernisation consists in the use of low potential nuclear warheads, also in the presence of a clash with conventional weapons.

February 8th – France. President Emmanuel Macron presents the new law for military programming 2019-2025, which envisages an increase in military expenditure of about 300 billion euros in the next seven years.

March 1st – Russia. Speech of President Vladimir Putin to the Federal Assembly, the two united Houses: in the part devoted to rearmament, he stresses the development of missile capacities and a new generation of weapons.

March 4th – Germany. The SPD power base approves the agreement for a grand coalition with the CDU. On the 14th, the Bundestag gives the green light to the fourth Merkel government: Olaf Scholz (SPD) takes over from Wolfgang Schäuble at the Finance Ministry.

– Italy. The elections confirm the Peninsula's political imbalance, with the victory of the two "populist" parties, the Five Star Movement in the South and Matteo Salvini's League in the North.

April 12th – China. In the South China Sea, Chairman Xi Jinping participates, in uniform, in a naval parade in which the biggest all-time fleet is on display, showing off the components of its *nuclear triad.*

April 13th-14th – Syria. During the night, the United States, France and the United Kingdom launch missiles on Bashar al-Assad and his regime, accused of having used chemical weapons against its people. German non-participation triggers a debate on the European deficit in the centralisation of foreign and defence policy.

April 17th-May 4th – Argentina. A 12% devaluation of the peso in ten days obliges the central bank to make three consecutive increases in its interest rates, raised from 27.5% to 40%, without succeeding in staunching the currency haemorrhage. On May 8th, Buenos Aires will ask the IMF for a 30-billion-dollar loan.

May 8th – United States. President Donald Trump withdraws unilaterally from the 2015 Vienna agreement on the Iranian nuclear programme and announces he will restore sanctions against Tehran, also threatening European companies. London sides with Berlin and Paris in defending the agreement with Iran.

May 23rd – Italy. The President of the Republic Sergio Mattarella appoints as prime minister the jurist Giuseppe Conte, the candidate proposed by the League and the Five Star Movement. Four days later, Mattarella vetoes Paolo Savona as the Minister for Economic Affairs and Conte announces his withdrawal from office; but on the 31st a compromise is found over the appointment of Giovanni Tria as Minister of Economy and Finance and the new Conte government is born on June 1st.

June 10th – Italy. The neo-Minister of the Interior Matteo Salvini refuses to let the Aquarius, a ship chartered by Médecins sans frontières, with more than 600 migrants including women and children on board, dock in an Italian port. The "closed ports" line will continue in the following months.

July 6th – United States-China. Washington launches its attack, announced in March, on Beijing. A volume of 50 billion dollars' worth of Chinese exports is hit with 25% customs duties. The Chinese government responds with customs duties of a similar order.

August 10th – Turkey. In just one day, the Turkish lira loses 14% of its value against the dollar.

August 20th – The protest in front of the Swedish parliament of Greta Thunberg, a sixteen-year-old environmentalist, launches the international youth movement against global heating called *Fridays for Future*.

September 27th – Italy. A 2.4% deficit/GDP ratio is fixed as one of the budget aims.

October 28th – Brazil. Jair Bolsonaro, of the Brazilian far right, is elected President of Brazil with 55.3% of the votes.

November 16th – Germany. The Volkswagen automotive group plans a 44-billion-euro investment in the next five years, mainly in electric cars, in a context of global competition in which no less than 1,000 billion is expected to be invested in just a few years.

November 17th – France. A demonstration on the Champs-Élysées, in Paris, against the increase in a fuel tax marks the beginning of the protest of the so-called "yellow vests".

December 18th – Japan. Shinzo Abe's government approves the new guidelines for defence programming, which envisage an expense of 242 billion dollars in the next five years, the conversion of the two Izumo class helicopter carriers into de facto aircraft carriers and the introduction of Cruise missiles.

December 19th – Italy. After long negotiations with the European Commission, the government reaches a compromise in order to avoid the debt infringement procedure and reduces the predicted 2019 deficit from 2.4 to 2.04% of GDP.

2019

January 31st – The Foreign Ministers of France, Germany and the United Kingdom announce the creation of the special-purpose vehicle Instex, with the aim of allowing trade with Tehran without using the dollar, so as to protect themselves from the effects of US sanctions against Iran.

April 4th – Libya. The militias of Khalifa Haftar, the chief-of-staff of the Tobruk government, march on Tripoli and besiege the capital.

May 19th – United States. Google forbids Huawei access to the Android operating system, complying with the Trump administration's "ban".

May 23rd-26th – European Union. In the European elections, the forces of the Europeanist forces – EEP, S&D, ALDE and Greens – remain amply majoritarian, while the sovereigntists remain below the 25% threshold. However, the victories of the League and Rassemblement National, the leading parties in Italy and France, weigh in the general fragmentation of the vote.

May 24th – United Kingdom. Theresa May announces her resignation, admitting in tears her failure over Brexit. On July 24th, she is succeeded by Boris Johnson.

May 27th – Car industry. FCA proposes a merger between equals with the French group Renault, with the contribution of the Japanese Nissan. The proposal will subsequently be withdrawn.

June 9th – Hong Kong. Anti-government and anti-Chinese demonstration; the wave of protests, which began in March, will continue and intensify in the months to come.

July 16th – Italy. The League votes against the appointment of Ursula von der Leyen as the President of the European Commission, while the Five Star Movement votes in favour of it. The Italian fracture over the *European line* is evident.

August 8th – Italy. The League leader and deputy prime minister Matteo Salvini asks for "full power", leaves the majority and demands an early election in the autumn.

August 20th – Italy. Prime Minister Giuseppe Conte announces to the Senate the end of the League-Five Star government and defends Italy's European and Euro-Atlantic position, challenged by Matteo Salvini.

September 5th – Italy. The second government led by Giuseppe Conte is formed. It is backed by the Democratic Party and the Five Star Movement, with Matteo Salvini's League in the opposition.

October 1st – Iraq. A wave of social protests against the cost of living, unemployment, deficiencies in social services and corruption begins. The government responds by deploying the army, killing hundreds and wounding thousands.

October 9th – Syria-Turkey. Ankara launches a military raid in the Kurdish-controlled border areas in Syria.

October 14th – Chile. A series of anti-government demonstrations begins, triggered by the increase in underground ticket prices: the state of emergency will be declared on the 18th.

October 31st – Car industry. The PSA Peugeot-Citroën and FCA announce an at par merger between the two companies.

November 15th – Iran. A wave of social protests, with a massive workers' presence, will take place in about one hundred towns; they are motivated by the 50% increase in the price of petrol and the triplication of that of gas. The repression will be very hard, with 150-200 killed and thousands of arrests.

December 2nd-13th – European Union. The COP25, the UN summit on climate change, is held in Madrid; the newly appointed President of the European

Commission, Ursula von der Leyen, announces the new European *Green New Deal*, a big plan for "green" investment.

December 4th – India. A wave of demonstrations begins against the Modi government's citizenship law, accused of discriminating against the Muslim minority.

December 5th – A movement of strikes and demonstrations begins against the pension reform, which envisages the abolition of 42 special pension schemes and the raising of retirement age. The mobilisation will be backed by both Marine Le Pen's far right party and Jean-Luc Mélenchon's radical left party La France insoumise.

December 31st – China. The first case of coronavirus is recorded in Wuhan, in Hubei province.

2020

January 3rd – United States-Iran. American forces kill the Iranian general Qassem Soleimani with drones and missiles while he is driving away from Baghdad airport. This political assassination is openly claimed by the Trump administration.

January 7th – Austria. The new coalition government between Chancellor Sebastian Kurz's conservatives and Werner Kogler's Greens takes up office.

January 21st – Italy. In Bologna, during a campaign for the regional elections in Emilia-Romagna, the leader of the League Matteo Salvini is filmed while he rings the intercom of a Tunisian family accusing it of drug dealing.

January 23rd – China. Quarantine in Wuhan, where coronavirus is spreading rapidly, begins.

January 26th – Italy. Regional elections in Emilia-Romagna: its outgoing president Stefano Bonaccini (PD) prevails with 51.4% of the votes over the candidate of the League Lucia Borgonzoni.

January 31st – The United Kingdom leaves the European Union officially.

February 21st – Italy. A second patient infected by coronavirus dies in Lombardy; in the next three weeks the spread of the virus will take on dramatic speed and dimensions. The epidemic explosion will induce the health authorities to impose heavy measures of lockdown of the population and restriction of economic activity, initially limited to the original breeding grounds, with a population of 16 million people, but subsequently extended to all the national territory. In the main European countries, the epidemic will follow a similar evolution to Italy's, with a ten-day lag.

March 11th – The World Health Organization states that the Covid-19 coronavirus infection is a "pandemic".

March 15th – United States. In order to limit the effects of the *pandemic of the century*, the Fed, for the second time in a month, cuts interest rates bringing them to almost zero and launches a 700-billion-dollar quantitative easing programme.

March 19th – European Union. The ECB adds another 750 billion euros to its quantitative easing.

May 18th – France-Germany. Chancellor Angela Merkel and President Emmanuel Macron propose a five hundred-billion-euro "Recovery Fund" financed by common debt contracted on the markets by the Commission.

May 27th – The European Commission puts forward its proposal for recovery, called "Next Generation EU": 250 billion in loans are added to the 500 billion of subsidies proposed by the Franco-German axis, for a total of 750 billion euros.

Index of Personal Names

J-K

L

M

N-O

P

R

S

Books published by Éditions Science Marxiste

English

Texts

Arrigo Cervetto	CLASS STRUGGLES AND THE REVOLUTIONARY PARTY
Arrigo Cervetto	THE DIFFICULT QUESTION OF TIMES
Arrigo Cervetto	THE POLITICAL SHELL
Arrigo Cervetto	METHOD AND THE SCIENCE-PARTY
Arrigo Cervetto	UNITARY IMPERIALISM, VOLUME I
Arrigo Cervetto	UNITARY IMPERIALISM, VOLUME II
Nicola Capelluto	THE CRISIS IN GLOBAL RELATIONS
Renato Pastorino	THE UNPRECEDENTED TASK
Renato Pastorino	THEIR POLITICS AND OURS
Guido La Barbera	THE NEW STRATEGIC PHASE
Guido La Barbera	LOTTA COMUNISTA: THE ORIGINS 1943-1952
Guido La Barbera	LOTTA COMUNISTA: TOWARDS THE STRATEGY-PARTY 1953-1965
Guido La Barbera	LOTTA COMUNISTA: THE BOLSHEVIK MODEL 1965-1995
Anthology	REACTIONARY TERRORISM, IMPERIALIST EUROPEANISM, COMMUNIST INTERNATIONALISM

Analyses

Federico Dalvit	EUROPE IN THE GLOBAL COLLISIONS

Documents

David B. Rjazanov	THE ORIGINS OF THE FIRST INTERNATIONAL
G.G. Cavicchioli (ed.)	OCTOBER 1917 100 Years, 100 Militants of the Revolution
G.G. Cavicchioli – E. Gianni (eds.)	1919 THE COMMUNIST INTERNATIONAL 100 Years, 100 Militants of the World Party
Anthology	ENGELS Revolutionary Science and Passion

Publications for young people

Arrigo Cervetto	LENIN AND THE CHINESE REVOLUTION Lenin – Inflammable Material in World Politics and other Writings
Friedrich Engels	ANTIDÜHRING & THE ROLE OF FORCE IN HISTORY Arrigo Cervetto – The Discovery of Politics
V.I. Lenin	WHAT IS TO BE DONE? Arrigo Cervetto – The Decisive Struggle
V.I. Lenin	"LEFT-WING" COMMUNISM, AN INFANTILE DISORDER Arrigo Cervetto – The Time of Lenin's Clarity
V.I. Lenin	IMPERIALISM, THE HIGHEST STAGE OF CAPITALISM Arrigo Cervetto – The Marxist Theory of International Relations
V.I. Lenin	THE STATE AND REVOLUTION Arrigo Cervetto – The Restoration of Marxist Theory
Karl Marx	WAGE LABOUR AND CAPITAL / WAGES, PRICE AND PROFIT
Karl Marx	THE CIVIL WAR IN FRANCE Arrigo Cervetto The Politicol Form at Last Discovered
Anthology	MAY DAY IN WORKING-CLASS HISTORY

Anthology	THE COMMUNIST CHOICE Understanding the Present, Changing the Future
–	OUR INTERNATIONALIST STRUGGLE The Direction of the New Strategic Phase

French

Collection Textes

Arrigo Cervetto	LA DIFFICILE QUESTION DES TEMPS
Arrigo Cervetto	LUTTES DE CLASSE ET PARTI RÉVOLUTIONNAIRE
Arrigo Cervetto	LE MONDE MULTIPOLAIRE 1990-1995
Arrigo Cervetto	L'ENVELOPPE POLITIQUE
Arrigo Cervetto	MÉTHODE ET PARTI-SCIENCE
Arrigo Cervetto	L'IMPÉRIALISME UNITAIRE Tome I, 1950-1967
Arrigo Cervetto	L'IMPÉR IALISME UNITAIRE Tome II, 1959-1980
Arrigo Cervetto	LA CONFRONTATION MONDIALE
Guido La Barbera	LA CRISE DU CAPITALISME D'ÉTAT
Guido La Barbera	L'EUROPE ET LA GUERRE
Guido La Barbera	L'ORDRE INSTABLE DU MULTIPOLARISME
Guido La Barbera	L'EUROPE ET L'ÉTAT
Guido La Barbera	L'EUROPE, L'ASIE ET LA CRISE
Guido La Barbera	CRISE GLOBALE ET RESTRUCTURATION EUROPÉENNE
Guido La Barbera	LA NOUVELLE PHASE STRATÉGIQUE
Guido La Barbera	LOTTA COMUNISTA – LE GROUPE D'ORIGINE, 1943-1952
Guido La Barbera	LOTTA COMUNISTA – VERS LE PARTI STRATÉGIE, 1953-1965
Guido La Barbera	LOTTA COMUNISTA – LE MODÈLE BOLCHEVIQUE, 1965-1995
Renato Pastorino	LA TÂCHE INÉDITE
Renato Pastorino	LEUR POLITIQUE ET LA NÔTRE - Una nouvelle génération de communistes en Europa
Nicola Capelluto	LA CRISE DES RELATIONS GLOBALES
Paolo Rivetti	LES SYNDICATS DANS LA RESTRUCTURATION EUROPÉENNE (2008-2015) et en annexe: Considérations sur les luttes politiques en France (2006-2012)
Roberto Casella	BATAILLES ET PRINCIPES POUR UNE POLITIQUE COMMUNISTE

Collection Classiques

Marx – Engels	MANIFESTE DU PARTI COMMUNISTE En appendice notes sur les premières éditions du Manifeste et sur sa diffusion
Lev Trotsky	LES GUERRES BALKANIQUES 1912-1913
Friedrich Engels	NOTES SUR LA GUERRE FRANCO-ALLEMANDE DE 1870-1871 Préface de Lev Trotsky

Collection Analyses

Nicola Capelluto – Franco Palumberi	ÉNERGIE ET PÉTROLE DANS L'AFFRONTEMENT IMPÉRIALISTE
Roberto Casella	LE SIÈCLE DES GÉANTS DE L'ASIE – I. LA CHINE (1995-2012)
Roberto Casella	LE SIÈCLE DES GÉANTS DE L'ASIE – II. L'INDE (1998-2012)
Gianluca De Simone	GRAND MOYEN-ORIENT Crises et guerres de la nouvelle phase stratégique
G. Motosi – P. Nardini	LA BATAILLE MONDIALE DE L'ACIER
Federico Dalvit	L'EUROPE DANS LES COLLISIONS MONDIALES

Collection Documents

G. Munis	LEÇONS D'UNE DÉFAITE, PROMESSE DE VICTOIRE Critique et théorie de la révolution espagnole 1930-1939

Paul Frölich	AUTOBIOGRAPHIE – Parcours d'un militant internationaliste allemand : de la social-démocratie au Parti communiste 1890-1921
P. Frölich – R. Lindau – A. Schreiner – J. Walcher	RÉVOLUTION ET CONTRE-RÉVOLUTION EN ALLEMAGNE 1918-1920 De la fondation du Parti communiste au putsch de Kapp
Paul Frölich	IMPÉRIALISME, GUERRE ET LUTTE DE CLASSES EN ALLEMAGNE 1914-18
Anthologie	MARX Scientifique et révolutionnaire
Anthologie	LÉNINE Conscience et volonté révolutionnaires
Anthologie	ENGELS Science et passion révolutionnaires
Anthologie	Le Premier Mai. Dans l'histoire du mouvement ouvrier
G.G. Cavicchioli (dir. par)	OCTOBRE 1917 100 ans, 100 militants de la révolution
G.G. Cavicchioli – E. Gianni (dir. par)	1919 L'INTERNATIONALE COMMUNISTE 100 ans, 100 militants du parti mondial

Bibliothèque jeunes

Anthologie	LE RACISME EST CHEZ NOUS
Lénine	QUE FAIRE? Cervetto – La lutte décisive
Lénine	L'IMPÉRIALISME, STADE SUPRÊME DU CAPITALISME Cervetto – La théorie marxiste des relations internationals
Lénine	L'ÉTAT ET LA RÉVOLUTION Cervetto – La restauration de la théorie marxiste
Lénine	LA MALADIE INFANTILE DU COMMUNISME (LE « COMMUNISME DE GAUCHE ») Cervetto – Le temps de la clarté de Lénine
Lénine	MATÉRIALISME ET EMPIRIOCRITICISME Notes critiques sur une philosophie réactionnaire Cervetto – La critique libérale de Bernstein
Lénine	CE QUE SONT LES « AMIS DU PEUPLE » suivi de LE CONTENU ÉCONOMIQUE DU POPULISME Cervetto – La théorie de la politique de Lénine
Lénine	LE SOCIALISME ET LA GUERRE
Lénine	LA RÉVOLUTION PROLÉTARIENNE ET LE RÉNÉGAT KAUTSKY Cervetto – Le fondement scientifique de la lutte des classes
Cervetto	LÉNINE ET LA RÉVOLUTION CHINOISE Lénine – «Matières inflammables de la politique mondiale»
Engels	ANTIDÜHRING Cervetto – La découverte de la politique
Engels	LA SITUATION DE LA CLASSE OUVRIÈRE EN ANGLETERRE Cervetto – La vision historique de la transformation sociale
Engels	SOCIALISME UTOPIQUE ET SOCIALISME SCIENTIFIQUE suivi de LUDWIG FEUERBACH ET L'ABOUTISSEMENT DE LA PHILOSOPHIE CLASSIQUE ALLEMANDE
Marx–Engels	LA CONCEPTION MATÉRIALISTE DE L'HISTOIRE
Marx	LA GUERRE CIVILE EN FRANCE
Marx	CRITIQUE DE L'ÉCONOMIE POLITIQUE
Marx	TRAVAIL SALARIÉ ET CAPITAL suivi de SALAIRE, PRIX ET PROFIT
Marx	LES LUTTES DE CLASSES EN FRANCE 1848-1850 suivi de LE 18 BRUMAIRE DE LOUIS BONAPARTE
Marx–Engels–Lénine	UNE CAUSE DE L'HUMANITÉ TOUT ENTIÈRE – Anthologie
–	LE CHOIX COMMUNISTE Comprendre le présent, changer l'avenir

En partenariat avec éd. L'INTERNATIONALISTE

Anthologie	TERRORISME RÉACTIONNAIRE, EUROPÉISME IMPÉRIALISTE, INTERNATIONALISME COMMUNISTE

Anthologie	LA FONDATION DE L'INTERNATIONALE COMMUNISTE – MARS 1919
Anthologie	ORIGINES ET DÉFAITE DE L'INTERNATIONALISME EN CHINE 1919-1927

Spanish

Textos

Arrigo Cervetto	LUCHA DE CLASES Y PARTIDO REVOLUCIONARIO
Arrigo Cervetto	LA DIFÍCIL CUESTIÓN DE LOS TIEMPOS
Arrigo Cervetto	EL ENVOLTORIO POLÍTICO
Guido La Barbera	LOTTA COMUNISTA – EL GRUPO ORIGINARIO 1943-1952
Guido La Barbera	LOTTA COMUNISTA – HACIA EL PARTIDO ESTRATEGIA 1953-1965
Guido La Barbera	LOTTA COMUNISTA - EL MODEL BOLCHEVIQUE 1965-1995
Guido La Barbera	LA NUEVA FASE ESTRATEGICA
Renato Pastorino	LA TAREA INÉDITA
Renato Pastorino	SU POLÍTICA Y LA NUESTRA - Una nueva generación de comunistas en Europa
Antologia	TERRORISMO REACCIONARIO, EUROPEÍSMO IMPERIALISTA, INTERNACIONALISMO COMUNISTA

Análisis

Gianluca De Simone	GRAN ORIENTE MEDIO Crisis y guerras de la nueva fase estratégica
Federico Dalvit	EUROPA EN LAS COLISIONES GLOBALES

Documentos

Antología	ENGELS Ciencia y pasión revolucionaria
G.G. Cavicchioli (A cargo de)	OCTUBRE DE 1917 100 ANOS, 100 MILITANTES DE LA REVOLUCIÓN
G.G. Cavicchioli – E. Gianni (A cargo de)	1919 LA INTERNACIONAL COMUNISTA 100 ANOS, 100 MILITANTES DEL PARTIDO MUNDIAL

Biblioteca jóvenes

Marx	TRABAJO ASALARIADO Y CAPITAL / SALARIO, PRECIO Y GANACIA
Marx	LAS LUCHAS DE CLASES EN FRANCIA / EL DIECIOCHO BRUMARIO
Marx	LA GUERRA CIVIL EN FRANCIA Arrigo Cervetto The Politicol Form at Last Discovered
Engels	ANTIDÜHRING
Lenin	EL IMPERIALISMO FASE SUPERIOR DEL CAPITALISMO (Esbozo popular) Cervetto – La teoría marxista de las relaciones internacionales
Lenin	¿QUE HACER? Cervetto - La lucha decisiva
Lenin	EL ESTADO Y LA REVOLUCIÓN Cervetto – La restauración de la teoría marxista
Lenin	EL IZQUIERDISMO, ENFERMEDAD INFANTIL DEL COMUNISMO Cervetto - El tiempo de la claridad de Lenin
Cervetto	LENIN Y LA REVOLUCIÓN CHINA Lenin - "Material inflamable en la política mundial" y otros escritos
Antología	LA ELECCIÓN COMUNISTA Comprender el presente, cambiar el futuro
Antología	EL RACISMO ESTÁ EN NUESTRA CASA
–	NUESTRA LUCHA INTERNACIONALISTA Orientaciones para la nueva fase estratégica

German

Arrigo Cervetto	KLASSENKÄMPFE UND REVOLUTIONÄRE PARTEI
Arrigo Cervetto	DIE POLITISCHE HÜLLE
Anthologie	UNSER INTERNATIONALISTISCHER KAMPF Richtlinien für die neue strategische Phase

Russian books

Éditions Science Marxiste in collaboration with Prometey Publications, St. Petersburg

Arrigo Cervetto	UNITARNII IMPERIALISM, TOM I
Arrigo Cervetto	UNITARNII IMPERIALISM, TOM II
Arrigo Cervetto	MNOGOPOLIARNI MIR 1990-1995

NOVY PROMETEY Publications, St. Petersburg, Russia

Arrigo Cervetto	TRUDNIY VOPROS VREMENI
Arrigo Cervetto	POLITIČESKAYA OBOLOČKA
Arrigo Cervetto	METOD I PARTIA-NAUKA
Arrigo Cervetto	KLASSOVAIA BOR'BÁ I REVOLIUTSIONNAIA PARTIA
Arrigo Cervetto	VSJEMIRNOJE PROTIVOSTOJANIJE
Guido La Barbera	LOTTA COMUNISTA : GRUPPA, STOYAVSCAYA U ISTOKOV (1943-1952)
Guido La Barbera	LOTTA COMUNISTA: V NAPRAVLENII PARTII STRATEGII (1953-1965)
Guido La Barbera	NOVAYA STRATEGICHESKAYA FAZA
Renato Pastorino	BESPRETSEDENTNAYA ZADACHA
Gianluca De Simone	BOLSHOY SREDNIY VOSTOK. Krizisy i voyny novoy strategicheskoy fazy
Vladimir Nevskiy	ISTORA RKP(B). KRATIJ OCHERK
Lev Trotsky	BALKANI I BALKANSKAYA VOJNA. Pered istoricheskim rubezhom
Ivan Babushkin	RABOČIJ BOL'SHEVIK
Y. M. Steklov	PERVYY INTERNATSIONAL 1864-1872
G. G. Cavicchioli	OKTYABR 1917 GODA. 100 let. 100 bortsov za revolyutsiyu
G.G. Cavicchioli Gianni	1919-2019. 100 let kommunistieskomu internatsionalu. 100 militantov E. mirovoj partii proletariata
Federico Dalvit	EVROPA V GLOBALNIKH KOLLIZIJAKH
Antologhija	REAKTSIONNYIY TERRORIZM, IMPERIALISTICHESKIY EVROPEIZM, KOMMUNISTICHESKIY INTERNATSIONALIZM
Antologhija	OBRAZOVANIE KOMMUNISTICHESKOGO INTERNAZIONALA. MART 1919 GODA
Antologhija	KOMMUNIZM ILI VARVARSTVO? NAŠA INTERNATSIONALISTIESKAJA BOR'BA.

Greek books

DIETHNISMOS (Internationalism) Publications, Piraeus, Greece

Anthology	Ο ΜΥΘΟΣ ΤΟΥ ΚΑΛΠΙΚΟΥ ΣΟΣΙΑΛΙΣΜΟΥ (The myth of false socialism)
Arrigo Cervetto	ΤΑΞΙΚΟΙ ΑΓΩΝΣ ΚΑΙ ΕΠΑΝΑΣΤΑΤΙΚΟ ΚΟΜΜΑ (Class struggles and the revolutionary party)
Arrigo Cervetto	ΤΟ ΔΣΚΟΛΟ ΖΗΤΗΜΑ ΤΩΝ ΧΡΟΝΩΝ (The difficult question of times)
Renato Pastorino	ΤΟ ΠΡΩΤΟΓΝΩΡΟ ΚΑΘΗΚΟΝ (The unprecedented task)
Guido La Barbera	Η ΕΥΡΩΠΗ ΚΑΙ Ο ΠΟΛΕΜΟΣ (Europe and the war)

Anthology	Η ΚΟΜΜΟΥΝΙΣΤΙΚΗ ΕΠΙΛΟΓΗ (The communist choice)
Anthology	ΜΙΑ ΥΠΟΘΕΣΗ ΟΛΗΣ ΤΗΣ ΑΝΘΡΩΠΟΤΗΤΑΣ (A cause of all mankind)
Anthology	ΜΥΘΟΙ ΚΑΙ ΠΟΛΕΜΟΙ ΣΤΙΣ ΜΠΑΝΛΙΕ ΤΟΥ ΕΥΡΩΠΑΪΚΟΥ ΙΜΠΕΡΙΑΛΙΣΜΟΥ (Myths and wars in the peripheries of European imperialism)
Anthology	1991-2011 : 20 ΧΡΟΝΙΑ ΠΟΥ ΑΛΛΑΞΑΝ ΤΟΝ ΚΟΣΜΟ (1991-2011. 20 years that shook the world)
Anthology	Η ΕΥΡΩΠΗ-ΔΥΝΜΗ : Ο ΕΧΘΡΟΣ ΣΤΟ ΣΠΙΤΙ ΜΑΣ (Europe as a power: the main enemy is at home)
Anthology	Η ΥΛΙΣΤΙΚΗ ΑΝΤΙΛΗΨΗ ΤΗΣ ΙΣΤΟΡΙΑΣ (The materialist conception of history)
Anthology	ΧΡΟΝΟΙ ΚΡΙΣΗΣ, ΕΠΙΣΤΡΟΦΗ ΣΤΟΝ ΜΑΡΞ (Years of crisis – returning to Marx)
Anthology	ΤΟ ΠΡΩΤΟ ΠΡΑΚΤΙΚΟ ΒΗΜΑ (The first practical step)

Brazilian books

Edições INTERVENÇÃO COMUNISTA Niterói-RJ. – Brazil

Arrigo Cervetto	LUTAS DE CLASE E PARTIDO REVOLUCIONÁRIO
Arrigo Cervetto	LÊNIN E A REVOLUÇÃO CHINESA Lênin – «Material inflamável na politica mundial » e outros textos
Arrigo Cervetto	A DIFÍCIL QUESTÃO DOS TEMPOS
Arrigo Cervetto	MÉTODO E PARTIDO-CIÊNCIA
Arrigo Cervetto	O INVOLUCRO POLITICO
Guido La Barbera	A NOVA FASE ESTRATÉGICA
Lenin	O IMPERIALISMO FASE SUPERIOR DO CAPITALISMO
–	A ESCOLHA COMUNISTA
–	A ASCENSÃO IMPERIALISTA DO BRASIL
–	A NOSSA LUTA INTERNACIONALISTA

Workers of All Countries, Unite!

Internationalism

Journal of Marxist Analysis No. 27 - May 2021 - £2 *Proletarian Opposition to European Imperialism and Unitary Imperialism*

Historical Constants and Strategic Surprise

The agreement between Beijing and Tehran falls under the definition of *strategic surprise,* i.e., events that entirely appertain to the political realm and mark a change or an about-turn in the balance among the powers. New alliances, the breakdown of alliances, the overturning of coalitions, diplomatic openings or unexpected military sorties: these are the "regular novelties" of international politics that Arrigo Cervetto wrote about. However, if the agreement was an unforeseeable event in itself, the long-term objective economic and political trends that have determined it and made it possible are entirely investigable.

The invasion of Afghanistan by the USSR at the end of December 1979 was interpreted by the United States as a potential threat to the oil routes of the Persian Gulf, and it was a contemporary revival of *the Great Game,* which had set the British Empire against the Tsarist Empire in the 19th century. This is not the place to analyse whether the Russian threat at the beginning of the 1980s was real or just a pretext brandished by the American administration of Jimmy Carter and his Security Advisor Zbigniew Brzezinski. The opening up of archives, memoirs and historical research have demonstrated that the Russian sortie in Afghanistan was actually defensive in order to protect the USSR from the contagion of the instability of the Central Asian republics, and that the crisis was brandished and even fomented by Washington with a dual purpose – to put pressure on Moscow and thereby to condition its allies in Europe and Asia.

Our Marxist analysis of international relations at the time understood how to identify the lines of force that were hidden behind those events. It was doubtful that Moscow really had the strength to challenge the United States in the Persian Gulf; in warm seas, wrote Cervetto, "sharks swim better than bears". And the Gulf artery was "multidimensional", as it also concerned Europe and Japan: in making sure that the Strait of Hormuz would remain an *open door* – this would become even clearer in the crises of the 1980s – Washington was addressing Bonn, Paris, London, Tokyo and also Rome. In January 1980, the American strategy was summed up in what would go down in history as the Carter Doctrine: "Any attempt on the part of any external force to take control of the Gulf region will be considered as an attack on the United States' vital interests; this aggression will be repelled by all means necessary, including military force."

The agreement between Beijing and Tehran, a kind of *quasi-alliance* lasting for twenty-five years, calls into question the fate of that doctrine. Not by chance, a comment of the *South China Morning Post* suggests that the Carter era "belongs to the past". In discussions of a wider scope – including that of Gary Sick, who was responsible for the Middle East in Brzezinski's National Security Council (NSC) – America's interest in preventing any hostile control of the Persian Gulf dates back to the post-war period beginning with the time of Truman. This guarantee is considered in continuity with, and in succession to, the role the British Empire played in the region.

In the version of Justin Vaïsse, the author of a biography of Brzezinski, the Carter Doctrine in the strict sense dates back to 1977, i.e., before the catastrophic crisis in Iran that would lead to the fall of Reza Pahlavi and before the Russian invasion of Afghanistan. An NSC document elaborated for Carter was based on the idea of seeing a balance with the USSR in all the dimensions of power, not only the military one. In that context, the notion of *economic diplomacy* – i.e., the concept of the use of economic tools for political purposes – emerged. From this aspect came the conception of a strategic use of the energy connection, which was linked not only to the Persian Gulf.

Therefore, in Carter and Brzezinski's version, Iran was crucial to preventing the USSR from having access to the "warm seas". And from the very beginning our analysis saw the plurality of the interests involved, given the centrality of this energy artery for all the world's players. Over the decades since then it has been a question of following the American doctrine's transformations according to the changes in power relations, characterised first of all by the irruption of Asia.

In all the critical junctures, our point of observation has been identifying every sign of the appearance of China and India, following Japan, in the Gulf area. America's military interventions in Iraq, in 1991 and 2003, are the most obvious examples of these transformations. With George Bush Sr.'s first Gulf War, hot on the heels of the collapse of the USSR, Washington confirmed itself "at the centre of every balance", on both the European and the Asian front. With the second conflict, George W. Bush's "war by choice", the United States already intended to forestall China, confirming its grip on the energy routes in order to condition China's rise.

(*continued on p. 6-7*)

CONTENTS

Cet ouvrage a été achevé d'imprimer en juin 2021
par Galli Thierry Stampa – Milano
Dépôt légal: juin 2021
Imprimé en Italie